Where Have All Our Cowboys Gone?

Where Have All Our Cowboys Gone?

BRIAN JENSEN

TAYLOR TRADE PUBLISHING

Lanham • New York • Oxford

Published by Taylor Trade Publishing
An Imprint of the Rowman & Littlefield Publishing Group
4720 Boston Way
Lanham, Maryland 20706
Distributed by National Book Network

All photos courtesy of *Dallas Cowboys Weekly* and the players except: p. A and
throughout–Ron St. Angelo; p. 6 (bottom three photos)–Bettmann/CORBIS; p. 61
(top)–Kathy Young; p. 62 (bottom)–Rusty Marchman; p. 62 (bottom)–Ed Culwell; p. 176
(bottom) and p. 178 (middle)–Rod Aydehotte; p. 249 and p. 250–AP/Wide World.

Designed by David Timmons and Barbara Werden

Library of Congress Cataloging-in-Publication Data
Jensen, Brian.
    Where have all our Cowboys gone? / Brian Jensen
        p.   cm.
    ISBN 0-87833-265-0 (cloth)
        1. Dallas Cowboys (Football team)—Biography. 2. Football players—
Biography. I. Title.

    GV956.D3 J46 2001
    796.332'092'27642812—dc21   2001027503

∞ The paper used in this publication meets the minimum requirements of American
National Standard for Information Sciences—Permanence of Paper for Printed Library
Materials, ANSI/NISO Z39.48–1992.

Manufactured in the United States of America.

To Mallory and Bennett,
my pride and joy.

Contents

The Arrival of America's Team

The Lean Years

How 'Bout Them Cowboys!

Foreword

When a young player becomes a part of the Dallas Cowboys, he quickly develops an understanding of—and an appreciation for—those who have come before him.

I'm sure this is the case with nearly every NFL team, but, because of the success and heritage of the Dallas Cowboys, the feeling of tradition and history that surrounds this franchise is something that is very tangible—and very powerful.

The Dallas Cowboys have enjoyed 40-plus years of unprecedented success on the football field. At the foundation of that dynamic achievement is a collection of characters who played the game. These are the men who shaped this franchise's history, and they did so with an unusual blend of style, substance, and staying power.

This book documents the journey that many of those players traveled after they stepped away from the glaring spotlight that accompanies the star on the helmet.

Where Have All Our Cowboys Gone? is a collection of stories that tell us what it is like to move on and grow: how some have enjoyed triumph away from the field—and how others have been forced to display the heart of a champion under circumstances that are far more dramatic than those that go along with simply playing a game.

More than anything, this book reminds us that heroes are humans. They have fears and failings just like everyone else.

Brian Jensen is uniquely qualified to bring you these stories. He is an experienced journalist whose fascination with these players began, like it did for so many of us, as an impressionable young fan of the Dallas Cowboys.

Troy Aikman

Acknowledgments

The process of telling current stories of players past would not have been possible without the willingness of so many of the subjects themselves. I would like to thank those players who entertained the idea of participating by accepting the invitation for an interview and especially those who opened their hearts, minds, and lives by sharing private experiences, many of which were difficult to express.

Thank you Roz Cole, Mike Connelly, Sean Hamilton, and Rich Dalrymple for pointing me in the right direction as the search began to locate Cowboys around the world. Many family members of former players also assisted the effort, while some teammates encouraged others to join in.

Over the years the Cowboys organization has had more than its share of media scrutiny. During the research and writing of this book, the doors were always open. I would like to offer a special thanks to Ron Spain of the *Dallas Cowboys Weekly* for being so gracious in allowing the perusal of his photography files. Tom Landry, Tex Schramm, Gil Brandt, Jerry Jones, and Jimmy Johnson assembled a group of men from a variety of backgrounds and left an impression on each. You all provided inspiration for me as well.

On a more personal note, thank you Michel, Dawn, Bobby, Stacey, and other friends for your encouragement and support. To my family—especially Gail, whose passion for the written word keeps my bookshelves full—thanks for constantly inquiring about the progress of the project and talking me through the challenges. I only wish our parents were alive to share in the experience. Mom, the most accomplished book connoisseur I've ever known, would have told me it was the best read of her life—whether it was or not!

Where Have All Our Cowboys Gone?

Introduction

They filed in one after another. Faces familiar to so many of us despite the altering of age. A Hall of Fame running back here, a troubled linebacker there, Super Bowl MVPs in between. The whispers among those watching the processional grew into curious conversation.

Hey, there's Harvey Martin. I wonder what he's doing these days.

Isn't that Ralph Neely? Look, there's Don Perkins. Where have they been lately?

Has anyone seen Don Meredith?

It was a brief relief from the moment of mourning that had brought America's Team back together. Tom Landry had lost his battle with leukemia. The athletes he molded into great football players gathered to share the realization that he had also helped guide most of them into becoming great men—husbands, fathers, lawyers, company presidents, entrepreneurs. As military jets flew over the private graveside service, they wept. As thousands of adoring fans flocked to memorial celebrations, they stood proudly and proclaimed their love for Landry.

All the while came the whispers.

Do you see Lee Roy? Isn't he in the lumber business?

How about Walt Garrison? I haven't seen him since he did those chewing tobacco commercials.

Has anyone seen Duane Thomas? Or Golden Richards?

For over 40 years they have been the names, numbers, faces, and stories that captivate Cowboys fans worldwide—especially one particular fan.

In 1960, as the franchise was taking its first step into the NFL spotlight, a little boy in Dallas was taking his first steps, tightly grasping a blue blanket in one hand. Later in life, I would learn it was "Cowboys blue."

New Year's Eve, 1967, was one of the most memorable days in Dallas Cowboys history. No wonder all the adults at my seventh birthday party were screaming names like Meredith, Hayes, and Lilly while surrounding the television. To my friends and me, the NFL Championship game that became known as the Ice Bowl just looked like a cold place far, far away.

When the team turned ten, it received a Super Bowl berth as a birthday present. Mine was an "authentic" Cowboys uniform complete with the white plastic helmet and blue star. My best friend and backdoor neighbor, Mark Miller, was instantly a marked man. He was the opposing offense. I was Jethro Pugh or George Andrie, Chuck Howley or Cornell Green. He never gained a yard.

While Roger was dodging defenders, Dad and I were dodging broadcast blackouts in Dallas with trips to Tyler, Texas, slightly more than the 90-mile radius required. Sitting at a roadside park with plenty of others in our motor homes, vans, and cars, the reception was rough, but it was better than the "Cowboys Antenna," being sold as the high-flying solution, the we had tried so many times before.

A trip to DFW Airport to see the team arrive after the "Hail Mary" beat Minnesota became bigger than life when a simple "Hey, Drew," drew the smile of the man wearing a hat of horns from the Vikings he had conquered.

In 1977, a senior from the University of Pittsburgh won the Heisman Trophy and brought it to Texas as the Cowboys No. 1 pick. Meanwhile, a senior from Dallas' W. T. White High School somehow landed an invitation from his buddy Rick Rasansky to attend that year's rookie orientation at the Cowboys complex. A picture with Tony Dorsett and a handshake from "Too Tall" Jones jolted me into feeling as if I had graduated to the inner circle.

Manning a concession stand at Texas Stadium for our swim team's fund-raising project produced a perfect plan. As a pregame and half-time volunteer, the four quarters were mine to roam. Suddenly the portals above the north end zone became the best seat in the house. Hollywood Henderson's kickoff reverse for a touchdown, complete with the goalpost dunk, was a performance worth the price of admission.

Years later, after college and the beginnings of a career in broadcasting, a return to Dallas put that little kid with the blue blanket in the middle of the media madhouse that is the everyday experience of covering the Cowboys as a reporter and anchor for two Dallas–Fort Worth television stations. Through the firing of the living legend to a three-Super-Bowl bonanza and finally the farewell that February day at Highland Park United Methodist Church, a 12-year period that brought a boy once in awe of America's Team to a more realistic vision of their world, a world even players like James Washington now admit is a "fantasy land." It also brought that little boy closer to what the big boys he once idolized describe as "the real world"—life after football—real jobs with real challenges, real life problems with real difficult solutions.

Suddenly, the questions being whispered had answers.

Some were readily known because of top-level NFL figures seen by football fans every week. Mike Ditka and Dan Reeves having their high-pressure heart problems played out in high-profile performances for television commercials, on the sidelines as head coaches, or in the studio as network television hosts. Calvin Hill and Robert Newhouse continuing their Cowboys careers as player personnel counselors, reluctant, with the eyes and ears of their owner ominously close by, to reveal anything more. Jim Jeffcoat and Bill Bates back in the comforts of the Cowboys family as familiar assistant coaches.

Many were hidden behind the celebrity status that still surrounds the players of the past. At least one, Rayfield Wright, who directs the NFL Alumni regional office in Arizona, would participate only with remuneration for himself and all other former players. Others, like Clint Longley and Golden Richards, are purposefully protected in their own private worlds.

All had one core element that was surprisingly common. Unlike their counterparts of today, the heroes that put the shine on the Cowboys star actually had to learn the labor of polishing and buffing a new star once their playing days were done.

As Walt Garrison says in unison with the others, "Most of the guys that played when I did weren't financially secure when they quit playing football, like Troy (Aikman) will be or like Emmitt (Smith) will be, that make millions of dollars a year. Some of the guys I played with, including myself, we never made a million dollars in all our career. You have to get a job and go to work. It's not like you can just pal around with somebody."

"I worked every off-season doing something," adds Ralph Neely. "We didn't make enough money to retire, we just changed jobs."

Yet there they were, filing into the memorial service, the way we had remembered them so many times before—as Dallas Cowboys—and carrying with them the stories that answer the whispers, *Where Have All Our Cowboys Gone?*

The Building Years

Cabin Fever

Snow is falling outside a log cabin on a little island in the Great Lakes. The scraping and growling sounds being heard just a few feet away from the window don't create enough of a stir inside to disturb the occupants from the warmth of a winter fire. It is probably just a bear. Tomorrow it might be a deer. The next day it could be an elk or even an eagle. Attracting Michigan's wildlife is why they built the feeder near that window in the first place. George Andrie and his wife have come to their little cabin in the woods to retire.

"Our children couldn't believe it when we told them what we were going to do," admits Andrie. "They said, 'Why would you want to do that now? Most people your age go south and you're going north.' I don't think I ever got used to Texas, being there for 37 years, to living in the humidity and the heat."

It was the same George Andrie who, as a Cowboys defensive end, looked around the locker room before the 1967 Ice Bowl game in Green Bay and knew his team was in trouble. "It was cold, and I could see the effect it had on the rest of the guys," remembers the man who was raised in nearby Grand Rapids. "I didn't say a damn thing, one way or another, but I could see where we were getting psyched out. That's all they were talking about was the weather. We didn't have our mind on the game, even though we played a real good game and hung in there and could have won it and should have won it."

Andrie had plenty of good memories to go along with his 11 years in a Cowboys uniform, leading the team in sacks for four straight seasons while playing alongside Hall of Fame tackle Bob Lilly. The successful combination on the field created another career path off the field with "Mr. Cowboy" a few years later. "Bob got a Coors beer distributorship in Waco, Texas, and I worked with him for about two years and we got that thing running, established the market and stuff like this. But the beer business was a lot like football," adds Andrie of his first attempt at an after-football future. "I'd be gone at 6:00 in the morning getting guys off running their routes, and then I'd be there entertaining retailers after hours until midnight. It was about to kill me. Not only that but you can't drink water, you gotta have a beer, you gotta have your own beer if you're selling it."

Not happy with the direction he was taking his future or his family, Andrie went another route, starting his own business in advertising specialties, imprinting items for companies' promotional and advertising needs. "It's all family owned and all family operated," says the proud father of seven. "All the kids work in it, off and on. It was really nice to be able to involve them all. They're all doing very well, and they're all making a very nice living off of it."

Which allows Mom and Dad the opportunity to enjoy a lifestyle that 25 years in business should provide. "We look across the water and we can see Canada maybe a couple miles by boat over there," says Andrie, whose wife works on her dream of writing a book while the former football player spends much of his days hunting or fishing. "I put a little feeder up there in front of my office window. I had about a six- or seven-pointer come up this morning. I don't shoot those deer. I go to another part of the island. I can't shoot the ones that I feed."

Andrie can't imagine being anywhere else or doing anything better during his golden years. He is as far removed from football as he can possibly be, and that is strictly by design. "I played for 11 years, and when it was over it was over. I don't think we went to one game since I left, even while I was in Texas. As far as going back and watching games, that new owner (Jerry Jones) kind of indicated that he didn't want anything to do with us and never invited us to anything."

There is always the possibility that an invitation never quite made it to Andrie's hideaway. Not that the invitation would be very timely when the Andries make it to the mainland to pick it up.

"The only way to get off the island is a ferry," describes Andrie. "We're lost. I'm gonna tell you what, if you're gonna try to come up here and find us, you got to work at it."

Not necessary. Just look for the most content creatures in the great white north.

Kicking the Big C

Y ou think, oh, crap, why does this have to happen to me?"
It was the reaction Mike Clark expected when he heard the
words no one ever expects to hear. "It was a melanoma. It had gone
from my left ear internal and showed up in six spots on my lung, one
on my left kidney and two spots on my spleen. You just think, 'Man,
this is it.'"

But Mike Clark was getting too much of a kick out of life for those
words to block his enthusiasm.

Calling the Super Bowl VI win over Miami his biggest thrill with
the Cowboys and the Super Bowl V loss to Baltimore the worst memory, Clark says it was a game against the Browns on the way to the
first Super Bowl that was his finest football moment. "We played in
the mud and I got two field goals and we won 6–2," remembers Clark.
"That was the most satisfying because nobody could do anything and
I just happened to hit the two and it got us into the play-offs."

Yet, even as his most satisfying moment in football was flying
through the uprights in Cleveland, Clark had already logged countless
hours of flying away from the field. It was a passion that would lead
him on a remarkable journey around the world.

Joining the Confederate Air Force, Clark worked his way up to flying some of the B-17 and B-25 aircraft that were active in World War
II. But it took almost ten years for Clark to talk one of his most decorated passengers into coming aboard. "You know, Coach Landry was
an airplane captain during World War II," says Clark proudly. "I was
still flying when I was playing, and I said, 'Coach, you gotta go flying
with us.' He said, 'When you get your type rating in the left seat as a
pilot in command, I'll go fly with you.' So, one Saturday (in 1981) after
I'd retired, I went out to the practice field and I walked up to him and
handed him my license and a piece of paper that said, 'Type Rating—
Boeing B-17.'"

Tom Landry joined Clark for an hour-and-a-half flight to an air show in Denton, Texas. "Probably about 45 minutes of that he (Landry) was sitting in the right seat, in the copilot's seat, flying. He was very good. That was a big thrill for me."

Clark's interest in airplanes eventually took off as a career. With experience in marketing and interior construction to go with his knowledge of the flying game, General Dynamics (now Lockheed Martin) hired Clark to put together international trade shows and air shows. And the thrills just kept coming. "About 38 countries, although most of the shows were in England, France, Germany, and the UAE," explains Clark.

Unlike his days with the Confederate Air Force, the hardware at these shows aren't being sold as museum pieces. American fighter planes like the F-16 and the F-18, Russian MiGs, French airplanes, and ground equipment including tanks and a variety of missiles were commonly on display at the shows Clark put together.

"I was at one that they had a live demonstration at night. That was most impressive. Everything they used in the Gulf War, we saw examples of. From 30-caliber machine guns all the way up to ground-to-air missiles like the Patriot. They make big booms when they go off!"

Unfortunately, not all the booms Clark witnessed were planned. "In Paris, they had the MiG-29 crash. He apparently ingested a bird and it just blew one of his engines and the other one was in afterburner and it just rolled him over and went straight down. The pilot punched out and the next day he was up flying again," remembers Clark. "Then, there was a Sukhoi, another Russian airplane that did a big loop and came around and just didn't clear the ground loop. It bounced and exploded. Of course, the guys punched out, and they were okay. I never saw a fatality."

But Clark got the biggest kick out of a joy ride he took in a battle-ready tank during one of the shows in the Persian Gulf region. "We made friends with some of the Russian tank drivers. We toasted vodka and then got the tanks, and I got to drive several demonstration laps around the obstacle course. It's extremely simple."

Of course, that comes from a guy who for the past several years has been riding the country on his Honda Gold Wing touring motorcycle. One of his favorite trips was a 32-day Alaskan adventure that covered 9,000 miles.

No wonder the former Cowboys kicker chose an intense treatment to battle the cancer that was discovered invading his body in 1997. Clark took chemotherapy that included five different chemicals in three separate sessions, each at 24 hours a day for five straight days. "It totally knocked me to my knees," says Clark of his third and final session. "Worse than any training camp I'd ever been through; just weak and tired and you just wanted to lay there. It took me a long time to get over."

But he did, regaining his weight that had dropped from 238 to 207 during the treatments. Now he has another thrill to add to the list. "We're just sitting here enjoying everything that's going on."

It's been, by far, the biggest kick of Mike Clark's life.

The Long Run

It was only a hill. Not a mountain, not even close. But this particular hill looked more ominous than it should have because it was about to become legendary.

One of Tom Landry's most famous fundamentals in training camp was about to begin. The Landry Mile. A run through the hills of Thousand Oaks, California, that every player would have to complete in 6½ minutes or less. Quarterbacks, linebackers, offensive lineman. Everyone was included, from the biggest names to the no-names. Don't make it and the entire team would be penalized on your behalf—if you were still on the team. No one was spared.

Mike Connelly knew it was coming. As a center, he had never run a mile in his life. So he practiced and prepared for what he feared could be a career killer. Instead, it became one of the shortest runs of the rest of his life.

"After I did it the first year, I thought, I feel pretty good being in this good condition," says Connelly of his indoctrination. "So, I just kept running."

Now in his mid 60's, Connelly still hasn't stopped. "When I retired, I read an article someplace with some statistics about retired NFL players, and at that time it said the average ex-NFL life expectancy was 56 years. I thought, 'Wait a minute, I'm 34. I just retired, and that's not too far down the road.' So, I kept running." Connelly counts more than 30 marathons in his 30 years since retiring from football.

Appreciating the long run is also a big part of Connelly's career calling. As a stockbroker just building his portfolio when the stock market hit the down years of the early 1970s, Connelly advised his clients to buy on the theory of a marathon, not a sprint. Few of his former teammates stayed in the race.

"Don Meredith and I had the thought that maybe we could form a mutual fund and go around to all the sporting people to invest their earnings," remembers Connelly of a plan that never panned out. "We quickly concluded that the guy coming out of football thinks that because it's been easy for him, even though he may not have made a lot of money, they have these ideas that you put a couple bucks in and you make a ton of money. They have no patience. We were in business for about a year."

Connelly has many more success stories of those who ran alongside. "In 1979, I had a client buy 500 shares of WalMart. He said, 'Just buy it and keep it, I'm not selling it.' He paid 30 bucks a share for it, so that's what, 15,000 bucks? Want to guess what that became worth? Over 18 million dollars."

The Cowboys' first center may not have become their first millionaire, but he's on the list. "I'm shocked looking at my net worth," admits Connelly. "I never dreamed I could make that, but it compounds. It goes pretty slow at first and all of a sudden, it just grows like a big old landslide coming down the hill, and all of a sudden it gets bigger and bigger and bigger. I'm just glad I stuck with it."

Just as he was years before, coming down that final hill during the first Landry Mile.

On the Board

He was an undrafted free agent, playing safety for the 1962 Cowboys as a rookie. Philadelphia Eagles quarterback King Hill obviously didn't think much of Mike Gaechter's ability. Throwing to Tommy McDonald in the end zone, King laid the ball perfectly in the arms of—Gaechter! One hundred yards the other way, and the Cowboys rookie was on the board. "Today they measure goal line to goal line, so that record will never be broken," says a proud Gaechter. "Believe me, all records are meant to be broken, and they will be eventually."

That moment in the Cotton Bowl may have been Gaechter's first opportunity to put points on the board, but it would not be his last, nor would it be his most lucrative.

An Achilles tendon injury kept Gaechter off the field during the final year of his contract and forced him to begin looking for his future away from football. He again found a way to put numbers on the board. "I got into the billboard business," explains Gaechter. "It was just kind of like dumb luck that I got into it, I guess."

Like the interception that began his NFL career, Gaechter turned luck into luxury. Developing billboards in Dallas and San Antonio attracted the attention of his competitors, and Gaechter began selling what he had built.

The strategy worked well enough to take his game plan to Amarillo, Texas, and to Albuquerque, New Mexico. Once established in those markets, Gaechter sold again. "I kind of retired for a while."

But the bug to stay busy bit Gaechter again a few years later. It was something he picked off from his football days with the Cowboys. "Landry's defenses and philosophies didn't come natural to me; I had to really work at it," says Gaechter. The work ethic drove him back to the billboard business, and once again Gaechter had a touchdown drop in his hands. Buying the Waco, Texas, region at a time when the billboard market was down, Gaechter built it back up over the next few years. "We didn't have it that long, but while we did, it cash flowed a half a million a year at least," boasts Gaechter. "We paid like $200,000 for Waco and we sold it for 6½ million, maybe a little more."

Now Gaechter can retire more comfortably with another record return in his grasp.

Home on the Range

Most afternoons he rides and ropes in the arena at his Argyle, Texas, home, practicing for upcoming rodeos. Then it's on to his porch, where he's likely to whittle the evening away. Walt Garrison was a cowboy long before he was a Cowboy.

"I started rodeoing when I was in high school," says the proud Texan, who added to his image while sharing time with the rodeo and football teams as an Oklahoma State Cowboy. He also gives rodeoing credit for his success in life after football. "That's probably what helped me get my job with U.S. Tobacco. I started out doing commercials for them when I was still playing football with the (Dallas) Cowboys. NFL Films did a documentary on my rodeoing, and in that I was dipping snuff. The fact that I rodeoed and played football probably had the biggest effect on them wanting me to come to work for them when I retired."

For the next 23 years, Garrison was a spokesman for the U.S. Tobacco Company. He became as well known for delivering the line in his commercial, "Just put a pinch between your cheek and gum for that full tobacco pleasure," as he did for delivering a punch to an offense that helped the Cowboys give Dallas its first Super Bowl pleasure.

But Garrison also felt the pinch along with the rest of the tobacco industry as a result of the class-action lawsuit settlements of the 1990s. "We had to pay our part, which wasn't as big as the cigarette industry," Garrison explains, while showing some displeasure at the process itself. "I've used tobacco all my life, so it's hard for me to see how people that used tobacco and have used it 40 or 50 years with everybody telling you it's bad for you could then turn around and sue the people they bought it from."

The tobacco industry has actually been very good to Garrison. Sponsorships of rodeo events kept him close to the sport of real cowboys and, although he recently left that line of work, he may never let go of the rodeo reins. Well into his 50's, Garrison and his wife, Debbie, continue to ride and rope around the country. "She makes more money than I do. She's a little better," says an always humble Garrison. "But, I'm still team roping. As it implies, it's a two-man or two-person sport. One ropes the horns, and the other one comes in and ropes the back legs. The fastest time wins."

Speed was never a big part of Garrison's game at fullback with the Cowboys. In fact, the pace he set at training camp in Thousand Oaks, California, is still a big part of his lifestyle today. "I couldn't sleep during the day during two-a-days," remembers Garrison of his second camp with the Cowboys. "I'd just hang out and walk the halls and stuff. My dad was a whittler, so I just went and bought a knife and a piece of wood and started whittling. I'm still doing it." And doing it so well, the Imperial Charade Knife Company hired Garrison to represent them at gun and knife shows with live whittling demonstrations. "Horses, people, chains, balls, and boxes. Whatever," adds Garrison.

But don't go looking for the price tags on any of Garrison's creations. They are not for sale. "I don't sell anything. I've got 30 years of whittling out here," Garrison says of his collection. "If I'd start selling it, I'd be working for someone else. I give 'em to friends. They gotta be real close friends 'cause it takes a long time to whittle most of this stuff."

Friends like Meredith and Reeves are some of the fortunate few. "As a matter of fact both of them do" have an item whittled by Garrison. It has become almost as rare a find as a true cowboy in the fast-paced, high-tech world of the new millennium.

Walt Garrison is that rare find. He may have retired as a Cowboy, but he'll never be a former cowboy.

Lovin' the Lonely Life

He was the prototypical cornerback of the 1960s. A five-time Pro Bowler, four times an All Pro. Cornell Green loved being out on the island. Alone. "If you're not a loner type of person, you soon learn to be one," admits Green of the characteristic that helped him perfect man-to-man coverage.

Apparently, he learned to develop that trait so well, it led Green to another lonely profession—as an NFL scout.

"Ninety percent of the time you're alone," explains Green while searching for a story to tell of his travels throughout the nine-state region he covers for the Denver Broncos. "If a story happens, you have to make your own story, because nothing funny ever happens. You travel alone. You go in there, you watch tapes alone, you talk to coaches, then you're alone. You go out on the field when the players are practicing and the coaches are coaching, and you walk around there by yourself. Then you say bye, and you go on your way to the next town. You're out on the corner looking in. You're alone."

Most try to avoid a lonely life. Cornell Green obviously relishes it. "When I was a player, I was also a scout for the Cowboys. I did them both at the same time," Green points out. "I was the only person that did that. In the off-season I would go out and scout for the Cowboys. During the season I would go and put on a uniform."

Out on the corner, looking in. A view that Green says has not changed very much over the quarter century that he has been studying it. "It's still about the same. It's just a lot more technical now than it was when I first started with the Cowboys. Everybody is looking for an edge," adds Green. "There's more psychological testing and all that type of stuff. Everybody's got a different test that they give kids to see if they can play football. But, it still is—can the kid play or not—that's what it comes down to."

It is probably a good thing Green did not have to experience the exams firsthand when he was knocking on the NFL's door. He was a basketball player. The first time he ever had to make a tackle was his first exhibition game against Green Bay. And those tests may not have noticed Green's nose for the ball. He still owns the Cowboys career record for blocked kicks.

On the other hand, according to the All Pro player turned Super Bowl scout, there isn't much that anybody misses, test or no test. "It's not like what people think. I'm not the only one that scouts a player. Everybody scouts them. It's like with John Elway, everybody seen John Elway. It's not that one guy just saw him and said John Elway can play. It's a consensus of opinion. It's not really one guy scouting and finding a player nobody else seen. That don't happen. That only happens in the movies."

If anyone decides to make a movie about the Green-er pastures of Cornell's career, they will have to be prepared to travel—to Louisiana, Mississippi, Arkansas, Texas, Oklahoma, New Mexico, Arizona, California, and Nevada. And they better be prepared for plenty of stops along the way.

Green has seen his share of big-name players along the way. In fact, lately, some of those names have been repeating themselves. "Some kids, at this age, scouted some of the kids' dads and now I'm scouting their sons."

If the sons are as successful as the fathers, Green will be adding more than airline miles to his credit. Counting his playing days in Dallas and his scouting career with the Cowboys and Broncos, Green has nine Super Bowl appearances. He owns four Super Bowl rings.

Maybe it's not so bad being out on the corner looking in. Even if you are alone.

Slowing Down

He was the fastest man in the world, an Olympic gold medalist. He changed the way football was played in the NFL with his blazing speed. It has taken Bob Hayes almost thirty years, but he's finally slowing down.

"My mind is so tired," said Hayes, as he talked about the hurdles he has cleared since retiring as one of the most gifted athletes to ever don the Cowboys star. "I still do a lot of talking to kids and to people. I don't talk basically about my life. I talk to them about staying out of trouble, get an education, respect your parents, your teachers, your counselors, and stay away from bad company and undesirables. They can't help you."

Actually, the examples and the words Hayes uses in his conversation are all about his life. His experiences include trouble—trouble that put him in jail, cost him one career, and may be holding Hayes back from the one honor that's even more elusive than he was to NFL defenses. "I'm very disappointed in the Hall of Fame," says Hayes, with a crackle in his voice. "The ones they select, they all deserve it. But how many of them revolutionized a part of the game? As Tom Landry and Don Shula said, 'Bob Hayes changed the game of football.' Sam Huff, he said, 'Man, we had to change the whole scheme of defense because of Hayes.' Everyone says that. I had troubles 30 years ago. That's not it. I don't know what it is."

The Cowboys who played with or after Hayes agree. But finally, "Bullet Bob" can at least boast about the honor that the Cowboys franchise has bestowed upon only ten others: the team's Ring of Honor. "I'm lost for words," said Hayes—now a frail, 58-year-old football legend—during the announcement news conference, which came just two months after Hayes's battle with prostate cancer and liver and heart ailments nearly ended his race short of its goal. "I've wanted this for a long time and it's just a miracle for me. This is such a high honor for me."

It wasn't the first time since turning 50 that Hayes has determined to reach out and snare an honor that eluded him no matter how fast he ran. Education has also been a part of his stretch run. "I've gone back to Florida A&M and gotten my degree," Hayes says of the special education degree he earned at the age of 51. "I just had to finish it because when I go to speak to these kids, I tell them if you start something, if you're really serious, you've got to finish."

And Hayes has lived his lesson at home. The respect for parents he preaches is practiced daily since his return to his hometown of Jacksonville, Florida, where Hayes lives with and has spent the past several years taking care of his mother. "She's in her 80s. I'm the youngest and she wanted me around right now, so I had to come back and spend some time," says Hayes. "After I got drafted by the Cowboys, I stayed out there for 36 years. I've come back to spend time with my family and get to know my nieces and nephews."

Life after football has been more of a marathon than a sprint for Hayes. In and out of business with several companies, including some owned by former teammates, he retired after selling part ownership of a computer business. "It was called Junk Mail. We called on financial institutions to sell insurance, real estate, savings and loans," says Hayes. "It wasn't an Internet company. There wasn't no Internet then."

More recently, along with his own ailments, Hayes has had to endure the passing of his college football and track coaches as well as Tom Landry. He served as pallbearer for all three. "I had the greatest coaches in the world," an emotional Hayes remembers.

And they had the greatest athlete in the world.

The Perfect Fit

He may not be a native Texan, but Chuck Howley certainly sounds like one. "You get a little Texas stuff on your feet, I guess you have to hang around," says the proud linebacker from West Virginia. "We came here in 1961. I didn't really dream this would be our home, but we dearly love it here."

The feeling is mutual. It's part of the humble Howley heritage that fits a man who is still the only Super Bowl MVP selected from the losing team. "I get a lot of fan mail as a result of that," Howley admits. It may have been the Super Bowl V performance against the Baltimore Colts. It could have been the six Pro Bowl appearances, six All Pro selections, or six interceptions in the 1968 season. Or it might be his Ring of Honor inclusion that keeps Howley a hot property. "I had a card here last year from a boy over in China. It's kinda humbling when somebody that far away can still want your autograph. He was just asking on a little 3x5 card for my autograph, and I sent him one of my cards instead. He wrote me back and said I was the hit of the neighborhood."

Howley has always been a hit, especially in business. Long before his retirement from football, Howley began his next career with Chuck Howley Uniform Rental. "Quite a few players played and then looked for things after retirement. I took it as it came," explains Howley of his foresight in preparing for life after football. "The opportunity arose, and so when I wasn't practicing or playing football, I was there helping run this particular uniform company." And ran it successfully for 30 years, as uniformly as he carried out his consistent play as a Cowboy. "I had to carry what I felt was the same enthusiasm for my football playing days into my businesses to take care of the customer the way I felt the customer should be taken care of. I get a big kick out of pleasing customers. I believe that they can find that product someplace else. As long as I take care of them they're gonna take care of me, I guess."

Now, Howley is taking care of the direct sales side of the business. "Polo shirts, T-shirts, silk screening, public safety, fire and police uniforms, everything but firearms."

He's also taking his taste for Texas a step further. "I do a little ranching. We raise quite a few cows and horses. We run about 5,000 acres up there with about eight to nine hundred mother cows and about 100 horses," says Howley. "It's been one of those things. That's my golf game. I go there on weekends and we work cattle or we work horses. That's kinda where I get my chance to let off steam or relax a bit."

Maybe Howley is a real Texas cowboy after all. "Well, not really," he says. "The guys are still trying to get me to rope. It's a slow process."

Cross Examined

Tom Landry talked to me about, at the end of my career with the Cowboys, being kind of a player/coach. I thought about it, and I said, 'Tom, I'm an old quarterback and a young lawyer, so I'm going to stick with the law business.'"

He was, and always will be, the first starting quarterback in Cowboys history. Eddie LeBaron may also have been the first to cross his legendary coach and get away with it, because of a compelling case. "I guess the most unique play I was involved in and I think about it occasionally," admits LeBaron, four decades after the fact, "was when I threw the shortest touchdown pass in league history. It was against the Redskins. We got down to about the 2-inch line. Tom had sent in a running play. The Redskins got into an 11-man line, so I just called an audible and dropped it over the line to an end for a touchdown, a 2-inch pass for a touchdown. When I came out, he was a little concerned. He said, 'Why did you call a dumb play like that?' I said, 'It worked!'"

Concise. Accurate. They are characteristics that describe a confident quarterback and crafty counsel. LeBaron was both. From the time he used a job with a Dallas law firm as a condition to come out of retirement to join the expansion Cowboys in 1960, to his retirement from the legal profession almost 40 years later. In between he used the skills he learned in football to make the right call in the courtroom. "Quarterbacks, if they're good ones, get to be good decision makers," says LeBaron. "Decision makers, the good decision makers, are the ones that succeed in business. What it comes down to, in the heat of the battle, you have to make good decisions and if you do then you're gonna overcome obstacles and you're gonna go ahead."

Of course, LeBaron also learned that some of those decisions, even the good ones, did not always result in the right verdict. "We were playing the Pittsburgh Steelers in Dallas and were on our own 1-yard line. I threw a 99-yard touchdown pass, which would have tied for the longest pass in league history," recalls LeBaron. "They called the play back and called us for holding in the end zone, and they gave the Steelers two points. So, it was a 9-point turnaround. I think that's the only time in the history of the game that's been called. We lost by 2 points."

Maybe that is why LeBaron never felt sacked by a legal loss. "There's always another play, so you can't worry about the last play. You might get some learning out of it, and you might do it differently. The next play is the only one that counts. It's very true in business. You're always going to have setbacks, and you can't let that be an earth-shattering experience. You just learn from it and go on. There's always another third and 7."

Sometimes it is an unexpected play that helps you get the first down, as it was for LeBaron as managing partner for a firm in Las Vegas during the years of 1969 and 1970. One of his clients was eccentric billionaire Howard Hughes. "I never saw him," remembers the lawyer about his client. "We'd get orders from either his business manager or sometimes from the suite that he was in, some of the people that were up there. Basically we knew he was ever present."

Another pass at football in the front office of the Atlanta Falcons, as general manager, developing the family's Woodbridge vineyard, and seats on several boards including the Northern California Golf Association and a major oil company, were about the only plays that scrambled LeBaron out of the pocket of a law firm's protection. Retirement finally allowed him a chance to try a different role, which he currently enjoys, as a partner in a high-tech hedge fund and developer of residential housing.

Through it all, LeBaron has drawn on the days in Dallas, where he learned the one play that earned his team the 2-inch touchdown was the exception rather than the norm. It rarely paid off to cross Coach Landry. Instead, LeBaron has consistently run the plays that work. "Tom Landry was a great teacher and a great coach. I quickly found out that management and people are the best part of any business arrangement. You get good people and train them properly, and things are usually pretty successful."

It may not have helped Eddie LeBaron win many games as Cowboys quarterback. It has helped him win plenty of decisions since. Case closed.

Mr. Kodak Cowboy

He stepped onto the porch outside his childhood country home. The sight took his breath away. "In the spring when the wheat came out and the wind would blow, it would wave and look so smooth and silky and pretty."

During a family trip to California as a child, he was consumed by the colossal beauty before him. "When I first went to the ocean, watching the waves when I was nine or ten, I watched how they would come in and turn up and become real white and pretty and how the foam would come up to the sand and all that."

Bob Lilly was experiencing his first Kodak moments. "I always saw those things, I just never had a way to capture it," he adds.

Lilly's playing football provided the NFL plenty of Lilly moments that were captured by others. His 14 seasons with the Cowboys included a team record 11 Pro Bowl selections. He still owns a club record with three fumble recoveries for touchdowns. But the most replayed highlight of Lilly's career, looking like a Patriot missile bearing down on its target during the Super Bowl VI win over Miami, apparently is not the most memorable moment. "Every time I see Bob Griese (Miami Dolphins quarterback), he talks about me chasing him down, and I say, 'Nobody ever remembers that about me.' They remember the year before when I tossed my helmet 58 yards."

Yet Lilly has football to thank for the chance to create his own images for the world to see and remember. "I had never picked a camera up until my senior year in college. I made several All America teams, and one of them was Kodak's All America Team. That's when I got my first personal camera," begins the Cowboys first-ever collegiate draft choice of the perk provided each player picked for the camera company's honor. "Plus, they gave us each about 200 rolls of film that was prepaid, so I'd just shoot the film and send it in."

It was the beginning of what would become Lilly's passion and eventually his post-Cowboys career. "I had a darkroom my second year, and I've had one ever since. Now I've pretty well gotten out of the darkroom business and digitize all my films."

In between, "Mr. Cowboy," as he became known over the years, snapped several behind-the-scenes photographs that caught the Cowboy even he called Mr. by surprise. "In the meeting rooms I took my Leica (camera) in there, it was so quiet. I shot a few pictures when it was real dark. I had some fast film, and I would shoot some pictures while he (Tom Landry) was up there lecturing. I knew the first time I could get by with it, but he never did hear it," admits Lilly of a series of pictures that became public in his book *Bob Lilly Reflections*. "I really wasn't doing it for any mischievous reason. I was just trying to see if I could make a picture like that, and I did. They weren't great pictures, but they were pictures that showed him (Landry) in a little different light, I think, which was kind of neat."

The most treasured image an NFL player can see of himself is the bronze bust that resides in the Pro Football Hall of Fame. Lilly was the first of the Cowboys to become part of the Canton shrine's landscape, as well as the one at Texas Stadium that houses the team's Ring of Honor.

Other landscapes became award winners through Lilly's eye. "As far as wildflowers, I don't think you can beat Texas when you get a good year. That's one of my favorite subjects. Another is windmills. I don't have a lot of good windmills, but I love 'em," shares the man who admires Ansel Adams above all landscape photographers that have come before him. It was through his books and images that Lilly learned much of what it takes to turn what he sees into something he shares. "In landscape photography you not only have to have the lighting and the subject but you've gotta have the foreground, the background, something alive in it and you've gotta have a sky without contrails. Hopefully it'll have puffy clouds in it," explains Lilly, who at one time owned his own gallery to display his work.

Often the making of a masterpiece is more difficult than it looks. "Generally if a person gets ten good images a year you've had a great year. We judge everything by our peers, and we talk about No. 10s. We're to the point now where we don't even get our camera out if it's not an 8-plus," laments Lilly. Mother Nature seldom seems to leave the landscape alone long enough to capture her creations. "The wind is a big factor. We shoot with view cameras, and the wind blows your bellows, which wiggles your camera. You set up and sometimes everything's right but the wind's blowing your camera, so you wait and wait and wait and then, by the time the wind dies down, the conditions are gone. It takes a lot of skill to be an artist that paints, an awful lot to be a good artist. But at least they can get rid of those darn telephone lines and the contrails in the sky, and they can put in a sunset or something."

Actually, photographers can manipulate more today than ever before by using a computer canvas. Lilly continues to print some of his subjects the old-fashioned way. "You manipulate everything anyway as far as burn in, you dodge, and you print them." But he has also joined the new generation of digital photography. "A lot of times you take the picture you think is wonderful, you get home and it doesn't quite live up to what you thought it would. Digitally you can shoot as many as you want. If you fill up your disk, you can just erase a lot of it, just like using a computer," Lilly tells of the new technology. "It surprises a lot of people that I've learned to run a computer. They don't think of a defensive tackle as being a computer nerd, but I have thoroughly enjoyed it."

So are the fans of his football and photography. Currently his creations can be seen at his new gallery on the Internet website, BobLilly.com.

Ironically the action Lilly longed to capture when his playing days were over was the playing days of others. "I was interested in sports photography whenever I was playing ball. I went out a couple of times with the *Dallas Morning News* and took pictures. One time George Andrie and I were on the sideline and we took pictures at the Texas–OU game, and I got my picture double-page spread. I tried it after I retired from the Cowboys and everyone was shouting for me to come sign an autograph. I could never get away from that, so I gave it up."

Fortunately Bob Lilly never gave up on the images he saw as a child. "Like someone said, after 10,000 prints, you finally learn how to take a picture."

Custom Cowboy

He was a defensive lineman when the Cowboys needed an offensive lineman. So he played tackle until they needed a bigger guard. Tony Liscio fit whatever role was necessary to help Dallas turn the corner from losing seasons to the first above .500, all the way to the first Super Bowl title.

Three decades later, Liscio still customizes his craft. "My fixtures are all custom," says Liscio, an account manager for a company that supplies refrigeration fixtures and compressor racks for grocery store chains like Safeway, Tom Thumb, and Randall's. "It's nothing you take off a shelf, so you have to make sure you're putting everything together right. You're the only guy between the factory and the customer to get it all put together."

Liscio learned the flexibility and discipline necessary to be that guy when he arrived in Dallas just before the 1963 season and was immediately told he wasn't the guy he thought he was when he left Green Bay. "I was a defensive end up there. They never tried me on offense," explains Liscio. "The Cowboys had me scouted as an offensive lineman. They traded for me or bought me somehow right at the end of the exhibition season." And Liscio immediately started at offensive tackle. A serious knee injury with complications kept him out of football for two seasons. When he came back in 1966, Tom Landry had another plan for the custom Cowboy. "I thought I'd be like a backup tackle at my natural position," admits Liscio about his return. "Landry thought we needed bigger linemen and we needed more strength up the middle. I was a big guy, so he moved me into first-team guard."

Liscio developed into a solid player at whatever position he was asked to play. "My main thing was consistency. I didn't go for the big blocks that people could notice. Many times I was the highest graded blocker when I was playing on the team. I didn't have spectacular blocks, but I made the blocks to their satisfaction."

It is no wonder Liscio stepped out of real estate when the market "hit a hell of a recession" just four years after his retirement from football, into a business in which he had no prior experience or knowledge, and made it work. "It's very demanding, takes a lot of time and effort," he adds, "but it's just a job."

One that is custom fit for Tony Liscio.

Building Momentum

I t takes time and perseverance. It takes extra effort. It takes a strong foundation with a solid center. Dave Manders knows. He was and is that center.

"The people that came into the scene in 1961, '62, '63, and '64 had an opportunity to suffer with some losing seasons and then a 7–7 record in 1965 and then to go on and be winners. The ones that were fortunate enough to stick it out eventually got to that Super Bowl in '71," explains Manders of the evolution that took place in the Cowboys first decade.

It also became an example of what to expect in his after-football days. "The whole theme there, and I think it carried over in everybody's life, is that you may work and toil for a good many years before you start to realize the fruits of your effort. I always feel whenever we start out in business it may not be successful right from the start but if we work hard enough we can turn it around and enjoy some real fruitful years."

The fruitful times for Manders were sweetest during the Super Bowl VI win over Miami, "the best thing that ever happened," but there were plenty of sour moments along the way. "The fumble that I recovered against Baltimore in Super Bowl V that they didn't give to me and they gave to Billy Ray Smith instead," recalls Manders of a moment that keeps coming to mind. "Craig Morton and I tried to fight with Jack Petty (NFL official) and convince him, and he said, 'One more word from either one of you and you're out of the game.'"

Manders chose to leave the game on his terms a few years later. Again, the fruits took some time to grow. Work in the radio broadcast business that was a good part-time fit during his playing days became a full-time misfit.

There would be no snap decision on a solution. Eventually, Manders placed himself at the center of his own success, starting a commercial landscape company in 1977. "We didn't know if it was going to work. We might have to sell pencils or something," says Manders of his generic company name, Dave Manders, Inc.

It worked. Manders' company has handled landscape contracts for major corporations including EDS and Texas Instruments. They are his new Super Bowl efforts. "When you meet the president or CEO of Texas Instruments, for example, you just have to look at that person with a lot of admiration," describes Manders of his current league of clients. "When you work with the first-class companies that have high safety standards, quality standards, it's really a benefit to you as a contractor because your people pick up all these good traits as well."

Everything starts with the center, in football and in business. Dave Manders has always been comfortable in that role.

Twice as Good to Be First

In 1957, I was on the Packers team that played in the first game at Lambeau Field," says one of the expansion picks who experienced an equally memorable first, just three years later—starting at running back for the inaugural Dallas Cowboys. "Nobody can take that away from you. A lot of guys went on and made the Hall of Fame, but there were only 36 of us that played in that first game."

Being in the right place at the right time may have been Don McIllhenney's calling. "Some people think I've lived the charmed life," admits the 38-year Dallas resident who worked in real estate for the first decade after retiring from the NFL, but used a downturn in the early 1970s to join the upswing in another traditional Texas gold rush—oil.

"I did the standard deal, slept in the car, slept on the floor where you could when there was a boom going on and made some wells and had some excitement and had some disappointments," says McIllhenney of the business that has often been glorified by Hollywood. But he played football at a time when no-cut contracts were unheard of; exhibition games were auditions for everyone; grass and mud, blood and sweat, were the norm rather than the exception; and his most memorable game in a Cowboys uniform, in his favorite stadium, Chicago's Wrigley Field, included a touchdown that ended with McIllhenney throwing up in the end zone against the famous ivy wall. So many of the stories of how he delivered on deals, discovered and drilled both boom and bust, have a script-writing ring to them.

"My partner and I met some people. His deal was meet 'em in the coffee shop, and that's what we sort of did," tells McIllhenney of one such story. "We met some fine old gentleman that owned some acreage. One time we leased about 60,000 acres from these two old guys that just sort of liked us. I bummed a typewriter from somebody and I typed up an option for a 60,000-acre lease and we came back here to Dallas and turned it to some people and made more money than we'd ever made in our lives. It was just a deal."

Sometimes the deals were someone else's. Kind of like an NFL team designing a play or two that work. McIllhenney took what he had learned from Lombardi and Landry, figuring you either game plan against them or figure out what made them successful and do it even better. "Everybody keeps pretty much close to their chest what's going on when there is a good lease play," explains McIllhenney of how that concept worked on some wells in south Texas. "You gotta really kind of scour around and talk to people in the coffee shops and where they sell and lease equipment. You gotta learn all you can from who you can. We had heard some wells were producing real well, and we wanted to know where they were."

But McIllhenney was not getting anywhere from the scouting reports on this particular play. So he and his partner decided to take a look for themselves. "We went out about midnight, because it's off-limits going to someone else's well. It was a full moon, and we crawled up to their wells, went up to their tank battery, up on the walkway. We opened up the top of the tanks and, when oil just comes into a tank it makes a tremendous sound, just a thump and a roar," recalls McIllhenney as he realized the rumors of boom were true. "Standing on top of a tank battery like that in a clandestine maneuver as we were and listening to the roar of that oil going into a tank and then spilling off into another tank and imagining that could be yours or the next one might be yours, that's sort of fun and exciting."

As it turned out, the next one was McIllhenney's. And it was big—the closest thing to a good old-fashioned oil field blowout that his company had ever seen. "It blew all the tools out of the hole. My partner called to say that all hell had broken loose. My voice broke, I was so excited," said McIllhenney of the 1981 strike, his voice beginning to pick up steam again. "Oil was 30 to 40 dollars a barrel at the time because of the windfall profits, and we were making 2,000 barrels a day. I kept the run ticket from that. It's how much oil you sell and, I mean, it was several pages long."

Now retired, McIllhenney still will not admit the late-night covert operation gained his company a competitive advantage. "I can't say that big lease we took was a result of that or not. It was in the immediate area," hedges McIllhenney. "It probably led us to drilling another well or two."

Just like in football, not every oil play pays off. McIllhenney had his share of failures, including a spill he called "catastrophic"—one that made him give up drilling. But overall, Don McIllhenney would not trade his business days any more than he would want to go back on the trade that took him from Green Bay to Dallas for that first season with the Cowboys.

"I never worked for anybody my entire life. I never made a paycheck. I always worked on deals," McIllhenney summarizes as only he can. "I one time had somebody ask me, 'Have you ever done anything courageous? I sort of envy people that have done things courageous, guys who fought for their country and things like that.' I said, 'No, and I regret that I haven't.' He says, 'Well, what have you done in your business career?' and I told him, and he says, 'That is a degree of courage to have never drawn a paycheck and raised four children.'"

There are not many that can make a better claim. Even if they were first.

Just Dandy, Thank You

Keep up with those old Cowboys, that's a hard thing to do."
The voice on the answering machine sounded just like it did almost 20 years earlier while being broadcast through a television in the living room every Monday night. But the words being expressed did not carry the sarcastic tone usually associated with the Texas drawl. In fact, considering the source on the other end of the line, the message was pristinely accurate.

"I know it sounds silly, but I really haven't changed my idea or thoughts about doing this. I'm still to the point where I think I'd rather not."

It was Don Meredith. Calling from his home in Santa Fe, New Mexico, where he and his wife, Susan, have spent the last two decades living a very private life. "Don is sort of a recluse," describe some of the former teammates who have remained a part of Meredith's inner circle of friends.

He is not pitching the "dandiest" tasting iced tea anymore. He is not singing "turn out the lights, the party's over" to signal what he considered the end of a Monday Night Football game. He rarely participates in anything considered public. Even those who know him do not know for sure what makes up Meredith's day.

"He's doing the same thing he's been doing the last 20 years. Nothing," says former center Dave Manders with a hint of sarcasm. "He's deep in thought most of the time, or deep in something. He's a great guy. He really is."

"I know he's playing golf," was the common response shared by fellow Ring of Honor member Bob Lilly. "He's got a lot of injuries. The last time I talked to him, he had just played golf with President Ford. He said, 'You know, he's in better shape than I am. I had to wear a $2,000 brace on my foot so I could play. He (Ford) doesn't have any problems like that.' He used to play a lot of tennis and had to quit because of a physical problem."

The mention of Meredith still stirs a variety of responses to his low-key lifestyle. "He's doing what he wants to do. He and Susan do a lot of traveling worldwide. He's being around the people he wants to be around and when he wants to do it," says one former teammate. "I think a lot of people keep in contact with Don, whether Don keeps in contact with them I don't know. I quit calling Don basically because I get a recording and his wife usually ends up calling me back," adds another.

"He doesn't ever hardly leave New Mexico, so you have to go see Meredith. He don't come visit you," remarks Walt Garrison. "I don't blame him. Like he explained to me one time, he said, 'You know, I've been in football since I was in the seventh grade.' And after, what he played 8 or 9 years with the Cowboys, then 15 years of 'Monday Night Football.' I think he just tired of it. He's tired of the limelight. He was pitching horseshoes when I was out there."

"We've been down to Santa Fe to visit him," confirms the man who handed Meredith the starting quarterback duties in Dallas, Eddie LeBaron. "He's still a neat guy. He's one of my real favorite friends. He's still very outgoing."

In fact, according to a *Sports Illustrated* article in the fall of 2000, Meredith considers his quiet life in the mountains of New Mexico "normal." The interview with writer Richard Hoffer was only the second Meredith could remember granting in the past decade. He spends a few months each year in Palm Springs and regularly travels to New York and Europe.

Meredith even made a new millennium stop at his alma mater in Dallas. "You know why they're winning, don't you?" joked the former SMU Mustangs quarterback while watching a win over Kansas in the debut of the university's new stadium. "Because I'm here. It's been 20 years since I was here before."

It has been more than 30 years since "Dandy Don" walked away from Dallas just as the Cowboys were on the verge of becoming America's Team. Three Pro Bowl appearances and two championship games, including the infamous Ice Bowl against the Green Bay Packers in 1967, helped earn Meredith one of the first inductions into the Cowboys Ring of Honor.

A series of high-profile positions for the next several years, including his 15 seasons as a part of the original "Monday Night Football" broadcast crew, helped build his bankroll. How and what Meredith has made of his earnings since stepping into the private persona is part of what he keeps to himself. "I just don't feel comfortable talking about myself," mentioned Meredith as the stadium stories turned to questions about the former quarterback.

Answers from his closest connections, former teammates, and current friends, also come with a hint of hesitation. "I think he was the spokesperson, internally anyway, for RJR Nabisco," says one member of Meredith's inner circle. "I think there was a leveraged buyout a few years ago. That's when he kind of severed his business deals. I think he still buys real estate. I'm sure he has a stock portfolio and various things. Don's done very well." There was a brief pause before this particular conversation continued with a brief chuckle. "I don't know what he really does."

"The lifetime contract with Nabisco," adds another in an attempt to share the secret of his teammate's treasures. "And he also has one with Lipton and Susan's management of their finances. His wife, her management of him, she's the best thing that ever happened to Don."

"Meredith's a pretty good businessman. I think he invested in some real estate," continues another former Cowboy.

The answering machine reaches the end of the message. The voice is clear and concise. This time there is no sarcasm, no clever cliché. There will be no formal interview, no revealing the real story of his lifestyle since leaving the public eye.

"I'm sorry I feel that, don't necessarily apologize for that but, anyway, that's what I was calling to tell you."

Don Meredith has politely made his point. He is just dandy in his own private world, thank you.

Timing Is Everything

It seemed like the right place at the right time. Roger Staubach had been drafted in the tenth round the year before but would not be available until the end of his tour of duty with the navy. Don Meredith was probably about to pass his prime. For the first time in franchise history, the Cowboys used their first pick on a quarterback. As it turned out, the timing could not have been worse for Craig Morton.

"It was always a battle there," admits the sixth overall pick in the 1965 NFL draft. "It was either a battle with Meredith or Jerry Rhome or with Roger. My highlight was just trying to make sure I kept playing."

Morton has been battling bad timing ever since. Shuffling plays with Roger Staubach was an experiment that eventually earned Morton more bench time than playing time while Staubach's star rose as the starter. Morton saw two Super Bowls from the sidelines and shuffled off with his ring for a shot at another as a starter in Denver. But when Morton brought the Broncos "Orange Crush" to the brink of a championship six years later, his timing was way off. The Cowboys were there to crush his hopes with four interceptions, and Staubach had another star-studded Super Bowl ring.

"People always said, 'Well, you guys don't like each other,' but that was never the case. I competed against him," maintains Morton, who annually attends golf tournaments hosted or sponsored by Staubach. "Roger and I have remained really close friends through all these years, and he's helped me greatly throughout the years. He's as great a guy as he is a football player."

The end of Morton's playing days was another example of his tenuous timing—the 1982 strike year. "I've always been against strikes anyway. After training camp we were off like eight weeks, and my knees wouldn't let me come back again," admits Morton. "I wasn't really ready to quit because I thought my arm was still good and I was just starting to learn the game after 18 years. When you think you're smart enough to keep playing you have to retire."

Fortunately the man who still shares the Cowboys single-game record of five touchdown passes was smart enough to take what he'd learned into his post-playing professions. Especially about battling bad timing. He was head coach of the Denver Gold in a league (USFL) that folded. After a year as quarterback coach under former teammate Dan Reeves with the Broncos, Morton moved on to Oregon—wrong place, wrong time—both places, both times. "When I left Denver I'd invested lots in the real estate market, and then all of a sudden it just turns and then you have to start over again. I moved up to Oregon to take over kind of a fledgling spring league that just a week before we started playing it just never got to the point where we had enough money."

Five years followed working with Hoop Heaven building basketball centers in Oregon—wrong place, right time. "I enjoyed that, but I had to get out of there. It was just too tough to be in a rainy climate year-round."

With a new climate and a new business, Morton may have finally found the right place at the right time. He is currently the president of an energy company in Phoenix, Arizona, on the cutting edge of deregulation. "It's new to everybody, and you just need some really good experts involved. Like any team, you just have to get the best, and I think we have," adds Morton. "I think we have a pretty good niche market now, and we have something that has been proven to happen in other industries, and there's no reason why this one can't be equally as successful. It is a bigger industry, and people are hurting for power. It's going to continue because the big power companies haven't built enough of the generation stations the last number of years, and it's going to take a while to catch up again."

Morton ought to know. Since that first battle in a Cowboys uniform, he's spent a lifetime catching up to a career that could provide the perfect fit.

"I think the worst things that have happened in my life have been bad timing."

Making Amends

I cried. Like a baby, I cried. I walked up to him, and I just started crying."

It was a moment John Niland had hoped would happen at some point in his post–football life. He just never expected it to affect him the way it did. "Don Meredith came to town a while back for a reunion. He looked at me, I looked at him, and it was the first time I'd seen him since he retired. I wasn't panicky or anything, but I was crying when I walked up to him. I had tears in my eyes, and I apologized to him because I always remembered the block that I missed against Joe Krueger of the Washington Redskins. I was a second-year man. Joe came in and killed Meredith, put him out of the game on a stretcher, and he retired the next year, Meredith did. I always felt guilty about that. I just really felt a heartfelt apology," said a relieved Niland about letting down the guard on a burden he had carried for almost 30 years. "It was a rookie move, obviously, and certainly I tried my best, but I missed the block, killed the quarterback, he retired out of the game, and I was in tears. Now, Meredith stood there in his old jovial self, and it didn't faze him either way, but I could sense a little bit of emotion from him, too, as he received that information from me. I apologized, and we went about our business. I'll always remember that."

Niland could spend a lot of his time making up for some of the memories he carried away from his career with the Cowboys. "I've had a very colorful life, both good and bad," admits Niland about the days in Dallas in between his six straight Pro Bowl appearances. "I don't think football is very conducive to growing up. I could tell you some dirty stuff but I really wouldn't want to repeat it. I could write a book myself. In fact, I did write a book, and I'll print it one of these days."

Until then, Niland would rather talk about the growth and maturity that has taken place within him over the years, despite himself and his former career. "I looked at the Super Bowl picture recently, and I think that with the exception of like six people, they're all divorced or separated, and the national average is not even close to that. It tells you something," theorizes Niland. "The lifestyle of an athlete, I think, is very counterproductive to growing up and being an adult in many ways. The pounding they take and the emotional stress and strain. You have this tremendous high, then you have this tremendous low. You win, you lose, you're great, you're lousy. When you get off the field, you can't be normal."

At least not for a while, and Niland had plenty of abnormal moments on the way.

"You've got a P & L (profit and loss) statement right at the end of the football field. It's called a scoreboard. And you've got judge and jury right there, the referee. You've got millions watching on TV, thousands in the stands and ten coaches with cameras and VCRs. It's pretty hard to cheat," describes Niland of the business he came from and the adjustment necessary for the business that followed. "Now, when I come out of that world, into the real world, it's just the opposite. It was a panic, and it made me so angry. I've had customers lie to me. I felt like going over and kicking their ass. I did not do well when I had customers lying to me or some of my salesmen lie to me. I just want to say, 'You're cut; you're out of here. March it back 10 yards, you're gone.' At least in the sports world if a guy's not doing his job you trade him to Green Bay or something. In the real world you can't do that."

But Niland also credits a characteristic or two he picked up from football that have helped him have a better than normal career in sales and marketing for a manufacturer of industrial chemicals. It's a job Niland has quietly conquered over the past 20 years. "A good work ethic has worked well for me, and I've gotten real good at what I do," claims Niland, who had an opportunity to get some one-on-one time with Tom Landry to help understand some of the lessons he would learn. "I didn't particularly like him when I played. I didn't dislike him, don't get me wrong, I just didn't know him. He was a stoic figure," remembers Niland. "We sat on a log in Estes Park, Colorado, next to a fireplace, and just the two of us talked for a good part of an hour about everything but football. That man meant more to me at that point than any time I played for him. He became a very three-dimensional person at that point in my life. I was grateful for that."

Grateful enough to bring a tear to his eye.

Keeping the Peace

He stood in the center of the city and campaigned for something he strongly believed. It may have cost Pettis Norman a chance to continue his career with the Cowboys. It helped save the city of Dallas in the process.

"People still believe that I was traded because of my stand and leading a march downtown in 1970," admits the starting tight end in Super Bowl V. "I talked to Tex (Schramm) about how our team needed to begin to let African-American and white players room together. I went to him in the mid '60s and said, 'You know it's time for us to stop this.' I was the first African-American to live with a white guy (Dave Manders) on the Dallas Cowboys."

Norman then noticed the team was just one Dallas entity plagued with prejudice. "I then spearheaded a march on downtown Dallas. It happened on Mother's Day. We had several hundred people when no one predicted anyone would come. We simply had a very peaceful march, and I spoke out on what I thought was an affront to the African-American community, and I did the same thing to the city council. That off-season I was traded to the San Diego Chargers, and most people think that my trade was prompted by that march I led downtown."

Norman and the Cowboys were coming off their first Super Bowl season. He had been through the tough times that included many franchise firsts. "Coach Landry had promised us in five years that the Cowboys would be winners, that we would no longer be considered a team that lost more games than we won," remembers Norman of the 1965 season. "The last game of the season we went to New York and beat the Giants to become a .500 team. It just meant that we reached a major milestone that defined us in a whole different way—winners—because we'd been losers up until that time."

The major milestones were just beginning for Norman, who returned to Dallas after his playing days were over to develop and operate apartment complexes while dabbling in the restaurant business with several Burger King franchises. "I've been very fortunate. In the restaurant business, I got in and bought an existing restaurant and built a couple more and saw a trend developing that I thought would have a negative impact on the industry, so I sold the operation back to Burger King and retained the real estate to lease that out to them. In the apartment business I was able to get in, develop several units, bought several more and sold them just before the apartment market crash in the '80s."

But the milestone that cemented Norman's legacy was another apparent crash facing the city at that time. Fortunately, the reputation he'd earned as a mover and shaker during his football days in Dallas preceded his involvement as a community activist. "The turmoil in our city was at a boiling point. Everybody was angry with each other. Blacks were angry with the police department, the police department was blaming African-Americans for the shooting of police, and blacks were blaming police for shooting elderly African-Americans. This city just erupted along racial lines," describes Norman of the troubled times. "They had this 'Back the Blue' campaign. If you were Anglo, you had lights (automobile headlights) on, and if you were African-American you didn't. It led to the police chief lambasting African-American city council people who were recommending reforms. All of this really just kind of led up to that point in which I was firmly under the opinion that if we did not stop this process and begin to deal with this issue, we were going to have a race riot in this city. I think it was the most dangerous time that Dallas has ever had, at least since I've been here."

Norman knew how to handle the situation. He had been through the battle before. This time the stakes were higher than a trade to another team, and the political positioning was more difficult than a knock on the team president's door.

"I made recommendations to a friend of mine that he contact the mayor and ask to set up a committee to study the underlying causes for the racial problems in Dallas," explains Norman of a suggestion that was initially declined but within days was deemed necessary. "She (the mayor) appointed a committee called Dallas Together. It's a committee that has dealt with the racial problems in our city over the last decade and probably has done more than any one committee in helping us move to another level in dealing with each other."

Solutions ranged from realigning the system of electing city officials to more inclusion for minorities in economic development. Norman helped with a number of other committees and has continued carrying on an active role behind the political scene while building a new wholesale fuel business. "We sell fuel—gasoline, diesel, and jet fuel—to a lot of the fleet operations for cities and counties. We also have a company that transports fuel for refineries, and we're in the convenience store business."

Diversity. Pettis Norman practices what he preaches. Some would like to see him preach on a more public level again. "I've had many encouragements to run for office," Norman admits. "Every office that you can name—the State Senate, the U.S. House, the mayor—and I've steadfastly refused to do so. I've never had a desire. My motive has been simple: to advance us as a community and make it a better place for others to live as well as my family."

Norman has had his own personal trials along the way. "In 1991, my wife of 29 years and my childhood sweetheart just died very suddenly." Then there is the physical damage suffered during so many battles on the football field. "I'm at the age now where I have to take care of all those injuries and things that I thought nothing about when I played football. I'm having to deal with all those things right now. I had knee replacement in '94 and back surgery in 1999."

Nothing has knocked Pettis Norman down. He will always stand for what he believes.

To Be or Not to Be

He still gets recognized as the former running back who was the last original Dallas Cowboy to retire and was the first to be inducted into the team's Ring of Honor. But Don Perkins is also seen as Martin Luther King Jr., George Washington Carver, or Frederick Douglass.

"I was recruited back in 1987," says Perkins of the day he was approached by playwright Victor Izay. "He had written a play about the life of (the nineteenth-century slave-turned-author) Frederick Douglass. He didn't know me from anything, but he had seen a picture of me in the paper and said, 'Well, this guy looks like him. I wonder if I could teach him to remember the lines.'"

Remember, he has. Perkins traveled the United States performing the one-man play as well as appearing in productions of *I'm Not Rappaport* and *Driving Miss Daisy*. During one month in 2000, Perkins rotated performances of three separate one-man plays at the New Mexico State Fair, playing King, Douglass, and Carver all at once. For some, juggling that many characters could get confusing. "It's always terrifying when you know you've got a sizeable number of people out there, and you're trying to remember, 'Am I still Frederick Douglass or am I Dr. Martin Luther King and I have a dream?'" admits Perkins, who juggles more jobs than he did footballs.

He's been a sportscaster and frequent television guest. "I've been on TV so much, people still recognize me even though I'm gray haired." He's been a state government employee, which literally drove him to another career. "I thought I was going to go crazy as a bureaucrat, so I quit work for a while. I actually went to truck driving school and crisscrossed the country for several months." He works for the Albuquerque police department "as a crime prevention specialist. Essentially what we do is tell people how to make their homes safe, how to make their personal travels safe and make their businesses safe." He's been twice a husband, four times a father, and ten times a grandfather. "The thing that's most significant to me is I've always had and retained a good relationship with my kids." He's been a devotee of the Chinese discipline of T'ai Chi. "It's kind of a mind-body experience." He's served on several civic boards, "probably every organization from the University of New Mexico, the Boys Club, University Hospital and on and on and on."

The one thing Don Perkins rarely goes on and on about is—football. "I don't think I've ever looked back," explains the six-time Pro Bowler. "I've been too busy."

It's no act. Perkins never really expected to have a career in the NFL, much less a great one. Leaving the game as the Cowboys all-time leading rusher at the age of 31, after his second-best season as a pro, was a clear indication that records and numbers on a football field were not the achievements Perkins wanted as his legacy.

Three decades later it is still unclear which legacy to choose. "I would not pigeonhole myself," an understated Perkins says of his accomplishments. "I know I'm a lot more than a city employee. I know I'm a lot more than an actor or a former athlete or an African-American. I don't want to be limited. Life's bigger than that. Being the greatest actor in the world and a sorry father, or a sorry husband, or a sorry neighbor. Life is really about being the best person you can be."

It is a message that describes Don Perkins, but it is also a message he used to describe Tom Landry at his former coach's funeral. Being asked by the Landry family to speak at the memorial service was an honor Perkins did not expect any more than the honor of being drafted by the Cowboys in the first place. Yet, despite all the hours of practice from the variety of stages Perkins has performed throughout his days as a player, a public speaker, an actor, and a civic leader, the podium is the one place he has never been at home. "It's frightening every time," admits Perkins. "I've always been absolutely terrified to speak in public, and I do it all the time."

No one would ever know. His presence was commanding, his delivery flawless. He wasn't Frederick Douglass or George Washington Carver or Martin Luther King Jr. He was Don Perkins.

Wake-Up Call

*G*ood *morning, Mr. Rentzel . . . it's 8 A.M. . . . the temperature is minus 15 degrees with a 20 mph wind out of the north . . . we expect the windchill to reach minus 55 by game time . . . have a nice day!*

"Over 30 years later, I still remember that wake-up call like it was yesterday," says Lance Rentzel when reflecting on his most memorable moment as a Dallas Cowboys receiver. It would not be the last wake-up call to have a profound impact on his life.

Lance Rentzel was one of the Cowboys' first "golden boys"—the blonde hair, the Hollywood wife, the flashy style that made headlines both on and off the field. His touchdown catch on the first play of the fourth quarter in the 1967 NFL Championship game known as the Ice Bowl gave the Cowboys the lead over the Green Bay Packers. One series later, Rentzel admits he loafed on a route that could have resulted in another score to put the title on ice. Instead, the Packers responded with a game-winning drive of their own.

Playing opposite Bob Hayes, it was Rentzel who led the team in receptions for three straight seasons on the way to the Cowboys' first Super Bowl. It was also Rentzel who sounded the alarm with an arrest and guilty plea for indecency with a child during the 1970 season, all but ending a possible Hall of Fame future. "You can never get away from something like that," Rentzel admits three decades later. "What you can do is become a better person, treat people right, and own up to your mistakes. You don't make them again, and I haven't."

He may not have realized it then, but another wake-up call was ringing for Rentzel.

Leaving the Cowboys for Los Angeles, Rentzel's life was turning into one busted pattern after another. His football career came to a disappointing close with the Rams. "I would have liked to have played out my career in Dallas, but those are things I created. I will always be a Dallas Cowboy."

His next creation—a book and Hollywood script picked up by Paramount—never got off the line of scrimmage. Rentzel's timing was way off. An entertainment industry strike hit just as his attempt at a new career was in mid stride. It fell incomplete.

Ring, ring. This time the call came from a magazine cover and a friend working in politics. It was the call that put Rentzel on a route he would run like the champion he had hoped to become.

A graduate of the University of Oklahoma with a mathematics degree, Rentzel saw the cover of *Time* magazine's 1982 "Man of the Year" issue. That it was actually dedicated to a "Machine of the Year," the computer, rather than a person, caught his eye. Suddenly a new play was being diagramed in Rentzel's head—mathematics, computer technology—the game of the future.

A call from Morgan Mason, who was working with President Ronald Reagan's administration, then set the game plan in motion. Ready or not, Rentzel took off for Washington, D.C., to develop a database for the Republican Party. "At some point I crossed the line of promising more than the technology could meet. I'm promising 200-station e-mail networks on the convention floor, but there is no e-mail," Rentzel remembers. Reaching back to his days as an NFL receiver, he adjusted on the fly. "I tap danced my ass off to provide the solutions that didn't exist when I suggested them. We created information systems that provided the model for the party that is still used today. It worked out so well I never left Washington."

But the creative bug that bit Rentzel back in Hollywood never left, either. The project he left behind during the entertainment strike kept replaying in his mind as often as his favorite football highlights. "I've been privileged to play in the NFL and have accomplishments, triumphs, and experience of things few people do. But I can't imagine what would be more satisfying than to create something on a screen, go in and see it work, and know you've made something people want to see."

It's no wonder Rentzel's description of the Ice Bowl reads like a movie script. "I was looking up at people in the band. Five or ten were bleeding profusely at the lip. I thought that was odd until I realized the trumpets and clarinets were freezing to their lips and literally ripping the skin away. It was that kind of bizarre, surreal atmosphere."

Now the bizarre and surreal is part of his latest post–football project—a movie script and computer adventure game based on football and warfare in the 21st century. But unlike his days of darting through defenses on a pattern set by others, Rentzel is carving out his own path on the way to his newest creation.

"One of the first passes I caught in the NFL, Dick Butkus threw a forearm and broke my nose in four places," Rentzel recalls. "I was knocked out, and when I regained consciousness I looked up and Dick is smiling at me. He looked like the Brawny towel guy. He says, 'Rentzel, don't come in here anymore.' And I say, 'Why is that, Dick?' 'Because I'm gonna be in here.' I thought there was some clarity there. If you don't want to pick your nose up off the ground, don't come into the middle of the football field. You get into the entertainment field and there are a million ways to do things. Thousands are the right way. There is no clarity. You don't know where the linebackers are. The cheerleaders could be linebackers. In the NFL linebackers wear No. 51 and they're in the middle of the field."

Whether Rentzel's project is a success or not, he has clarity about the route he took to get there, the accomplishments and the failures, the triumphs and the trouble. Ironically it is now his young daughter who keeps him waking up with a new appreciation for everything he has done. "It's terrific to be on the football field and be good at whatever you do," Rentzel suggests. "And I was good at what I did. But what it boils down to is loving people and being loved in return. When your little girl says, 'I love you, Daddy,' what else matters—touchdowns, Ice Bowls, Super Bowls? Nothing else matters."

Lance Rentzel has answered the call. Have a nice day!

A Case of Murder

He may have been one of the least known Cowboys until the day he died. A punter, who spent just a half season with the NFL club after graduating from little Lamar Tech in Beaumont, Texas, Colin Ridgway is well known in the Dallas area now.

May 13, 1993. Police are called to a duplex in the University Park section of Dallas. A 54-year-old man is found shot at least seven times at close range in the head, arm, and chest. He is dead.

According to police reports, Colin Ridgway, a travel-agency executive, had just returned to his home after dinner out with his wife. Joan Ridgway said she parked her car, proceeded upstairs, and found her husband shot to death. There were no signs of forced entry. No weapon was found. The FBI concluded that someone with a close personal association with Mr. Ridgway had carefully planned the murder.

Police have accused Joan and two of her friends of being involved in a murder-for-hire scheme. She was questioned by a grand jury but was not indicted. An arrest was made as late as 1997, but charges were dropped on the eve of the suspect's trial. Almost ten years after his death, no one has been convicted of the murder of former Cowboys punter, Colin Ridgway.

El Kickador's High Spiral

We were involved in a hijacking of a plane. I was caught in the middle of a riot. I was involved in the death of one of my staff people. I've been bombed."

Danny Villanueva's life has been a sensational spiral reaching incredible heights.

Standing on the opposite sideline at the Cotton Bowl on Christmas Eve of 1967, Villanueva watched as one of his NFL idols moved slowly onto the field to line up for a field goal. "I remember it vividly," says the former Cowboys kicker and punter of the day his focus turned to his future away from football. "We played the (Cleveland) Browns and Lou Groza was there and he was old, overweight, he had a back brace on. We beat the socks off of them and I hit several field goals and he missed several. That left a lasting impression on me and my motto then became 'Better three days early than three days late.'"

A week later, despite being in the prime of his career with a Cowboys record 100 consecutive extra points made, Villanueva lived up to his new motto. He quit kicking footballs and started kicking down doors for Hispanics throughout the nation. "After the Ice Bowl game (December 31, 1967, in Green Bay) I went directly to work. Within a day I was working under the hot cameras after being in 42-below-zero windchill. My gut told me it's time to leave football. It's time to do this, and they told me I was going into a dead-end business."

The business was Spanish-language television. Villanueva had a feeling it would be anything but a dead-end. He was right.

Of course, Villanueva already knew more than most about what he was getting into. Long before the surprise trade that took him away from the Los Angeles Rams, a move to media was on his mind. He did not allow the Cowboys acquisition to take him away from the secondary career he had already begun. "We trained in Thousand Oaks, California," explains Villanueva of his new confines and the new challenge it presented his part-time position at a Los Angeles television station. "After our meetings, while the other guys, I don't know, would drink beer or something, I would jump in my car and drive all the way into Hollywood and do a show, live, then rush back to make it by curfew. I'd do the evening news at Univision. Then the season started, and after every game, say we would arrive from Philadelphia, when the guys would go home with their families, I'd go to another airline and take a red-eye into L.A., work all day, tape five shows, and then go back to the airport, take a red-eye back to Dallas and go to practice."

It was just the beginning of a lifestyle that would pay huge dividends for Danny, and they came quickly after his football career came to an end. "I went back to the Univision station in L.A. and moved up the ladder. I became news director, then I became news and operations, then I became station manager, then I became general manager, vice president, and president in rapid order. It was the same formula as football. You're limited in talent, you know. I was short, fat, and slow but nobody outworked me," explains Villanueva of a philosophy that at one time had him working seven days a week as a television newsman. "That was another one of my crazy ideas. I worked five days in Spanish, and I worked two days in English at NBC, trying to prove that you could be bilingual and you could work in two languages. I attacked it with the same intensity as I did kicking."

Each rung of the ladder was also a step on the way up a pay scale far removed from the $5,500 he earned to begin his NFL career. "I used to set these little goals: 'I want to make $1,000 a month.' Later in my career I said, 'I need to make $1,000 a week.' And then later, 'I want to make $1,000 a day," says the kicker turned Spanish televisionary. "I guess that's my kicking background, where I used to try to eliminate the valleys and let the peaks take care of themselves. But don't get the bad highs, don't get the shanks."

Villanueva has reached peaks beyond his belief. The increments grew to hundreds of thousands, millions, and even billions. His post–football career spiraled in wealth to heights few, if any, Hispanics have ever reached in the United States before. "I don't know where it ranks, and it doesn't matter. My mom told me you can work your whole life, and she told me you'll never pay it back. The fact that this country let us in and welcomed us in—you'll never, ever fully pay it back, but you keep chasing it and you keep trying."

What does matter is the impact Villanueva has had during the chase. He has been singled out as one of this country's true pioneers.

The youngest of Univision's founding partners, Villanueva was involved in a variety of industry firsts while building the Spanish-language network to a multibillion-dollar dynasty. "We pioneered what they used to call ENG, electronic news gathering, which was an alternative to using film," begins the media mogul. "We introduced videotape to doing news three years before the English-language stations did it. We were on the satellite two years before they were. Adversity is the mother of creativity, and that's what it was. We just couldn't afford to develop film, because we were in deep trouble. We were hanging on by the skin of our teeth from losing our company. We were almost out of business, so we had to do things that other people would never do. Videotape was one of them. The satellite saved us from having to send programs around the country. We just couldn't afford that. The satellite company gave us a one million dollar interest-free loan to entice us to go on their satellite and, man, that was like blood. We used that money to do a World Cup."

Villanueva continued to create television firsts that helped develop what we all see in our homes today. "Remember closed circuit? We were doing soccer and boxing matches on closed circuit before cable. We were the first UHF station in this part of the country, so we had to go around and ask people to please buy this black box so they could watch us on TV. We were the only company that went on the air with no viewers—guaranteed. Our first rating was a letter from the black-box manufacturer saying that they certified that they had sold 30,000 boxes in L.A. And so I'd say, 'You see, I have at least 30,000 homes. That's how we started this business. We sold it for 300 million dollars, and now it has a market value worth over 10 billion."

During the early 1970s, as the east L.A. riots were raging out of control, Villanueva discovered the value sometimes was not worth the price. "My assistant, Ruben Salazar, was killed in east L.A.," describes Villanueva of the volatile time. "There was an inquest, and we televised it full-time. I had to assume a role that was not a lot of fun. To the people who would have violence, I was a pacifist that they needed to silence. To the other side, I was a militant. I straddled the two sides. I took a very active role during that period. They scrawled 'spic station' on my door and they threw a bomb. I had an off-duty policeman with a rifle on my roof trying to protect my people at the station. They were very difficult times. It left a huge, huge impression on me."

It was not the first time Villanueva had experienced prejudice, although his early days in the NFL, when he was the only Hispanic in professional football, were accepted as a much more lighthearted affair. "I remember the Rams players saying, 'Red rover, red rover, send the Mexican over,' or 'All the black guys get in this bus, all the white guys get in that bus, and Danny, you take a cab,'" Villanueva says with a laugh. He was not laughing as much when the loudspeakers would sing with bullfight music every time he would take the field. "It used to drive me crazy. I used to look around and couldn't figure out what was that all about. They called me El Kickador."

He now has help kicking down deals as the Villanueva empire continues to grow. His sons, Danny Jr. and Jimmy, are successful with businesses that their father has helped guide in one way or another, including Spanish radio that owned the rights to the NFL's Raiders games. "Part of their promise to the Raiders was that I would do the Spanish-language broadcast. So I came back, and that was kind of my reintroduction to the NFL."

One son is a major investor in BigBallot.com, a company that handles the voting for NFL, NBA, WNBA, NHL, and Major League Baseball All Star activities as well as the 100 Greatest Players of the Century campaign, *Reader's Digest*, and *Sports Illustrated* balloting. "I'm the only guy over 40 on the board. They do about 800 million ballots a year. A newspaper said if Florida had hired his company, they wouldn't have had all the problems they did (in the presidential election of 2000)."

The other son was president of the Los Angeles Galaxy soccer team, which Villanueva owned. They shared a moment of déjà vu from Father's football days in Dallas. "I thought, 'I'm finally going to get a ring.' The irony is just inescapable. We were in Boston, not Green Bay. It was pouring sheets of rain, not ice. We had the lead, and time was running out. In front of my eyes, Green Bay flashed again, the Ice Bowl. I said, 'Lord, please not again. I can't go through this.' In Green Bay, I know we were making history with the weather and everything. I knew this game was special. I sensed that when we were there. This game was the first championship game in the history of Major League Soccer. I sensed history again. We were ahead and the weather was horrible and I got that sinking feeling. Sure enough, they tied us in regulation, and they beat us in overtime in the last minutes. This time it was more painful because it was my son."

Sharing the family fortune and an occasional misfortune drew Danny back to business with his boys after the sale of Univision in 1989. This time it was building the Bastion Capital Corporation, a financial firm, which created another high-flying fortune. "I was gonna retire and go do my other work (charity), and then my son talked me into this business, and what's the first thing we do? We buy our competitor, Telemundo," says Villanueva with a hint of shyness in his voice. It did not translate that way in the boardroom.

What Villanueva did next with his new network was as bold a move as ever, merging with Sony and Liberty Media in December 2000, to form a mega-media Spanish language entity. "It was about a billion, 50 million dollar deal. So, all those guys that told me I was going into a dead-end business, that everybody would be speaking English within a couple of years—I did okay."

Danny Villanueva did much better than okay. So will many others because of him. Scholarship endowments, foundations, and disaster relief are just part of what he and his family do with their wealth. "One project leads into another one. The 1985 earthquake in Mexico, we sent 15 million bucks down there to help. I founded a Christmas telethon here in L.A. 27 years ago, and it's still alive, still going. I just founded a foundation in Ventura County called Destino that we empower, and we're teaching philanthropy among Hispanic families and governance. I want to do some inner city work with minority entrepreneurs and women entrepreneurs. I'm going to begin pulling back and cutting down my time here (Bastion Capital) and then starting my work in the inner city, which will be my last mountain that I'm going to climb and then I'm done."

Unless, of course, another cause comes calling or another challenge is thrown before Danny Villanueva. Then he may have to send another high, hanging spiral of success or a towering end-over-end accomplishment through the uprights.

"I'll never stop. As long as I have breath, I'll do my charity work. I'm going to give it all away. I'm gonna go out like I came in—bare naked."

Driving It Deep

It was almost like a well-struck golf shot. The moment of impact felt as if nothing was struck at all, yet the ball sailed high, hovered for what seemed an eternity, and finally dropped to the ground and rolled down a fairway lined with yard markers. The 84-yard drive is still listed in the Cowboys record book as the longest punt in franchise history.

Ron Widby appreciates the golf reference as much as his kick that conjures up the comparison. "After I retired, I went straight into the golf business as a golf professional. I knew that's what I wanted to do," explains Widby, who would always spend his Mondays off during the NFL season on a golf course. "So for me, the transition out of football wasn't that hard." The transition out of his second sports career has taken him almost 30 years to get through.

"I got close but never made it to the big show," says Widby of his professional golf career. Two attempts at qualifying for the PGA tour came up short for Widby. He tried to put it behind him and move on as a salesman for a roofing company. But as Widby approached 50 years of age and the success of the Senior Tour grew, the bug bit again.

"I worked for the Reunion Pro-Am tournament when it came to Dallas," recalls Widby. "They gave me a sponsor's exemption to play in the event here. I got to play in two others and played with guys like Miller Barber; Chi Chi Rodriguez's brother, Jesus; and Billy Casper."

Widby played well enough to compete but never had a day on the Senior Tour like he had that record day against the New Orleans Saints. "I was never in the top 10, but I was never in the bottom 20. I was always in the middle. I made good checks. I wasn't disappointed." Not even after twice failing to qualify for a spot on the Senior Tour. "I got to the finals the second time. The fact that I did come really close, not having the golf background like most of the guys had, being golf professionals for years, I think that was an accomplishment."

Widby knew from experience that he still had a few swings left. When former Cowboys center John Fitzgerald got Widby an invitation to a Celebrity Tour event in Dallas, Widby didn't shank the opportunity. "I won it," says a proud but humble man. "After that, I got invited to the one in Chicago, and I finished third there. But the next year I didn't get invited anymore, and I haven't been invited to play in the last few years."

Don't expect Widby to spend much time worrying about the snub. He was a punter in the NFL. He's used to being forgotten. Actually, he kind of likes it that way. "We moved up here to Wichita Falls, Texas, because I got tired of the big city. I don't play golf much anymore because we're into horses now. Even though I didn't make it, I came close, and then I found a good line of work in the roofing business, and I'm starting a new business with my horses."

From now on Ron Widby may have to describe his record-setting punt in a completely different way.

The Arrival of America's Team

The Necessary Link

A young woman in Philadelphia turns on the television to watch her favorite cable program. An English professor at UCLA picks up the phone to call the university's administration office. A doctor at a major hospital in New York City is alerted by the in-house communications system of an urgent call in the ER. A Yankees fan tunes in to a pay-per-view telecast of his beloved pinstriped heroes. Somewhere along all of those lines, Herb Adderley provided the necessary link.

"We do installations, all types of wirings, connections, disconnects, anything to do with cable construction, laying the cable underground, or laying it overhead on poles. We also do telephone work," says the owner of Adderley Industries, Inc. "We wired close to a quarter of a million homes in Philly, we have a big account in hospitals in New York, we do college campuses, and now our main deal is Cable Vision in Brooklyn. They paid $50 million to televise 48 of the Yankees games, and we do all the work for them."

Adderley has a history of linking success. When traded to the Cowboys in 1970, he left Titletown, USA, with two Super Bowl rings, five Championship trophies, five Pro Bowl appearances, and five All Pro selections. His new team had the reputation of "not being able to win The Big One." Adderley believes he was the missing link.

"There were a lot of racial problems in Dallas when I was there where guys separated themselves. It was nothing like Green Bay, we were all like one big family. In Green Bay there was no color thing," explains Adderley, who provided the Cowboys a solution. "My biggest contribution to the Cowboys was off the field as far as bringing the players together as one and letting them realize that, 'Hey, we're only here for one reason and that is to win. In order to win we have to be friends off the field and speak and get along.' The closeness of the team came together off the field and then on the field. You could tell the difference."

The difference helped turned Dallas into winners. The first Super Bowl appearance followed Adderley's first season with the Cowboys, and their first Super Bowl title came the next year.

Adderley's assistance with minority issues did not stop with his retirement from football. The communications industry in Philadelphia needed some help in the early 1980s and again, Adderley was the link. "They needed a minority in order to help smooth things out because years ago they had set aside monies for minorities that were qualified, so I got qualified and went in as a minority and we got a lot of business—millions of dollars in business—to get started because of that," admits Adderley.

But, he adds, the growth that followed can be linked to the job that was done after the gift was granted. "We started out with two trucks in Philadelphia and ended up with 200. We built a reputation in Philly so the minority thing was like it didn't matter, because we were judged on the quality of work."

Yet, when Adderley judges the source that links his past success to his current career, the cord does not attach to Dallas. It is clearly a line that runs through the north. "The things I learned in Green Bay from Vince Lombardi are the things that I use today. I don't use anything from the Cowboys," Adderley states in an abrupt tone. "The Cowboys didn't help me, you understand, I helped the Cowboys. I was a Hall of Famer before I put any Cowboys uniform on. I didn't make the Football Hall of Fame for what I did for Dallas."

Herb Adderley still shares the Cowboys team record for interceptions in a game. He owns a Super Bowl ring emblazoned with the Cowboys star. They may not have created the connection between Adderley and the Hall of Fame, but they will always be part of what links the Hall of Fame cornerback to Dallas.

Bambi's Business

In San Diego, I used to walk around the house mumbling, 'Watch it, catch it, tuck it, and run it,'" said Lance Alworth in a 1999 article published by the *Union-Tribune*. "In Dallas, I growled at the cat, made faces in the mirror, and kicked the trash can."

Alworth made a rapid return to the comfort of California after just two seasons with the Cowboys. The receiver whose graceful moves and soft hands earned the nickname "Bambi" and induction into the Pro Football Hall of Fame is not as smooth expressing anything about his days in Dallas. Yet, three decades after scoring the first touchdown in the Cowboys first Super Bowl win, earning his only championship ring, Alworth also enjoys the rewards of something else he picked up while playing for the silver and blue—a booming business.

He is the owner of All Aboard Mini Storage, a concept he developed after first seeing self-storage units in Dallas. Based in California, the company boasts millions of storage square footage throughout the country.

"My whole life is like a fairy tale," Alworth told the *Union-Tribune*.

As long as Bambi is roaming the redwoods of California and not the trees of Texas.

Top Secret Defense

For ten years he went up against an arsenal that included the most dangerous weapons the National Football League had to offer. Most of the time he figured out a way to disarm them. Defense strategy on a football field was always second nature to Benny Barnes.

The real deal wasn't quite so comfortable.

"I'm there on base and I just happened to venture into this one area that we were having a few problems in and all of a sudden this buzzer goes off and it was a lockdown," describes Barnes of a harrowing moment on a military base in California. It was just a few years after he retired as defensive back for the Cowboys. Barnes was working with a contractor that had the janitorial services for the base, and part of his duties required clearance in some highly sensitive, top-secret areas.

"It was almost like that *Get Smart* (the TV show) thing where all these doors start coming down, you hear all this noise, people are running all over the place scrambling and wherever you are you're stuck there," says Barnes with a brief chuckle in his voice. "It was kind of scary there for a minute. I see all these people with guns and I don't know if it's a terrorist or what's going on."

What went on was simple enough. Barnes and his crew had tripped an alarm while making their rounds. "I made sure that I didn't venture back in that spot again. I'm staying in the open."

Not quite the game plan Barnes believed in the last time he was engaged in a defensive disaster drill. Despite having flags thrown and whistles blown after getting tangled up with Lynn Swann in Super Bowl X, Barnes went back to the battlefield for more. Against Denver in Super Bowl XIII, it earned him the ring many feel the interference call just two years before had taken away.

It also gave Barnes a story to tell the kids at Contra Costa Junior College, where he has been in charge of the athletic department's equipment and facilities for the past decade. He is also the football team's self-appointed consultant and counselor.

"As I tell kids, you're gonna have those games, you're gonna get beat. It's gonna say a lot about you on how you come back, because there's not a guy out there that hasn't been beat or been called on a bad play," says Barnes of a message that is almost as therapeutic as it is informative. "It really helps me to talk to them now when their head is down."

And they listen because they know Barnes, not only for his Super Bowl ups and downs, but they also know him as a former Contra Costa longshot who made it big in the NFL.

"As a free agent, having the opportunity to come to a team that just won the Super Bowl, as I tell them, nobody was more surprised than I was," says Barnes. "I kind of looked at it as a great summer job to be able to go to camp and get paid and play something I love doing. And then, the thrill of being told, 'Hey, we're going to keep you.' But, I tell them now it's even tougher to make it. You've got to be Superman among supermen to make it."

Of course, it also takes Superman to get through a top-secret defense system without setting off the alarm.

Plain Vanilla

He walks out of the Dallas home he and his family have lived in since he became a Cowboys linebacker. He travels in a radius of only ten miles or so. Bob Breunig has just toured the life he has led for the past 20 years. "The good news is my story is vanilla."

It is actually the Breunig style more than his story that could be considered somewhat plain. He played ten seasons at linebacker, most of those in the middle of Tom Landry's complicated "Flex" defense. He has the second highest single-season tackle total in team history. Three Super Bowl appearances in Breunig's first four seasons would indicate a bowl full of memorable highlights. But it was being consistent, not being spectacular, that earned him three Pro Bowl selections. The rest of his teammates had already reserved the spectacular.

"When Dave Edwards retired after my rookie year, I was moved to start in his place. I remember running through that tunnel (at Texas Stadium) the first time the defense was introduced, and I was in the huddle with some of the guys, some of which I had been watching since grade school," shares Breunig of becoming a bigger part of America's Team. "Lee Roy Jordan, D. D. Lewis, Charlie (Waters), and Cliff (Harris), I think even Mel Renfro was still playing then and 'Too Tall' (Jones) and Harvey (Martin) and Larry Cole and all the rest of them. It was a pretty neat deal to be able to get in the huddle with those guys."

At the same time, Breunig huddled with another legend, Roger Staubach, off the field, entering the real estate business with the Cowboys quarterback. It would take all of Breunig's brawn to battle through some tough times after spinning off Staubach's partnership 12 years later in a slightly different direction. "He has built a very successful service business where they provide services to people who either use real estate, a la tenants, or people who own and operate properties on a corporate level. We are really considered local real estate private investors. We want to own and operate real estate for a profit," explains the current owner of the Breunig Commercial Group.

"But, the real estate industry went through a literal depression in Dallas during the late '80s and early '90s. Perseverance, dedication, doing the right thing and making good choices, being honorable and exercising character in difficult times—all of these things that we were taught as young men under Landry's tutelage were really necessary to endure a very difficult time in real estate."

As vanilla as it may sound, it worked. "We started buying buildings in the early '90s on the basis that we felt they were a good bargain. That proved to be true, as the real estate industry has come roaring back in terms of demand for occupancy and space," says Breunig of the buildings he has owned or built into a booming business. Most of the properties are within a quarterback sack of his home field. However, he says, "It isn't owning a couple of houses down the street. We've been involved with some very serious transactions. It has been prosperous, and we are grateful."

Breunig begins to rethink his assessment of a less than spectacular life after football. "Many of us have lamented through the years," rationalizes a man who gives time and resources to many charitable groups including Young Life, Urban Alternative, the Fellowship of Christian Athletes, and Happy Hills Farm. "It is hard to recreate coming out of that tunnel getting ready to play the Washington Redskins. It really is."

The closest Breunig has been able to come is with his children. They have added the much needed spice to his life. "Mary and I have four really diverse kids. My first was not athletic necessarily. He was an academic decathlon kid, a National Merit Scholar, in the jazz band, class president and all that stuff. Then here comes my second kid. He was a basketball player. I could hardly dribble when I was a kid. I never played basketball. I got to get involved in it and enjoyed it from a parent's standpoint and appreciate what he did. My third son played football. He is a linebacker, which I am probably more familiar with. Then I have a daughter who is a cheerleader. I've got to do a little bit of everything. I pinch myself at times. It almost comes off as awe. Married with four kids and everything went fine, lived happily ever after. I didn't get hit by a tractor. I didn't have to get crippled," reflects Bob Breunig.

Then comes the realization of a lifetime. "Geez, it's not exactly vanilla. I've just been fortunate."

Ground Zero

Looking out over a barren piece of real estate, Larry Cole sees something. It is not visible to the naked eye. It won't even appear with the help of the strongest lens. But given time, Cole will share the image for all to see.

"I like the creativity of taking a raw piece of ground, romancing it, and turning it into something special," says the custom home builder. "I like to conceive it, put it together, and achieve it with problem solving along the way—which is like playing defense in football. You just cut through the crowd. You take pride in the final product."

During his days as a defensive tackle, pride in the final product came in the form of play-off appearances. Cole's Cowboys claimed postseason berths in all but one of his 13 years, including five Super Bowls and two titles. Individually, No. 63 never garnered enough attention to earn a Pro Bowl invitation. But then, Cole was never comfortable doing anything but quietly making plays. "I'm the operations guy, the production guy. Give me the game plan, and I execute it. I'm not an ego guy that needs the glorification," says the man who never seemed bothered despite often being forgotten amongst the likes of Bob Lilly, George Andrie, Jethro Pugh, Harvey Martin, Randy White, and Ed "Too Tall" Jones. He laughed it off then, and he still enjoys the anonymity now. "I don't play the celebrity thing. I'm more humored by it than I am living with it. I leave it for the guys that have talent. I don't play ex-football player. There's nothing in my office that has anything to do with anything but what is in my life now. I like to be known as a developer. It does make you a more interesting person when they find out you've played football."

Especially when that one highlight appears year after year. The one Larry Cole created completely by accident. The one everyone seems to remember him by. "It was the first time in my life that we actually came from behind and won in a miracle game," remembers the subject of that jubilant moment during the 1972 play-off game against the San Francisco 49ers. There he was, the usually stoic fourth-year lineman, wallowing on the ground, drawing as much attention as his actions would allow. It was the kind of display Cole was never known for before and never would be again. "My kids' friends make fun of Dad rolling on the ground," he admits with a hint of embarrassment. "When I was an older veteran, like 12 or 13 years in the league, some of the rookies couldn't believe I had that kind of emotion—I was so deadpan—but I was young and excitable as a kid. I also point out, for dignity purposes, the other person rolling on the ground was Hall of Famer Lance Alworth."

Cole has since found his dignity in the ground he develops. Instead of wallowing in the wealth of a $15,000 bonus earned from the Super Bowl win over Miami in 1972, he invested the money in a townhouse project that required more of a defensive game plan than he had hoped. The struggles continued when banking bottomed out in Texas during the 1980s but Cole kept coming up with ways to build back up. His latest project, Remington Park in Colleyville, Texas, includes the development of 209 lots on 129 acres and involves investors like Roger Staubach.

So, exactly what did Larry Cole see when he looked over the land before him? "It's art with a bulldozer—being able to see, I'll put a pond here, a road there, move it here, build up a neighborhood—that's what turns me on."

Bearly Surprised

It's always nice when you get a bit of a surprise," says Pat Donovan of the moment that remains the highlight of his days as an offensive tackle for the Cowboys. The announcement that Donovan had been voted a Pro Bowl starter was certainly unexpected, even by the man spreading the word to his team. "Tom Landry sounded surprised when he announced it," remembers Donovan with a chuckle in his voice.

The best surprise was yet to come.

"The year before it had been in Detroit in February, and I remembered everybody complaining. I came home and my parents were in town in Dallas and they had heard it on the news," says Donovan, who was puzzled at the level of excitement until he heard the rest of the news. "It was a great celebration to find out that this was the first year it was going to be in Hawaii."

Donovan could appreciate the natural beauty of the islands more than most, having grown up in Montana. It is what drew him back to the town of Whitefish, near some of the country's most scenic national parks. It's also what keeps unexpected encounters in his current career as a real estate developer from becoming surprises he can't handle.

"We had a bear on the golf course this summer. He was at least 500 or 600 pounds," explains Donovan of the wildlife that often inhabits the area surrounding Iron Horse, a Tom Fazio–designed golf course and community of 820 acres and 335 home sites developed by Donovan and his partner. "We're not far from Glacier Park, the last habitat in the continental United States for grizzly bears. The guys were working on a little drainage project around the greens, and he was out there for about 10 days, maybe 100 yards from us. He'd walk out and sun and eat grass, that's what they do when they first wake up out of hibernation."

Donovan may have been successful in his day against the Bears, but he didn't throw a body block or attempt to use any of the hand-to-hand techniques he'd learned with the Cowboys on this particular bear. "To go out and wrestle the bear wouldn't be advisable. This bear was calm because we were leaving him alone, that's what they like the best. What caused the bear problems years ago was what happened in the national parks here, Glacier and Yellowstone both," explains Donovan. "They used to have garbage dumps outside the lodges, and they'd go out and just dump after-dinner garbage, kitchen scraps, on the ground. They had this bleacher-style seating set up around these amphitheatres and the bears would come in the evening and eat the garbage. That was one of the main attractions at the park lodges. In the 1970s, everybody became a lot more enlightened and realized that wasn't very good for the bears. So they stopped feeding them. But the bears were so habituated to human contact, they saw humans as a food source, and so the bears were very aggressive about approaching people and getting food. Now, the bears are largely self-sustaining in the natural environment, so you don't see bears that are very comfortable coming up to people anymore. They have a healthy respect both directions."

Whether it's fly-fishing for rainbow trout or elk hunting, golf, or hiking, Donovan has a healthy respect for the outdoors. Not that he always shared that respect during his playing days in Dallas. "I was snow skiing all through my playing career, which was in your contract that you weren't going to snow ski," admits Donovan, who began taking trips with offensive line coach Jim Myers' daughter and her husband. "Every year, for about five years, Jim would say, 'I heard you were skiing this off-season.' And I'd say, 'No, I didn't go skiing.' So, one year he brought in this photo with me in it. I said, 'No, see I'm not skiing there, I'm sitting around.' He didn't actually have photographic evidence."

Now the Cowboys have written evidence. Surprise, surprise!

Trophy Talker

His name is etched on the greatest statues and trophies in all of football—the Heisman, the Lombardi, the Hall of Fame. Tony Dorsett is often called upon to strike the pose at the podium. He talks the trophy talk because he walked the winning walk.

"It's just so simple," says Dorsett about the eloquence he delivers to dinner crowds around the country as smoothly as he darted through defenses in the NFL. "I tell a story or two. I just relate it all to football, and the word spreads if someone sees you at an event."

When opponents saw Dorsett break into the open field, they watched his numbers pile up to levels rarely seen in football. Now the numbers on the rise have dollar signs attached. Dorsett is proof that bronze does turn green.

"I started out at about 10 grand to speak. The plan was to get in about six months up to about 15 grand and then within a year get to 20 grand a speech," explains Dorsett of a speaking fee fueled by each additional award. "I'm trying to slow down and stay at home as much as I can, but it's tough because you never know when it's gonna dry up."

Drying up is something Dorsett understands from his attempts in the business world. Restaurant partnerships, investments—both good and bad—and television jobs have come and gone since he left the Cowboys. Stumbling into bankruptcy and bouncing back to the top has been part of his long run away from football. "We invest in a lot of upstart Internet companies, and I have an advertising specialty company that's doing very well right now," explains Dorsett. "I've had some success, but just like anything else, I've taken some hits."

Unlike most, Dorsett has always had the talent to turn a direct hit into a glancing blow. It was a running style that placed him just steps away from the top of the league's all-time rushing list. Now, it has become a business style that allows T.D. to take a hit and bounce forward for another possible score.

"We were involved with a company just like Broadcast.com. The company does the same thing, streaming radio stations on the Internet. They're at about 300 stations that stream, and when Broadcast.com went public they only had about 90 stations. What did he (founder Mark Cuban) get, like 5 billion?" Dorsett asks while shaking his head in wonderment over one that got away. "Guys that get there first are the ones that get it good. Especially now that dot-coms have died down."

Just as quickly Dorsett reverses field and flashes his childish grin. "We've got one coming out that's a full pleasure travel agency. I'm just thinking this one is going to be off the hook, man. It's gonna be really, really big."

So far, the really big events in Dorsett's life have involved family and football. He still looks like he could step on a field and throw down a stutter-step that would leave current NFL linebackers grasping for air, just as they did 20 years before. Dorsett gives much of the credit to being remarried with two young daughters. "I'm approaching 50 years old, and I'm moving around like I'm a 25-year-old."

But it is the son from his first marriage who brought Dorsett back to the field for Super Bowl XXXIV. Anthony Dorsett, following in his father's footsteps, started in the NFL's ultimate game as a member of the Tennessee Titans. Dad was there to share his experience and wisdom.

"We talked all week long about the distractions, and I tried to prepare him for all that stuff, the tickets and all the stuff you go through. Get that stuff taken care of as fast as you can," advised Tony. "Don't read all the hype, just stay focused on what you're supposed to be doing. Then when that final moment came, I wanted to get introduced again." Instead it was Anthony who was prepared for his moment, while Dad could have used an encouraging word.

"I was standing there on the sideline, and I'm trying to be all cool—Big Papa, been there, done that. They started playing the national anthem, and my eyes got so full," said Dorsett, still filled with emotion. "I got to think back to when he was a little scrawny, skinny little kid with glasses and then to see what he's grown up into and seeing that he's enjoying himself. You want to see your children do as well or better than what you do, and to see my son experiencing that, I didn't even think about myself. I was just thinking about him and how happy he was."

Dorsett would have his eyes fill with tears again just a few months later. It was another unexpected reaction to something affecting his other family. "I can remember very distinctively when I first found out about it. I was down in Washington, D.C., receiving an award, and right before I was going on a reporter came up to me and told me what had happened, that Tom Landry had died. I became very emotional. I didn't really expect it would be that way," shares Dorsett. "Here was a guy that drove me at times in training camp and it's like, 'What am I doing here when I could be somewhere else doing something better?' Once you retire and you're away from the game, you're looking at it from a different vantage point, you understand and realize the things he was trying to instill in us and taught us as players and men that I use even today. He's a guy that touched a lot of people's lives."

As has Tony Dorsett. The vision of No. 33 breaking the line of scrimmage, cutting to the sideline and racing 99 yards for a touchdown against the Vikings. The sleek-looking running back gliding down the line against the St. Louis Cardinals, unable to find an opening to the end zone, spinning back the other direction with a burst that gets the score. And to think, Dorsett expected those images to be burned into our minds in something other than silver and blue.

"When I was a kid, I was a big Steelers fan being brought up in the Pittsburgh area. I always wanted to wear that black and gold someday. I can remember leaving the University of Pittsburgh and I was receiving an award at a big banquet up there and I looked over at Dan Rooney and I said, 'Mr. Rooney, please don't let me go.' I was real sincere about it. I wanted to play right there in Pittsburgh and play for the Steelers," explains Dorsett. But he quickly covers his words with the same smooth style. "When I look back at it, it could have been a real big headache. I have no regrets about being a Dallas Cowboy."

And no regrets that many of the milestones that earned him the hardware and post–football financial security were eclipsed. His Cowboys rushing records removed by Emmitt Smith; his all-time NCAA numbers pushed aside by the University of Texas running back and Heisman Trophy winner Ricky Williams. "It was good for Tony Dorsett. It brought Tony Dorsett back up front and personal," rationalizes Dorsett. "It let a lot of people of the Ricky Williams era know who Tony Dorsett was as an athlete."

All anyone in any era needs to do is tune in. They will see or hear Tony Dorsett somewhere. He is still what the trophies and statues stand for.

"I've had the opportunity to go out and make a pretty good living; if it was any better, they'd have to make me a twin."

Get the sculptors ready.

One on One

Close your eyes and listen closely. The voice you hear sounds like that of actor Morgan Freeman. But the story does not seem like much of a movie script. "I've just been leading a dull, nonexciting life," are the words being told.

Open your eyes and you see Billy Joe Dupree doing the talking.

"What you see is what you get," says the former Cowboys tight end, who is as hard on himself during the post-football days as he was in his 11 NFL seasons. It is just one of the characteristics Dupree has carried from one career to another. "I spent my playing days, as well as years after I retired, in front of the public one on one. It kind of eliminates that rock-star type environment and gets the one-on-one type arrangement of tangible and touchable entities."

Dupree has used his ability of avoiding the spotlight with one-on-one relationships to touch plenty of tangible activities along the way, from construction to real estate development to business consulting to his current role as community program manager for the City of Dallas. "The development of the youth in the inner city," explains Dupree of his duties with the city. "What they're trying to do since I've been there is to initially develop a little bit more self-esteem, in a sense, if it's not there, and also give a kid a little more of an outlook on some of the things that may be outside their community, just to be familiar with what goes on in the rest of the world."

The world Dupree has lived in since earning three straight Pro Bowl appearances and a Super Bowl ring has provided his wife and two sons the opportunity to earn college degrees along the way. "That was my primary objective after football was to make sure my kids got educated and on their way, and by far that has to be the most rewarding thing after athletics that I've experienced."

Although Dupree is sincere about his family, if some of his comments sound politically correct, maybe he is taking advantage of another one on one to prepare for the rest of his world. "I think the last election I got involved in was George W. Bush's first gubernatorial election. I went on tour speaking for him," admits Dupree.

Dabbling in politics as a volunteer in the past has obviously sparked an interest for the future. "In about '84, I was propositioned to consider running for a congressional seat here in the state. I initially thought that was a good idea, but the reason I retired from football and went to work for somebody was to spend some more time with my family. That wouldn't have done it. It dawned on me that I just came out of athletics, which was a glass house, and I was thinking about going into politics, which is a crystal house. The basic difference is that if you pick up a rock and throw it at the glass house, you might break a window. The crystal house, you pick up a pebble and throw it out there and that thing will come crashing down all around you. I just didn't want to subject my family to that, and that's something I may consider later on. I think I've got some years left."

Sounds like a Hollywood script in the making. Billy Joe Dupree won't need Morgan Freeman to play the part.

Colorado Creations

With the Rocky Mountains forming a natural frame, heavy machinery rips through the canvas of dirt and rock below. Dave Edwards watches the work as a Colorado community begins to take shape. "We're putting in the infrastructures, putting in the streets. Everything has to go underground because it's so cold," explains the former Cowboys linebacker of his latest job in the construction business. "I work for the excavator."

A few hours later the large chunk of matter being manipulated is marble from another small mountain town. This time Edwards has come up with the creation and is the only one working the project. "I got started doing a little wood whittling with Walt Garrison back with the Cowboys. When I moved to Colorado, I got into doing some alabaster, which is a soft stone, and then I did a couple of things in marble," says Edwards. The subjects usually end up being animals.

Making his hobby with marble has been the toughest test yet. "You gotta have, first of all, the desire to do it. Then you got to find the tools that will handle it, like grinders and an air compressor that's like a mini-jackhammer. Finishing it you just have certain ways of sanding it down. You have to have diamond-tip grinders and stuff like that. You start chipping away at it, and once you've got it finished, you try to polish the marble as beautiful as possible."

Edwards has never been a very polished person. Linebackers during his day weren't supposed to be beautiful. Times change. "I played for 13 years and finally they said, 'Hey, we've gotta check you into the old folks home because Hollywood (Henderson) is in town.'

"The day I decided I'm retiring, in 1975, I'm sitting on the bench over there and they were trying old Hollywood out for returning kick-offs," says the man still tied for second among Cowboys defenders for career fumble recoveries. "They kicked off, and I said, 'Look, that boy is going for a touchdown—and his number was 56. I said, 'There is no way that I can cope with that, man.'"

Since then, Edwards has had to cope with hopping from job to job, often with a bad hip. "I got to where I couldn't walk around, and it was just worn out. I'd been hit on it several times, and it got to the point where I had to do something, so I had it replaced," shares Edwards of a procedure paid for by the NFL players association. "I didn't have health insurance. It was a miracle."

It may be a miracle that Edwards is still standing at all. Shortly after arriving in his new home state of Colorado, Edwards learned a hard lesson about his new land. "It was a bright, sunshiny day in August, and I thought, 'I'm going to go for a ride on my mountain bike.' I took my shirt off and was catching some rays climbing up this peak. I got towards the top, and I saw a dark cloud was coming in from the other side, and I saw a guy coming down. I said, 'Hey, where you going?' He said, 'Can't you see that?' I thought it was just a cloud, so I kept on going. After about three hours of climbing, the weather started changing. When I got to the top, it was snowing."

Having no cold weather supplies and no means of communication, Edwards had little choice but to head back down the mountain. It was a journey that tested him like few physical challenges before. "When I started down, I was trying to hold my speed down to keep the wind-chill factor from freezing my hands that I had already froze in the Ice Bowl, but they started freezing up. I couldn't mash the brakes. I had to pull over and kind of get under a rock, thinking that I might have to stay up there all night. It would have killed me. I finally got down and by the time I got to my car, I had lost feeling in both my dang hands and up to my dang wrists. I had hypothermia."

Fortunately the feeling returned so Edwards' hands could keep working their magic. Along with sculptures and excavations are paintings of his most memorable moments in silver and blue—one that earned Edwards the most meaningful of four career game balls from a 6–2 win over the Cleveland Browns during the Cowboys first Super Bowl run. "I made a couple of interceptions, and it was the springboard for the success of the Cowboys when they started the long run of winning, going to Super Bowls and stuff. I painted a picture of the last interception, of me holding the ball and the other guys hugging me and stuff like that, which is pretty important to me."

As is a poster of another Edwards work of art, which was recently released at a charity event for literacy. "It's an oil painting, a scene of the Cowboys when we played against the Colts (Super Bowl V)," describes the artist. "The Colts made four attempts to score and didn't. It's a shot of seven of the Doomsday guys and there's a flag in the back that somebody had put in the stands that says, 'Dooms day for the Doomsday Defense.'"

All seven of those teammates appeared, autographing posters at the gathering in Dallas. It sent Dave Edwards back to continue his creations in Colorado on a Rocky Mountain High.

The Career Couch

His ten-year NFL career was over. Despite being told to stick around and stay in shape after he was placed on injured reserve, John Fitzgerald knew it was over. A half dozen knee surgeries made him sure of it. He just did not know what to do about it.

"I was really up in the air, not knowing," admits "Fitz." "I had an idea I wanted to stay in football and coach or do something like that. Coach Landry finally talked me out of it."

Coming up with successful solutions when faced with doubt was something Fitzgerald had found himself in the center of before. "1975, when there were so many rookies that came in and made the team, we weren't supposed to do very well," recalls the former Cowboys center. "We went out to L.A. in the Championship game and beat them when we were supposed to really get crushed. I took a lot of satisfaction out of that."

Fitzgerald began looking for the same satisfaction in his post–football future. The next conversation took place on the career couch. "I got tested by an industrial psychologist to see what I would best be suited for," says Fitzgerald rather sheepishly. "You sit down there, and a guy asks you a whole lot of questions. You come back in three weeks, and he tells you all the exact same things that you told him. Then he says, 'Have you ever thought of doing this for a living?'"

As a player, Fitzgerald was a likeable lineman, a guy who got along with just about everyone he ran into, or over. When a former teammate wants to know the whereabouts of another, he often phones "Fitz." "I don't know why I know where everybody is. I think it's more just my personality of wanting to know where guys are or every once in a while I pick up the phone and call somebody out of the blue." Maybe that is why a group of friends suggested that his search for a post–football career center around insurance sales. "That was 1989, and here we are," adds Fitzgerald, who bought into the oldest licensed commercial property and casualty insurance agency in the

Dallas–Fort Worth area. He is one of three partners in the company. "I'm the producer, the salesperson. I go out and find clients and produce income. I'm not a person that would be good sitting in an office going over invoices and accounts receivable and that type of thing. I enjoy getting out and sitting in front of clients in their offices."

It is not the football business, far from it. But it fits "Fitz" just fine. "Comparatively speaking, it's pretty mundane. But in all honesty you don't want a whole lot of wild swings, at least in my business you don't. There are enough economic swings already that you have to put up with," he says as he thinks about a business that has now surpassed his NFL longevity. "I've dug this hole so deep I'm staying in it."

Oh, by the way, the career path John Fitzgerald was counseled to take that day on the couch was the same as the one he took. "I guess it's just the conservative old offensive lineman's life."

Looking Past the Future

"I lost a million dollars in a day," begins Richmond Flowers of the story that picks up where the CBS movie *Unconquered*, about his and his father's struggles during the racial strife of the Deep South in the 1960s, left off. "The second half, the life after athletics, has been about as tumultuous."

Richmond Flowers Sr. was the attorney general of Alabama in 1964 when Governor George Wallace stood on the steps of a schoolhouse promising segregation forever. Saying that it was illegal and immoral, that white people suffered just as blacks did, and that the Constitution was a document for everybody earned Flowers an eight-year prison term. "I grew up with the most hated white man in the state of Alabama," says his son, former Cowboys safety Richmond Flowers.

The senior Flowers served 18 months of his sentence and was eventually pardoned by President Jimmy Carter. The younger Flowers was a second-round draft pick of the Cowboys in 1969. It did not take long for the son to mirror the father in times of trouble.

Despite earning his law degree from the University of Alabama and working with Jim Neal, of Watergate prosecution fame, on the successful voluntary manslaughter case against Ford Motor Company and the exploding Pinto, Flowers walked away from the legal profession. "I think the practice of law was kind of like watching paint dry. It just wasn't my cup of tea," explains Flowers. "It's not what it looks like; it's just paperwork and deadlines. I've just been kind of a dreamer my whole life."

But even Flowers could not believe his dreaming would turn into the nightmare that followed. Stepping into the futures industry put Flowers on a financial escalator that saw his income rising into the millions in a short period of time. The fall was even faster. "In the soybean drought of 1983, I got caught on the wrong side of that with a limit position in soybeans and lost everything I had," describes Flowers. "I lost my family, I lost all my money and landed not knowing where to go next. It's those times when God takes you behind the woodshed and knocks some sense into you."

Flowers had been a regular visitor to that woodshed watching his father's fight. "When I start feeling sorry for myself, I go, 'This ain't nothing compared to what my dad had to do.'"

He had also received his share of sense from Tom Landry's school of hard knocks. "We were playing Cleveland the year we ultimately went to the Super Bowl for the first time (1970)," remembers Flowers of one such lesson. "We had them backed up in their end zone, and they had to punt. D. D. Lewis got hurt, and they sent me in to take his position. I never knew what D. D. did. I think everybody just assumed I knew. I just figured you went in and blocked the kick. I get in my three-point stance. I ran a 4.2 40, so I'm pretty quick. I got a perfect start and the guy kicks me right in the head with the ball. We recovered the ball on the 2-yard line. I came off the field fully expecting to be hoisted perhaps on Coach Landry's shoulders or certainly invited to dinner with he and Alicia. He looked me in the eyes, I'll never forget it, and said, 'Son, if you ever go on the field again not knowing what your assignment is and know what you're supposed to do you will not be on this football team.' As it turned out, my job was not to block, it was to make sure the ball did get kicked because if I had gone in there and missed that ball and roughed the kicker they would have gotten out of that end zone. We ended up kicking a field goal and that play won the game for us. But, that's how disciplined Coach Landry was."

Discipline and a newfound faith helped Flowers rebuild. Spending over a decade as a network marketer with the NuSkin Company afforded Flowers a chance to renew relationships with his family and prepare for his next big dream—Chiliware, a software company designing desktop applications for the Linux operating system. "That name came from Dallas. We thought about it sitting in a Chili's restaurant one time," Flowers says with a laugh.

His belief in the product's future turns to a more serious excitement. "We're only 1 percent into a change the likes of which this world has never seen. That evolution is even greater than the evolution that occurred at the turn of the century when we went into the Industrial Revolution. We really haven't had a period in history the likes of that until now. It's just literally a gold rush out there, and you've gotta get in the game, but it's a lot of risk."

Flowers knows it is still a long shot, but he's been through both sides of that story before. He just hopes he's in the right place at the right time for a change. "How does an old kook 53 years old figure out how to get in there? I don't even know how to hardly turn my computer on, but I'm in there," admits Flowers. "We're certainly in a big arena when you start looking at the big gorilla we call Bill Gates. Hopefully, he won't know I'm around for a while, and we'll squash him."

If his family history is any indication, Flowers will certainly give it everything he's got, regardless of the price.

Bridging the Gap

Pomp and Circumstance" was not the song he expected to hear at age 40, but it signified one of the proudest moments of his life. Andy Frederick, wearing cap and gown, was walking across the stage at the University of Texas–Arlington to receive his degree in engineering.

"When I first got done playing ball, I worked for Merrill Lynch for several years and discovered I couldn't sell. Trying to be a broker and not being able to sell was not too good," says Frederick with a hint of sarcasm. He can laugh about it now. "The last two months I worked for Merrill, I spoke to the analysts in New York, and they were really stressing infrastructure reconstruction and environmental concerns, and that essentially falls into the category of civil engineering. So, I just went back to school and earned an engineering degree."

Frederick credits his football career, which continued with the Chicago Bears after his final season with the Cowboys in 1981, for providing the financial resources that allowed him to resume his education. His athletic acumen also provided the mental makeup he needed to go back.

"It mainly goes to the discipline of making yourself do something that may not be fun to do. Football is a lot of that, because most people have to work at physical skills. Some people are gifted with it, naturally, but most aren't, so you have to work at it pretty hard to develop them. It carries over into engineering and school in general." It was not the first time Frederick built a bridge to success, and it would not be the last.

"Winning the Championship game to go to the Super Bowl" was Frederick's favorite moment as a Cowboys offensive tackle. It happened first in his rookie season and was a first for his football career, bridging the gap between hard work and reward. "We never had a winning football team all through high school. I don't believe the high school has still had a winning football team," explains Frederick of the frustrations along the way. "I went to school at the University of New Mexico. We never won the WAC (Western Athletic Conference) championship or anything."

Now the wins and losses are determined by structural success and failure. Working with an engineering firm in Dallas, Frederick specializes in bridge design. "Right now, for example, we're replacing a 75- to 100-foot bridge that went in sometime in the '50s with approximately a 900-foot bridge that's going in right now. That took several years from the very beginning, the initial phase, to get to the construction," says Frederick before adding another duty to his ever-expanding list. "I've probably inspected about 1,200 bridges for the state."

Little inspection is necessary to realize that the gap between his football days and his future will continue to widen, but somehow Andy Frederick keeps figuring out the structure required to bridge that gap.

The Universal Language

I couldn't even understand one word English," says the Austrian-born kicker for the 1971 Cowboys. "The other team was cussing me, trying to throw me off. Finally, Bob Lilly and D. D. Lewis stand up and say, 'Listen guys, hold your breath and save it. This guy don't understand not one word.' I didn't."

But Toni Fritsch understood enough about the job he was brought to America to do. Lining up for a game-winning field goal against the St. Louis Cardinals, in only his eighth contest in the NFL, Fritsch ignored the language that was foreign to him and performed like the European soccer star had in his homeland so many times before. And even though this football was American and the kick had to go over the bar and through the uprights instead of under the bar and into the net, the result was the same. The Cowboys began a 10-game winning streak that included their first Super Bowl Championship. "That was the turning point," says a proud Fritsch. "Even Roger Staubach says it."

That Fritsch succeeded when most told him not to try has become his lifelong story. "When I come here everybody say, 'Toni Fritsch, why you go to America? You have everything here. You have fame, fortune, you have music, you a big soccer star,' you know. I said, 'Let's go, let's challenge it.' That's all my life."

Learning the game and then the language gave Fritsch his share of challenges, but it also gave him his share of opportunities. Leaving Dallas for Houston earned Fritsch another ten years of life in football with the Oilers and USFL Gamblers. Houston remains his adopted home, where he owns Texas Rental and several Rent to Own stores, but he was careful to always remember his roots. "I kept close, close contact with my home, Vienna. I stopped counting crossing the ocean at 150 times," says Fritsch, who returned to Austria as general manager for the same pro soccer team, Rapid Vienna, he once played for. He was also called back to share his expertise on the first German-language version of "Monday Night Football." "We got it beamed over, the game of the week, and we cut it in the studio, took off the announcers and the commercials and put our voice on. It wasn't easy to translate quarterback in the German language."

Little did Fritsch know the mixing of cultures would develop a pipeline from Houston to Vienna that would produce his biggest challenge yet, with a much more unusual combination. "I invite my good friend George Foreman (the heavyweight boxer) to Vienna in the days when the time wasn't so good, when he started preaching, when he changed his life," explains Fritsch. "He write songs about his life, why he changed his life, and he said, 'Toni, is it possible we can have the Vienna Boys Choir, the Mozart Boys Choir, the Vienna Philharmonic Symphony play and you have people who can write the music for them,' and I do, you know. So, I put a CD together for him. I'm the producer. He don't want gospel. We will put it in a classical way with tenors. I think we call it 'George Foreman, A Message to You and the World.'"

It is another one of those challenges that has many questioning Fritsch's sanity. But it is another language he understands better than most. "When you grow up in the city of Vienna, it's a world of music, with Mozart and Strauss, with the classical you have six operas around you. You have to have it. And when I think, he (Foreman) sold 11 million grills, we can sell some CDs," Fritsch adds with a laugh.

Before the doubters start throwing barbs Fritsch's way, they may want to remember the lesson learned by the Cardinals that Sunday in St. Louis. Whether it is football, music, or words, Toni Fritsch understands more of the language than anyone seems to think.

Disaster Defense

As a seven-year member of the Dallas defensive line, Bill Gregory did his best to create a disaster situation for the opposition. It may have also helped him qualify for his after-football career with IBM.

"Right now I'm in disaster recovery," says Gregory, who went back to graduate school and to earn his MBA. "A classic example, the tornado in Fort Worth (March 2000). Companies are out of business because their buildings are gone or partially gone, their computers are not accessible, or it's as simple as they don't have a place to go. Disaster could take a lot of forms. My particular piece of it is providing an alternate facility in case of a disaster for companies to basically continue running their business. I provide a facility, a desk, a chair, and a phone for individuals in that company, and technology if they need that."

Gregory's Cowboys career had a bookend of security. The only active rookie during the 1971 season, the defensive lineman from Wisconsin earned a Super Bowl ring. His final days in Dallas earned him another piece of Super Bowl hardware following the 1977 season. Two other visits to the NFL's biggest game kept Gregory from thinking about anything but football for his future. "I had spent my 'normal adult life' playing a game as opposed to getting experience in the business world. Then I was traded to Seattle, and after three years there I was cut and basically told I wasn't good enough anymore."

Gregory quickly gained his first experience in disaster recovery—his own.

"The biggest challenge was just, okay, what do you do and how do you begin the rest of your life and going through that whole process of adjusting to the 'real world' and being able to do that in a relatively short period of time," explained Gregory of the panicked feeling that fell over many mid level players who retired from football past the age of 30.

Fortunately his foresight to work on a graduate degree helped the recovery. "When I was put out to pasture, I could present a resume that had an MBA on it, plus the undergraduate degree. But, I felt like I needed a company that could afford me the opportunity to play catch-up with my lack of experience in the business world, and one that was a good company with a good reputation."

For Bill Gregory, creating havoc for Silver and Blue has been replaced by the security of Big Blue.

Scientific Safety

The gray goatee and frazzled tufts of hair around the rim of an otherwise bald head fulfill the stereotype. Scattered thoughts interrupting mid sentence during conversation also fit the image. But a picture of the man sitting in front of a computer screen in his Dallas office is probably not the one most would place in the frame labeled "Mad Scientist."

"My degree is in math and physics, and I am a scientist, essentially," announces Cliff Harris, cofounder of the Energy Transfer Company. It is his second soirée into the energy business after leaving football for the windfall of the oil industry in the early 1980s.

"I made more money in the oil business in the first year than I probably made my whole career with the Cowboys," admits Harris of the allure that allowed him to leave the Cowboys despite coming off his sixth straight Pro Bowl season. It was just the beginning of a success story that has more ingredients than a laboratory experiment. "The oil business was booming. At the same time a friend of mine came to me and said, 'Cliff, because of your relationships, I want you to get involved in the insurance business.' This insurance company hired me essentially as a consultant just to go and make introductions into large corporations. Things were rolling until the mid '80s when oil hit the skids. It crumbled along with the real estate industry. A lot of people lost all their money. I lost a chunk of mine."

It was the first time his nickname "Crash" fit off the field. But the decision to dive into the insurance industry kept the benefits coming until another friend from the gas business experienced the high-dollar draw of deregulation and talked Harris into joining forces for a shot at similar success with electricity.

"The company is set up to maximize opportunities created through deregulation. They are opportunities that allow you to move electricity over wires to utilities that before deregulation were not available to you. Today they are, if you pay a fee for them. From that come opportunities. The same thing happened in the gas industry.

Pipelines were not available and then they became available so that you could move them gas. So, we delved into the world of energy once again. It was a risk, a big risk."

Harris took enough calculated risks with the Cowboys to produce four straight All Pro selections. His formula as a free safety did not produce big individual numbers although he does hold the team record for play-off fumble recoveries and is third all time among Cowboys in that category for his ten regular seasons.

"One of the most rewarding games was when I felt like I performed for Coach Landry," Harris recalls. "We were playing the Giants, the Guy-ants is what Coach Landry would say. He coached there and had a passion for it. He told the team if you want to make All Pro, play good against New York, it's the media capital of the world." Harris took it to heart. "Half my game balls were from New York. In the first one we were behind 14–0 at halftime. Coach Landry came in and made a spirited, emotional halftime talk where he said, 'You guys aren't professionals, you're amateurs drawing pay.' We came out in the second half, I intercepted one of the first passes that Fran Tarkenton threw, ran it back 65 yards down to the 5-yard line, and we scored. Intercepted another pass, ran it back to the 10, we scored. Got a fumble on the 3-yard line. We ended up by just a series of plays, good plays that I made, winning that game."

For the most part, his style was designed to be in the right place at the right time and hit the opponent hard enough to stop the play long before his objective was reached. It was a style based on a complicated equation that Harris explains as if teaching a college statistics class.

"I've always approached, even football, scientifically and diagnostically. Football is really related to percentages. This is the Landry structure and system. If you know the facts, which you do, about a team's offensive formation—the down, the distance, the formation, the time, the score—all those elements are given. Then you have an equation that has an unsolved component on the other side, and that is what's going to happen. If you throw into that equation all the knowns, then you eliminate from past history of this team, through scouting reports, through studying of film, you can eliminate a high percentage of the potential plays, come up with a fewer number of plays. Then if you incorporate into that keys and designed defenses, you eliminate more plays, and you can come down to very few plays that have potential to happen. Within a matter of a fraction of a second you can make a decision, because you've eliminated most of the possibilities, and you can determine real quickly what you expect to happen. Then you throw into the equation instinct and experience, and you become an All Pro or in the Hall of Fame, hopefully, or if you guess wrong, a touchdown gets thrown over your head."

That Harris is annually considered for induction to the Pro Football Hall of Fame is a credit to his creation. "It fit perfectly with my personality, makeup, and basic instinct of my nature. It was designed for me because what I would do during the game would be to learn not only all the statistics, facts, historical performances of the team, I'd learn the quarterback. That was my opponent." Unfortunately for Harris, very few quarterbacks vote. It may be the miscalculation keeping him out. "How do you judge that? What's the criteria that you use to make a great free safety or a great quarterback, a great receiver, great running back? Sacks, is it tackles, or is it winning? My deal is the same that I have up here (Energy Transfer). Don't give me the credit—let me win. I want the team to win and go to the Super Bowl. I went to five. I think I had a big part in the role of free safety and the different style of free safety than before I came into the league, and then after I left the league you could see that there was a different style free safety."

Harris shares more than his style in the new company that includes an Internet division created by Cliff. The other half of the Cowboys dynamic duo of safeties is back alongside his running mate. "Charlie (Waters) and I are close friends. We're also competitive with each other, which makes for enhanced performances by both of us whether it be football or business," says Harris of Waters. The tandem was inseparable during their nine years together on the field. The mixture still creates a constructive concoction. "Charlie's involved in a different part of the company than I am. We don't have those intense daily-coordination, reading-each-other's-mind situation that we did when we played. I knew where he was going to be, where he should be, and he did the same thing with me. Today he's got his deal and I've got my deal. Seeing Charlie every day does remind me of the past life that I lived."

Especially coming in together as rookies on a team filled with defensive stars. It was Harris that got into the mix first. "In the first year of the team I made the starting lineup in the first game," remembers the free agent from Quachita Baptist. "Bob Lilly told me in the huddle, he didn't even really know my name I don't think, he said, 'Hey, rookie, we're going to the Super Bowl this year and I don't want you to do anything to screw it up.' I said, 'Yes sir, Mr. Lilly,' and sure enough we went to the Super Bowl that year."

Cliff Harris did not have to be a scientist to figure that one out.

Lucky and Good

I was probably the most prepared man in the world to win the lottery," says Thomas Henderson, almost a year after depositing a $10.7 million check for winning the Texas Lottery. That assessment may seem odd coming from a man who drugged and drank his last fortune away, laughed in the face of authority, spent time in jail for sexual assault and even more time in rehab centers. That, he says, was "Hollywood." This is Thomas talking.

"November (2000) was my 17-year anniversary of being a clean and sober man," Henderson admits with sincere pride in his voice. "By now I'm completely confident I will die a sober man. That is my mission. The number one in my life is my sobriety. That's before my children. It's before God. It's before anything, because if I'm not sober, I'm worthless."

Even before Henderson cashed in the $200 to $500 a week he invested on lottery tickets with the one that hit, he was anything but worthless. Ironically, most of the income was a direct result of the headlines he made as "Hollywood." "I am a national lecturer, selling films to rehabs in prisons," explains the owner, president, producer, director, and subject of Thomas Henderson Films. "I've just been fortunate. When you don't have any bad habits, particularly the alcohol and drug bad habits, and if you have sort of the capacity to make good business decisions, it's pretty easy out here."

It helps that Thomas can turn on the "Hollywood" charm while turning off the "Hollywood" addictions. He is still the smooth-talking storyteller who used to entertain his teammates with locker-room laughter and lewdness. It is a talent that translates well to prison inmates and drug rehabilitation patients who are the target audience for films like *Staying Sober, Staying Free and Learning How to Live, Getting Out and Staying Sober, Staying Free,* and his most recent work *Do the Right Thing When No One Is Looking.* He is currently contemplating a new film called *Alcohol Doesn't Come with Instructions.* "At least one of my films is in almost every prison in the

United States. That's been my main business," says Henderson, who penned a best-selling book *Out of Control* but never writes a script for any of his on-camera or lecture works. "It's a pretty good diet for the soul. It's all improv. I know the subject. I know the character."

"Hollywood" is the character, Thomas the translator. On film or on stage, the message is mesmerizing. "I mostly want to affect other people's lives. What turns me on, what fries Thomas Henderson's chicken, is having a willing student to listen to me about where I've been and what happened and what it's like."

It is a story that has been told over and over since the return to his hometown of Austin, Texas, in 1990. Thomas immediately put his money where his mouth is. A pet project of purchasing and rebuilding the abandoned high school football field that provided Henderson a place to play out his childhood athletic dreams was completed in the mid 1990s, before his lottery luck. Raising money for a new athletic track in the community followed, and Henderson has established his own charitable organization, East Side Youth Services and Street Outreach.

Then came life after the lottery.

A cell phone in Henderson's office rings. "Hold on, that's my money guy," he says as he reaches over to answer the other call. Henderson can be overheard talking about a financial matter which is confirmed when the conversation ends. "I just made a hundred grand. The market is up today."

Suddenly, Thomas sounded more like "Hollywood," boasting that his appearance fees have doubled and his businesses now include the HHH 56 Investments firm—the initials represent his two daughters (Thomesa Holly and Dalis Henderson) and his supposedly forbidden nickname. There are many concerned that it is just this type of instant success that threatens to stir Henderson's inner demons, just like his flamboyant dunk over the crossbars after taking a reverse kickoff down the sideline for a score brought a Texas Stadium crowd to its feet. "I hate that I'm saying this," interjects Henderson in a moment of humility, "but the dunk wasn't original. A guy at Langston University named Eugene Howard did that once. But, I was probably the only guy to get to do it on national television."

Henderson believes he is the guy to show the nation how to handle the high price of public prosperity without ruining his recovery, although he quickly discovered the delicate balance that Thomas will have, not just with "Hollywood," but the rest of the world. "I'm not ever sure you're prepared to have what I would call famous wealth, where people know exactly how much money you came into. I think there is a part of this that is pretty eerie and pretty scary and also makes you a great target for every sort of request imaginable," admits Henderson of his early experiences following the financial windfall.

One such example has become a lecture topic. "People I thought were dead have called. I had a lady come to my office who has a God that I'm not familiar with, some Yassa, some connotation of God that I'm not familiar with. She was dressed in a real religious garb, white satin something to the floor, the headpiece. She was in her 80's. She has a day care, a church, so she wanted a million dollars. I made a mistake when she says, 'Can we pray?' I said, 'Well, okay,' very reluctantly. She grabs her daughter's hand and my hand and starts speaking in tongue. In the middle of the prayer this lady says, and I quote, 'God order him now, God . . . order him right now, God . . . to write me a check for a million dollars . . . right now, God.' She came back a couple days later and told me that God had told her to tell me to give her a million bucks. I said, 'Well, my God told me to give you a thousand and tell you to quit begging.' So I gave her a thousand bucks. She still shows up, unannounced. You know the old saying, if you give a man a fish, he'll eat it; you give him a fishing pole, he'll fish. I should have given her a fishing pole."

According to Henderson there was an angel of sorts trying to give No. 56 that metaphoric fishing pole during his days in Dallas. But it took another unexpected encounter, over ten years after his own wings were clipped, to discover the identity. "It's a moment that I will always cherish. It was in Scottsdale, Arizona, at the Princess Resort. I couldn't sleep, at like 5:30 in the morning. I just got up from my bed and started walking around the place. I come to this breakfast area and low and behold—Tom Landry. It was for a Fellowship of Christian Athletes event, of which I'm really not a member. He was sitting there by himself. It was almost like it was a preordained meeting. I walked over and sat down and we had the doggondest conversation. I apologized to him for my behaviors. I told him I never really had any bad intentions. I was just sort of a feisty stallion who didn't know how to live. And he apologized to me and said that if he had known what he knew now—then—he would have handled me differently. So, I was able to make amends to Tom Landry. I was able to make peace with him long before he passed away."

That peace had an immediate impact on Henderson's heart and soul. So many of his teammates had followed Landry's plan without understanding all of its elements. Henderson balked at the basics and laughed off the lessons. He revolted against the rules. It may have taken a strange path with a terrible toll, but Thomas Henderson gets it now.

"The Cowboys remains the greatest experience I've ever had. I didn't subscribe to it, but I learned every work ethic value, every moral value, every team concept value, every organizational value, every quality control value that I have in my bones comes as a result of being a Dallas Cowboy and working for Tom Landry." Henderson pauses as the realization builds within. "I didn't know what I was getting when I got it."

Almost like winning the lottery. Hopefully, Thomas Henderson is more prepared this time than "Hollywood" was then.

Extra Points

My father used to say, 'When you're gone, the only thing that is going to be left is your memory. So, it better be good.'" Efren Herrera has taken his father's wisdom and put it to work.

From Mexican restaurants to Spanish-language radio, computerized control systems for liquor inventory to air purifying systems in bars, speaking engagements to specialty gifts, public service to golf course computer assistance, Herrera has been building a variety of memories. Fittingly, for a field goal kicker, three of his post–football moments stand above the rest.

"The Miller Lite All Star commercials," Herrera points out as his first favorite. "We used to fight among each other why we liked it—it tastes great and is less filling and all that stuff." For several years Herrera toured the country promoting his part in the great beer debate.

His next discussion was much more politically correct. "I was special assistant to (former congressman and HUD secretary) Jack Kemp on the West Coast. He hired me to work under drug elimination and prevention," explains Herrera with pride in his voice. "We created this thing that was the vision of Jack. He saw that part of the reason why kids get into gangs is that they want to belong to a group or a family. A lot of these kids were getting lost during school days or maybe perhaps not at nighttime but perhaps between 3 o'clock and 7 o'clock in the afternoon because there was no guidance." Herrera says that Kemp, a former NFL player himself, asked him to help develop a solution to the problem by drawing on his athletic background.

"We had this goal to be able to create the Inner City Games so kids would be in some sort of activity where there would be some sort of sports to feel good about themselves. We service within the inner cities between 100 and 200 thousand kids. They compete in everything—soccer, baseball, boxing, volleyball, football—you name it, we have a program. We have writing competition, essay competition, math competition; we're gradually integrating part of the schoolwork."

It is a program that continues in the Los Angeles area, and Herrera hopes it eventually becomes a national event. Working in politics was both a rewarding and eye-opening experience for the former Cowboys kicker. "Doing the things that are not good for yourself but for the masses," describes Herrera. "When you are inside and you see what is taking place and how this thing has developed and how it is going to take place and what is going to be a part of history, it's mind-boggling."

But Herrera's history keeps pulling him closer to the competition. Planning is one thing, playing another. "I was looking for something to compete in. The drive that most of the players have doesn't go away. It is very difficult, even if you compete in the business world and you do some good stuff. This is a place that is kind of empty, the competition. There is some similarity in business, but it is not the same because you have sports all your life and it makes it real difficult." Herrera has stopped swinging his leg at a football in favor of swinging his clubs at a golf ball. He hopes to have similar success.

Herrera has already played the Celebrity Golf Tour and is working on a possible shot at the Senior circuit. "I will be turning 50 and look at it and say, 'Well, you got two years and you will be 50, and so maybe if you work real hard on this,'" says Herrera, who admits he may not have the time or the talent to make it to that level. "I don't want to be one of those people that will think back and say, 'If I could have. I know if I would have, I could have.' I figure I will take a little time and do that, and then if I don't feel that I am capable of being competitive and feeling good about, I enjoy golf."

So far, despite the variety of efforts, Herrera has not found anything he enjoys as much as his days in the NFL. "Making it to the Super Bowl was the biggest thing I ever accomplished," admits Herrera, who led the Cowboys in scoring each of his three seasons, which ended with the Super Bowl win over Denver. "I was All Pro, I led the NFL in scoring (with the Seattle Seahawks after leaving Dallas), I was one of the best percentage kickers in the league. All that stuff was just part of my job. Being there and making it and knowing what it takes to be able to go to the Super Bowl, there is no question, was the highlight of my career."

Of course, if his post–football career is anything like many of the Cowboys scoring drives while Herrera was around, Efren has yet to take his final extra point.

Whirlwind Quake

I woke up that morning, I'm thinking I'm gonna die. I knew it was my last day on earth."

There was not an earthquake shaking him out of bed. He had experienced that before. It was not a nightmare caused by the collision of a hard-hitting safety. He always survived those. The anxious moment making Butch Johnson jittery this particular morning was caused by something he had never known before.

"I had never swam 2½ miles in the ocean. I had never rode a bike 112 miles. I had never ran 26 miles," reveals Johnson. At age 44, he was about to do all three in the ultimate test for triathletes, the Ironman in Hawaii.

"When I went to do it, scare you to death, man. I'm training in Colorado and swimming in a pool, and I'm looking out over the ocean because I haven't done any ocean swimming. Here I am, it's Wednesday before the event, and I'm thinking it's a Sunday event, the event is on Saturday, so I'm already off. I go out to the ocean, they have these huge buoys like 20 feet tall, and I look out and I say, 'Where's the turn?' Because you go out and come back in the water and the guy says, 'Okay, count this. One, two, three, four. Okay, now wait a minute, wait a minute, wait, wait. See that wave? Wait, wait, wait. Okay, see that one? There's one (buoy) behind that.' I said, 'Oh, holy shit.'"

Johnson fought through the overwhelming wave of doubt just as he had 20 years earlier as a third-round draft pick out of UC–Riverside on a Cowboys team with Drew Pearson and Golden Richards already on the roster. "When I was a rookie I really believed that the chances of me making it to the NFL were probably slim and none, and Slim just left town," jokes Johnson. "We played a preseason game down in Memphis, Tennessee. I had never run kickoffs or punts in college or high school, and the first time I ran a kickoff I ran it back 90 yards for a touchdown." He would become one of the Cowboys top return men and remains the team's all-time leader in play-off punt returns and yardage. "It was the first time I had ever touched one. I just had to run scared and not let them touch me. I can remember running this thing back, I'm thinking, 'Damn, maybe I'll make the team now.'"

Standing now on the beach in Hawaii, Johnson was about to swim scared. This time the decision not to let anyone touch him hurt the cause.

"It's 4:00 in the morning. You get in the water at five, and the guy that was helping me because all of a sudden I'm in a panic says, 'Okay, get on this side of the buoy, and you'll be away from the people,'" begins Johnson. "Well, if you swim with all the people, they pull you along, so really it's a lighter swim than what it should be. I'm on the opposite side where there's nobody. I'm actually swimming this whole thing by myself. I am dying. I'm saying to myself, 'Just get me out of the water, okay, let me just get through this deal.' So, I come out of the water, and I'm just happy. I'm just like, 'Okay, I can get to the bike now.'"

Bouncing from one event to another has been a big part of Johnson's life since leaving football. "My life's been kind of a whirlwind since I've started it, and it hasn't stopped."

From partnering with former Cowboys teammates on Kentucky Fried Chicken franchises in Texas to developing a company's sports marketing division with flag football events nationwide to owning car dealerships in Denver. "At that time, there were only like 25 minority-owned car dealerships in the nation," he explains. "I was one of 20 guys that trained for three years and went into franchising. By the time we bought the first five in 1981 we were the largest minority franchisees in the nation. I was walking with kings and not losing the common touch." Johnson continues to walk the walk in government circles, lobbying for community projects and programs for African-American concerns.

But the concern facing Johnson as the race continued was could he ride the ride.

"I get to the bike and it becomes ridiculous. I hop on thinking, 'Okay, we're off and running.' Riding this bike through mountains and plains, it's 130 degrees, 35 MPH gusts of wind coming off the ocean and really there are mountain ranges in Hawaii so you're going up and down these mountains. I'm about 20 miles into it, and I realize, 'Damn, man, I got 100 miles to ride.' There's 35 MPH head winds coming at me, and I'm thinking, 'Geez, let me have a turn and get that tail wind.' It doesn't happen. Going over the first edge, I'm flying down, going 65 miles an hour and I'm thinking I'm home free. I get over the next hill and hit the ocean and—bam—I'm going 10 MPH down a hill that looks like Mount Everest, and I'm thinking, 'Oh, my God, how did I get myself into this?' You're dead by the time you get out of the water anyway, once you get off the bike you have no legs. I just traveled 112 miles. I was sitting there grinning and laughing and joking around."

It was the grin, the laugh, the flamboyant way Johnson carried himself during his days in Dallas that earned him the adoration of Cowboys fans. On the field he became known as a receiver who would sacrifice to make the catch. That was by design. In the end zone he became known as the "California Quake." That was actually by accident. "To tell you the truth, I had scored a touchdown against Mel Blount in this preseason game at the end of the fourth quarter," describes Johnson of the day the quake first shook. "This lady is standing in front of me, and if you really look at crowds when something happens, they jump up out of their seats, waving their hands in the sky showing a touchdown and they're vibrating. Really, what I was doing was vibrating back to her. I was doing the same thing she was doing. And that's the truth. A reporter came to me the next day and he says, 'What is that, an orgasm spike?' Since I was from California and I'd been in an earthquake, the first thing that came into my mind was the California quake. That's how it was created. It was really to avoid being called the 'Orgasm Quake.'"

A touchdown the following week on national television turned the sudden shake into a marketing model that is still used today. "It's always been a strange phenomenon to me, because I really only did that five times. That's it," admits Johnson, who was banned from the display by Dallas's front office but continued to create shockwaves with the quake. "I got a dance number, got in a tuxedo and did a poster, and all of a sudden guys started doing posters and they started expanding their thought process of what they could do to market themselves. In a conservative arena with probably the best team in America, the most conservative stadium, there was not beer served in the stadium at that time, I broke barriers. I was just ahead of the game. There are a lot making millions of dollars now because of that."

Yet, there he was, two thirds of the way through his first triathlon, and Johnson was about to face a barrier that even dollars could not help him climb.

"By the time I made the third transition—you get delirious, I think. You change and go through your transition, and I said, 'Oh, time for the run.' Once again people are cheering, 'Oh, keep going.' I'm thinking, 'Ahh,' and this adrenalin rush comes on. You turn the corner and you got 26 miles to run and the people are gone. I should be dead. You watch people falling out where they extended themselves too much. But you learn a lot about yourself," says Johnson, who finally crossed the finish line, another accomplishment out of the way. "Probably the reason why I did that was I wanted to challenge myself physically and what do I do, go out and play three-on-three basketball?"

Johnson expects more of himself. So do the fans he has found across the country who continue to connect his success with the Cowboys to his success in business. "There is a class of people who watched us, ten years younger and ten years older, I believe. That group ages with you, and they relate to you," says the man who is cashing in on the network his name recognition helped create. "There are millions and millions of people who grew up on you and now they're vice presidents and presidents."

Expect the whirlwind to cause another quake as Johnson grows into his next decade of challenges. It is part of the plan to keep the athlete in him satisfied.

"I told myself every decade I was going to do something really different. In my 50's I'm going to do the Eco Challenge, there are 10 different events in the ecology. You do cliff climbing, you do rapids, you do kayaking. It's a team of four or five. You do jogging, you do bike riding. You have one woman and four guys. That's my 50's thing. The 30's was football and it was skiing. Once I got to a point that I felt comfortable enough with it going off cliffs and hills and popping it and doing my thing, I backed off of it," adds an older but wiser man. "If you played sports and you played at that level, you will be carried away if you don't watch it."

Butch Johnson would probably like that for his last day on earth.

Main Event

"**S**ince I've been out of the game, I can honestly say I haven't missed it one minute." Ed Jones has not had time to miss football. "Too Tall" has been too busy putting on a show.

"I provide corporations with entertainment for conventions, any of their corporate needs, and also provide casinos with musicians," says Jones of the company he began, with his brother Cliff, while still playing for the Cowboys. Team Jones, Inc., has booked many of the top performing artists in the world, from Michael Jackson to Barry Manilow, Tanya Tucker to Luther Vandross, Bill Cosby to Santana, for a variety of events.

Originally designed to promote their own events, Team Jones has evolved into more of a corporate service company. "We promoted concerts all over the country where we'd go in and hire a radio station to advertise for us and sell tickets not knowing if people are going to buy tickets or not. A lot of times you find yourself sweating up until the time of the show. I don't have to do that anymore," explains Jones, who did not want to abandon the idea of having his hands on the event, he just wanted to be able to enjoy it along the way. "I love music. I will always be around music. It's an event every time I do something like that. You don't ever know going in, they all are different, what level of fun you're gonna have, but I can honestly say the positives far outweigh the negatives."

Jones's positive influence on Dallas's Doomsday II Defense helped the Cowboys to three Super Bowls in his first five seasons. He still holds the team record for career fumble recoveries. But at 6-foot 9-inches, Jones became the legendary "Too Tall" for the havoc he created in the face of quarterbacks and kickers throughout the league. Blocked passes and blocked kicks were his forte. They are also the moments that remain his most treasured times in football.

"We played the Bears and beat them 10–9," Jones describes one such instance during the 1981 season. "I blocked the extra point in the fourth quarter that enabled us to win that ballgame. That feeling ranks right up there with the feeling I had when we won the Super Bowl in '77. It was an incredible feeling for an individual to have a hand on actually winning the game. Or when we beat the Giants when we clinched the division (1985). I blocked two passes that Jim Jeffcoat returned for touchdowns. Even though he was the one that made the nice run and scored, I feel like I had a hand on us winning that game."

Jones was so good at getting his paw in the opponent's way that he took a break from football to try his hand at professional boxing. Many thought it was an aberration, especially when he returned to the NFL a year later. Jones knew otherwise. "I never lost that burning desire to be involved with boxing, and I knew then, when I came back to Dallas in '80, that when I got out of the game that I would be back involved in boxing again."

For "Too Tall" it was simple. He enjoyed boxing too much to give it up. In fact, if Jones had had it his way when he was younger, he would have taken his swings in the ring rather than football all along. "It's my favorite sport, thanks to my father. I remember when I was a little kid when fights weren't televised on TV, you could only hear them on radio. I remember sitting on his lap listening and watching his expressions when he was listening to one of his favorite fighters fighting. I could kind of read his expressions and tell if he was going to be in a good mood after the fight. I guess that's where I kind of started gaining interest," reveals Jones.

His passion for pugilism continued to grow as he got a chance to pull his first punches. "I grew up in the country, and I remember he (Father) and some of his buddies, any time kids got in trouble fighting, they would take chalk and draw a ring outside, and we'd have to get inside that chalk and fight it out. It all started back then, and this is something we continued for years. It was always a lot of fun. Nobody got hurt. It was just a way of disciplining us. It's just been a passion of mine ever since. I wanted to fight in high school. I was a baseball and basketball player, and my coach heard of me fighting in a Golden Glove event, big write-up about it in the paper, and he approached me and told me I was going to either have to give up basketball and baseball, or boxing. That was a no-brainer. There was no way I could give up basketball and baseball."

Now that Jones has retired from participation in any professional sport, he is back in the boxing game as owner of the Too Tall, Inc. Boxing Team in San Diego, California. "It's a full management team. We do everything. We have in-house lawyers, in-house PR people. All the guy gotta do is fight," explains Jones. "I have established contacts worldwide. I have scouts everywhere looking for talent, and I evaluate them and decide who we're going to go with, along with my people."

It is a business that satisfies Jones's passion while fitting well with his entertainment and event enterprise, but he is not Don King. Jones is more interested in finding and fertilizing the opportunities of young fighters than jumping on the bandwagon of big-name boxers. "Right now the most important thing to me is to keep these young men with unblemished records. I don't want to move them too fast."

Jones describes his team as a work in progress. "At the present time, I don't have a heavyweight in my stable. When you don't have a heavyweight, you better keep that fighter with an unblemished record so that by the time he's say, 18 and older, you can start telling the networks and these cable stations that put on big fights, take a look at this guy. Otherwise, there is no money there for them now that you don't have anybody that's a draw where they can make the big bucks. They can make a good living but nothing like the numbers that a lot of fighters in the small weight classes made years ago."

Ed Jones may have a tough time understanding what it is like to be an unknown, much less one that is small. A decade after stepping away from his career with the Cowboys, "Too Tall" is still too recognized to go anywhere without being noticed. "That's something that is truly amazing at times, even though I've had to live with this for years," admits Jones. "But still, when I'm in places like New York, where you've got the Jets, Giants, Knicks, Nets, Mets, Yankees, I can have a cap on or coat, walking down New York and somebody says, and you hear people even driving by, not just walking the street, 'That's 'Too Tall.' That's just truly amazing."

Being almost 7 feet tall is part of it. Being an All Pro defensive end for America's Team adds even more attention. "I was visiting with Wilt Chamberlain before he passed and we were just sitting talking at a function together and we were kind of throwing that out. Obviously, everybody knows who Wilt was because of his height and he had just a totally different look. I'm strictly an athletic football look. He said, 'Man, I'm going to tell you something,' because he was a big Cowboys fan. He said, 'That's something you'll have to deal with the rest of your life, because if you were a Boston Celtic, a New York Yankee, or a Dallas Cowboy,' he said, 'you will always be recognized.'" Of course, it can get a bit bothersome sometimes. "I remember one Halloween I dressed up and unless you knew my walk there's no way you knew who I was, but people kept figuring it out because they knew my walk. That's scary. That is too much."

As much as Jones does professionally in his post–football career, he is careful to keep plenty of time for family and friends. Always known as one of the more social Cowboys during his playing days, Jones frequently travels with large groups and participates in family reunions at least twice a year. "I talk to people that say, 'I have immediate family that I haven't seen in eight years,' and I can't imagine that. I thank my mom for that, who is no longer with us, but I thank her for that."

Jones is thankful for being one of only three players to play for 15 seasons with the Cowboys. He had more starts and more games played than anyone who's ever donned the Dallas star on his helmet.

But Ed "Too Tall" Jones is more thankful for his ability to walk away and never look back. "To see a number of them that's very frustrated because their careers ended prematurely, mainly to injuries, see how they're dealing with it, how some of them are handling it, it's very tough for a lot of them. I haven't missed it one minute. I guess it's just knowing I'm at peace with myself. I don't miss the game at all. I'm a big fan. I'm down when Dallas loses like other fans are. I'm really down. I'm sad for a while. But, I don't miss being out there."

In the Middle of the Hunt

I t has great longevity and great ability to stay where you put it. It doesn't warp or twist. It has resistance to decay."

The description given by Lee Roy Jordan when asked about the specialty products his lumber company sells could have easily been words used to define the stability of the Cowboys middle linebacker.

For 14 years, Jordan was the man in the middle. He still owns the majority of Cowboys career records for tackles and shares the interception record of three in one game (vs. Cincinnati, 1973). It should come as no surprise that Jordan's business has also withstood the test of time.

"You have to be a leader to be a middle linebacker," says Jordan of his success. "I think you like being in charge, you like the pressure on you. You accept the challenge not only for yourself, but for those around you that you feel like you can ask or inspire to perform at a higher level. It translates into business. You have an intensity level that makes you work hard and consequently inspires most people around you to do likewise."

Jordan admits he was simply "looking for a way to make a living" when a deal to become a car dealer fell through and his banker suggested he talk to a man on the bank's board about California redwood and western red cedar. "He introduced us, and three months later I was the proud owner of two lumberyards," continues Jordan. "I just kind of got in and learned it from the outside, from the bottom up. It was a product this gentleman felt could be distributed here in this part of the country (Texas)."

Yet, it is a product with a relatively expensive price tag, so Jordan had to stand tall through some tough times. It was something he had learned during his football days in Dallas. "Coach Landry was a great teacher in his planning and persevering. If he hadn't had great confidence that we would succeed if we kept improving in every area that we could improve in, he would have given up long before we won a Super Bowl. I think all of us would," admits Jordan. "I think the human mind and the human spirit is just that way. If you work at it long enough, you will figure out a way to get the job done."

Jordan has also figured out that success usually occurs in areas of expertise. That lesson took a little longer to learn. "If I'd followed my own advice, I would have not gotten into other businesses. I try to tell people, stay with what you know. Don't venture out and invest in other things that other people are promoting because most of the time it doesn't end up, it already hasn't ended up good for me."

The southern Alabama gentleman who played for Paul "Bear" Bryant at the University of Alabama before becoming the sixth overall pick in the 1963 NFL draft does venture out as often as possible in another area he knows very well. "I love quail hunting," Jordan says with an extra excitement in his voice. Especially when sharing the added Texas flare, "horseback quail hunting. You can cover a lot more territory because in walk hunting you just cover what a person can walk and cover and on horseback they move rather smoothly and your dogs can cover a much wider range of territory."

Jordan covered a lot of territory as a middle linebacker in Landry's innovative "Flex" defense. Adding the element of horseback riding with his love of hunting has been another perfect fit. "You're involving the horse along with the southern-type-gentleman quail hunting experience. A dog points, we get off the horses, get our guns out, load our guns and go get in position behind the dogs, hopefully get a covey rise, birds rise and we get a shot off," explains Jordan. "You unload every time you go back to the horse, put your gun back in the scabbard, mount up, and go ride again."

Fortunately for the anchor of the original Doomsday Defense, only a few long-term physical ailments followed him from his Cowboys career, allowing Jordan to "mount up and go ride again." "I've got some irritation and bone spurs along my spine from all the running into people for 23 years or so. Every once in a while I have kind of a pinched nerve or one of those spurs digging into a nerve or putting pressure on a nerve," admits Jordan. "But as far as the knees and hips, man, I do really good." That is, until the horseback hunter met up with an even more extreme form of finding birds. "A friend of mine used to hunt on Honda trail bikes," tells Jordan of his most embarrassing and dangerous moment. "One time I hit a stump or something and let the bike fall over. I fell on a limb that had a sharp point to it and punctured the right side of my leg, my right calf, kind of punctured it to the bone. I had to pull the sticks and wood chips out of there and kind of bandage that up, then we had to get out of there and get back home to a doctor a few hours later. It was just kind of scary."

Scary might be the adjective used by a former San Francisco quarterback about the damage Jordan inflicted for several years on his way to five Pro Bowls and a permanent place in the Cowboys Ring of Honor. "I had the opportunity to intercept a few passes of John Brodie's in some key situations in NFC Championship games or play-off games," remembers Jordan. "Those particular things are highlights that are big for me and probably were for the team at that particular time." And still are for those who follow Jordan and many of his former teammates to the Big Country Celebrity Quail Hunt in Abilene, Texas, every year, where stories are swapped with every shot—stories of football, business, and family. "I'm extremely crazy about my family. I've got a great wife of almost 40 years and three boys who like me enough that all three of them are working in businesses I own or have owned."

It is another example that proves Lee Roy Jordan always has been and always will be in the middle of the hunt.

Solid as a Rock

He was a fourteenth-round draft pick who spent most of his Cowboys career as a backup to Robert Newhouse at fullback. But when Scott Laidlaw was called upon, as he was during the late-season drive to the 1978 Super Bowl, he was solid as a rock. Now, Laidlaw makes sure the rock is solid for structures that stand much taller than anyone in the NFL.

"We did all the stonework on the Bell South Tower in Nashville, which is often called the 'Batman' building," says Laidlaw, co-owner of Laidlaw Stoneworks. "I'm currently doing one that's called the Nashville Main Library Building. It's a 51-million-dollar overall job that I'm doing most of the limestone on the outside, so for me, it's probably about a two-million-dollar job."

It hasn't always been that good for Laidlaw away from football. His first attempt at business threw the former running back for a loss. Lured by the temptation of an athlete's ego, Laidlaw was talked into a deal that involved Western apparel. His college degree was in architecture. It wasn't the only part of the deal that did not fit.

"My partner backed out of the deal, and I stayed in it. What am I going to do in retail sales? They ate me up, took all my money," remembers Laidlaw, who eventually declared bankruptcy. "I went from that level of three-time Super Bowl participant on a team that everyone wanted to be on, down to nothing. Now what am I going to do?"

The rock was only chipped. It was not broken. Laidlaw began working as a promoter for a Dallas construction company and found that, with the knowledge drawn from his Stanford architecture degree, he could do more than promote. "I'm an overachiever," says Laidlaw of the characteristic that best fits his style then and now. "I wasn't the biggest, fastest, strongest football player, but I don't know how to quit."

So Laidlaw built his own foundation after sharing high-profile projects in Dallas that include such name buildings as the Crescent, Momentum, Lincoln Center, Sunbelt, Onyx, Anatole, and Wyndham. The cylinder-shaped Wyndham carries a story of stone that sparked Laidlaw's interest in Mother Nature's treasures. "The material is called Indian Sunset Red," says Laidlaw of the hotel's high-rise exterior. "Those blocks were actually scheduled to be sold to a harbor as jetty material. They cut it up and polished it and the owner loved it. They were actually going to get rid of the blocks as waste, and it ended up going up on that building. You won't find any more anywhere because it was just a strain of that quarry, and that's all it gave before it went to a different color."

A different look also appealed to Laidlaw as his opportunity emerged. Selecting a location to carve his own niche seemed simple enough, at least the way Laidlaw looked at Nashville, Tennessee. "The way I looked at it, it was Dallas in the early to mid '70s. There's a very similar growth pattern here to what there was in Dallas. I kind of like that."

Every building should have a rock in its foundation like the one Laidlaw laid down for the Cowboys.

Plowed Over

I was laying there bleeding. I'm thinking I'm either going to have to get up and do something or I'm gonna lay here and bleed to death."

For Burton Lawless, the decision was as instinctive as the first step of a pulling guard on a Super Bowl sweep. But the hit that sent Lawless to the ground on this particular afternoon took his thoughts and his life completely away from football.

It didn't seem like anything but a normal Friday during May in the central Texas countryside. Lawless had worked the field cultivator for his friend many times before, and even after picking up the plow from the service center where a simple repair to the hydraulic cylinder was completed earlier that day, the drive to the field went without a hitch. Until it came time to lower the huge plow arms that stretch 40 feet wide when in operation, but ride in an upright position similar to football goalposts while en route.

"I pulled the pin out and when I saw the arm come past the point where it usually stops, I took off running," describes Lawless of the moment that changed his life forever. "As I took off, the tire on the outside of the plow hit me in the back of the neck and knocked me flat down. The point of the plow cut my head real bad."

That's when Lawless made his life-saving decision, somehow lifting his near-300-pound frame back into the tractor's cab to call for help. Moments later, his friend Brady White had Lawless on the way to the hospital, when suddenly Burton realized it wasn't the cut that would cost him his NFL career.

"We went about two miles and I said, 'Brady, you gotta stop. My neck is hurting me too bad,'" remembers Lawless, who would spend the next 17 days completely paralyzed from a broken neck.

While the feeling and movement in all of his extremities would eventually return, Burton knew that just three years after leaving the Cowboys for the Chicago Bears, he would be forced to leave football forever. "I was learning to walk again, and when you get right down to it, football don't mean a whole lot when you're trying to learn how to walk. But, in a way that was a blessing in itself because when you just leave the game retired there's always the question in the back of your mind can I play another year? There was no question in my mind," says Lawless with a matter-of-fact tone. "It was over then."

Memories that include being part of the 1975 "Dirty Dozen" draft class and starting Super Bowl X as a rookie are rarely in the forefront of Burton's mind anymore. It was all plowed over that day in the country. "It changed my life drastically," admits Lawless as he takes a break from volunteer efforts for several agencies in the Waco, Texas, area that have become his life's work. Whether it's the Boys and Girls Clubs, Compassion Ministries, or Ronald McDonald House, Burton's new direction has become more important to him than memories, more important than a career. "I rededicated my life to Christ, and what I want to pass along to people is that they're going to get knocked down in life. It's just a matter of how you respond to it."

When Burton Lawless got knocked down, he got back up despite a broken neck. It was a choice that seemed as simple as finding the right lineman to block. He knows he was blessed to have a choice.

"If I would have been killed out there that day, I would have had a great life. Period."

D. Day

"I am a recovering alcoholic and drug addict."

The words come without hesitation. They reveal no shame. D. D. Lewis is on a long road trip from Dallas to Illinois. It is nowhere near the longest or bumpiest road Lewis has traveled since taking five trips to the Super Bowl as a Cowboys linebacker.

"I ended up losing my family, any money I had, any property, any respect, self-respect, everything," shares Lewis of a story that got worse at every turn. "My daughters were estranged from me. My wife divorced me. I got caught with a DWI in Dallas. February 10, 1986, I got sober."

D. D. Lewis started 135 straight games at weakside linebacker. It is a streak that equals Bob Lilly's, tied for third all time in the Cowboys record book. No. 50 went about his business on the field in a quiet, unassuming fashion. So quiet, the rest of the NFL passed him over for Pro Bowl consideration each of his 13 seasons. So quiet, his teammates were unaware that while Thomas "Hollywood" Henderson was on one side of the linebacking corps in a drug-induced rant, Lewis was on the other side ignoring some of the same signs of addiction.

"I didn't know it myself. How would they know it? It was a very well-kept secret. I mean, an amphetamine before a game seemed like it just helped you talk more after the game," he says without the assistance of substance now that the secret is out. "Marijuana and cocaine, Demerol or Percodan. I was hyped on Percodan for eight years."

For almost ten years, Lewis has worked in sales and customer relations, hyping materials from the Potash Corporation of Saskatchewan. Resources from mines in Canada provide potassium chloride, and phosphates from North Carolina and Florida, along with nitrogen from plants around the country combine for a variety of fertilizer ingredients, foods, plastics, and other products. "We go around and train the industry, metropolitan fire departments and emergency responders, in the product itself. What it is, what it does, and how to handle it if you have a leak or an emergency situation."

Lewis also shares the story of other dangerous chemical combinations, the ones that could have ended his life. "I am just so grateful that I didn't die. I have seen people die with this disease, kill themselves, keep getting DWI and go to prison, run over people, have wrecks and paralyze themselves," Lewis tells high school kids and business associates as part of the company's community awareness program. "Remaining sober on a daily basis is a big challenge for me today."

On the football field he seemed to handle most of the challenges thrown his way. No linebacker in Cowboys history has more play-off interceptions than the little guy on the outside. "I intercepted two passes in our play-off game against the Los Angeles Rams in 1975. For me that was a personal high."

Yet from the earliest days he can remember, Lewis always felt like an outsider because he was the little guy. It was part of the personal problem that made him get high in the first place. "As a young man I felt that I was dumb, stupid white trash, lived across the tracks and was never going to amount to anything. Everybody in my family told me I couldn't sing—everybody else in my family could, they could sing and harmonize and I didn't fit in," admits Lewis of a difficult childhood. "But when I drank, I was 6-foot 5-inches tall, I could sing, I could dance, and I became a new person. I didn't think I had a problem in my life because I was comparing myself to the big boys who were under-the-bridge alcoholics."

During his football days the comparisons were to people like Henderson or other fellow teammates that would drink with Lewis. Only he would stay out all night.

The long road after retirement got even tougher. In the oil field supply business during the mid 1980s, Lewis rode the bumps of an industry that "went berserk, went nuts, and went down." When it all hit bottom, he realized he was no longer describing his life's work but his life as a whole.

"I had to find out who D. D. Lewis was for the first time. I got back in church and mended my relationship with God. Today I have fears, I have guilt, I have shame, I have anger, all those failings and sorrow just like everybody else, but I have a way through it today. I praise God for that. That, to me, is the greatest single thing that has ever happened to me."

So Lewis spreads the word within the role he now plays in the fertilizer business. It has done more for his growth than any of his products could possibly do to help the growth for which they are designed. He is remarried and his kids are back in his life. The road is still long, but it is much smoother than ever before.

"I need to have all that revealed 'cause I don't want everybody thinking D. D. Lewis is the greatest guy in the world. I am just like every other guy in the world. I am a human being and sometimes we fall and we make mistakes. We go down the wrong road. We realize it, we pick ourselves up and get back in the game, just like football," he says in summation. "The denial will kill you. We all feel so unique and yet, I try to tell everybody that we are so much alike it is unbelievable. We hide from everybody. We all put on masks and try to be something we're not or run from our feelings and won't let anybody love us. I try to break down that barrier and let everybody see that I am just an average Joe today. I know I am not stupid, I know I am not dumb, I can sing, I can dance, and I am just pretty much average—and what a great feeling that is to know today. It is wonderful."

Long Gone

Clint showed up at my house one day," remembers Charlie Waters, albeit a distant memory. "I had a house in Dallas near the (Cowboys) practice field that had some surrounding land. He showed up in a Cadillac with the back seat out and he had a Shetland pony where the backseat was and his head was sticking out. And he said, 'Can I board my horse here?'"

Clint Longley made a quick impression on the Cowboys he came in contact with—whether it was a wild request as a rookie, earning the nickname "Mad Bomber" for his off-the-bench barrage to beat the Washington Redskins in the 1974 Thanksgiving Day game, or the altercations that ended with a quick swing against fellow quarterback Roger Staubach two training camps later. His exit was just as sudden but much more complete.

"He's never been much for publicity, and he's a pretty private individual," says Howard Longley.

Clint's father could not have been more understated. Since sneaking out of Thousand Oaks the day of the surprise attack on Staubach, Longley has completely severed his Cowboys connections. A short stay with the San Diego Chargers was the last the league has heard of Clint Longley. Both franchises attempted to attract him to their 40-year reunions. Neither drew a response. Teammates, roommates, even his college alumni office list Longley as long gone.

He is not gone. He is apparently just not interested in entertaining the rest of the world's thirst for reliving his rocky history with Roger. Those who know him in his small east Texas town know him for his real estate dealings and his tenacity on the tennis court, not his crazy Cowboys career.

"He's skitsy about the Dallas press," more accurately states Clint's mother. It is a press corps that is often callous in its inability to forgive and forget. Cowboys fans seem more curious about

Longley's lack of sensitivity towards the cliché that time heals all wounds.

Besides, there may be a Shetland pony wandering a pasture somewhere in north Texas wondering why Clint Longley never came back.

Inner Beauty

He fought the battle of the bottle. He did away with the drugs. Now Harvey Martin was facing the toughest test of all.

"Stopping drinking and doing drugs was nothing compared to this," admits Martin. His fiancée, Debbie Clark, the woman who had helped turn his life around, was facing the end of hers. "She had brain cancer. It's just a debilitating disease. It strips the dignity of the person that has it. At the end, you look at your loved one and they are so ravaged you say, 'Lord, please don't let them suffer no more.'"

Harvey Martin understood about suffering. He faced serious troubles long before he met Ms. Clark. "I had some demons," says the former Cowboys defensive end of his days as a "functional" alcoholic and drug addict. "Anybody that's been through that realizes it will take over your life after a while. It took over my life to the point where I was not myself. I really didn't like the person I saw in the mirror, but I didn't know how to change it. I didn't know how to stop."

There were anything but visions of beauty staring back at the man Dallas knew as "The Beautiful Harvey Martin," a homegrown co-MVP of Super Bowl XII and a popular radio personality. "I'm still trying to live that name down," reveals Martin. "It embarrasses me when people go, 'Hey, beautiful.' You're a big ole hunking football player and people call you beautiful. It makes you blush."

It made "The Beautiful Harvey Martin" become an uglier version than even he could ever imagine, until some genuinely beautiful people entered his life to set him straight. "I fell in love with a wonderful woman, and I found myself being abusive, especially verbally abusive, really not treating her the way a man should treat the woman that he loves," explains Martin of the moments that took him to the proverbial bottom that most alcoholics and addicts must reach before beginning the hopeful journey back.

This time it also took a woman much stronger than the All Pro defender. "She had a lot to do with it. I got myself put in jail a couple of times for just being loud and abusive and drunk—things that you shouldn't normally do. A friend of mine who was a judge told me flat out, 'I think you need some help, Harvey, and I'm gonna send you to a place to get some help.' It was God's gift. It was wonderful."

That Martin can manage that kind of self-evaluation is a testament to how far back he has come. Once again eloquent in his expression, the Dallas native is complimentary of the opportunity he received as a third-round draft pick out of East Texas State. "Getting the chance to come on the team and have Bob Lilly sit down next to you and start giving you pointers as a rookie. These guys were heroes to me before I got on the team."

And thanks to many of the lessons learned, Martin feels like he can be a hero to them again as well. "When you were young and playing football and kinda wild, real wild, you didn't hear a lot of the things (Tom Landry) said. You heard him but you didn't really hear him. The older you get and you start reflecting, then it starts to make sense. A light bulb goes on in your head, and you're like, 'Oh, my goodness, this is what he was talking about. This is the lesson he was trying to show.' I was able to overcome what I had to overcome because of what I was taught. I had to go back to basics. I had to get the discipline back. I had to get that hard work attitude back. I was so glad I was able to rediscover what really makes me."

What makes Martin in business today is a sales position with a company that develops daily maintenance products for the construction industry and others. He passed through a brief acting career, time in the electronics business, and some real estate activities, but all that is in the past, among the moments he has finally put behind him. They are moments he readily shares, however, as a board member of the Greater Dallas Council on Drugs and Alcohol Abuse. He helps others, which in turn helps Harvey Martin.

There is no better example than his days with Debbie Clark. There she lay, the woman he so loved, being taken away just as Martin had finally found what truly made him beautiful. "I went through a year and a half with the lady that really helped me make my change, battling her disease. I was able to be there with her 24/7 and fight with her. I just loved her so much. A lot of people couldn't believe that I was doing what I was doing where she was concerned," shares Martin. "In that, I realized that I had come full circle."

The demons do most of their damage during the darkest of times. According to Martin, it doesn't get any darker than what he was witnessing. The true test of an addictive person's progress is how he handles the moment the temptations return. "I realized that a drink of alcohol is not going to take the cancer out of her head. And I realized that going and trying to find my old dope buddies was not gonna take the cancer out of her head. So what the hell was that going to solve?" The circle was complete. "She lost her battle on Super Bowl Sunday (2000)," adds Martin in almost a whisper. "I truly miss her."

Martin has not missed the opportunity to grow through his pain. Now he looks in the mirror and likes what he sees. "I wouldn't be the person I am today if I hadn't gone through some of life's experiences."

He may not want to hear it repeated, but Harvey Martin is beautiful again.

Deep Thoughts

I've been diving when somebody ran out of air. You just give them your air. You're trained to deal with it." Easy for Ralph Neely to say—he's experienced a variety of depths and has always been able to come up for air.

Neely was in deep despair as the Cowboys marched to their first Super Bowl Championship following the 1971 season. The All-Pro offensive tackle could only watch, his leg badly broken in a motorcycle mishap that cost him much more than a chance to retire early as a champion. "That was a $35,000 experience because my paychecks stopped. It was a non-football injury. They won the Super Bowl, and I only got a half a share of that," recounts Neely of a moment that is never far below the surface in his memory. "When I broke that ankle, I swore up and down that unless it had at least two doors and four wheels, I wasn't getting on it. I haven't been on a motorcycle since then."

There was actually a much deeper lesson to learn. Five years later, after battling back despite an attractive job offer away from the playing field, Neely finally earned the ever elusive title of champion. "All through college (University of Oklahoma) we went to Orange Bowls but never won," explains Neely. "Even in the high school play-offs we were never state champions. The first ball game where I won all the marbles in my athletic career was the last one I played (Super Bowl XII)."

It would not be the last time Neely would find his way up from a submerged situation.

"I went through some very tough financial times, like some other people in the early 1980s," says Cowboys guard Ralph Neely about some of his early struggles in the business life after football. He spent the first few years after his retirement from the NFL in real estate, apartment management, and banking. The timing was not good for

Neely and neither was the fit. Neely felt like he was on the verge of drowning. "I sold a Rolex watch to be able to have enough money to buy a car."

Fortunately, Neely knew how to swim with the sharks. Using characteristics he gained from the game he played for 13 seasons, Neely reached shallow water selling insurance. "Football let me meet and know, not just shake hands with, more people than most do in ten lifetimes. I think that enabled me to have good communicating skills and be comfortable in any environment, whether it's black-tie or sitting on the edge of a river fishing," says Neely, who finally found success in a post–football career that has now lasted longer than his days in the NFL.

All that experience exploring the depths, always returning to the surface, drew Neely and his wife to a more literal definition. Watching fish in their salt-water aquarium, the Neelys became enamored with what they saw. It was another breath of fresh air. Before they knew it, the Neelys were in the underwater world of scuba diving. Within the first three years they had completed 180 ocean dives. Now, all the ups and downs Neely has been forced to endure make sense. He feels completely comfortable going deep.

"I never dreamed that scuba would affect me this way," admits Neely of the pastime that has become his passion. "The thing that amazes me about the ocean is that you can look at one piece of coral and there's about a hundred thousand different things going on, different life organisms. The ocean is an amazing place. When you're down there seeing giant turtles or you're in a school of fish where there's about 5,000 fish just swirling around you."

The Neelys are advanced open water divers on their way to becoming dive masters, who reach depths in excess of 130 feet. With the encouragement of former teammate Bob Lilly, an accomplished photographer, Ralph has begun to photograph the undersea world, sending photos of recent trips to a handful of former Cowboys including Don Meredith, who Neely jokes was especially interested in one particular exotic species.

"There's a fish called a spotlight parrotfish. They get huge—6 feet. They start out as a female (dark crimson red) and then turn into a male (turquoise)," Neely explains. "Meredith said he'd like to be the other way. He said he's ready to change. He always wanted one to play with."

When the laughing stops, Neely continues to share the depth of his experiences, pointing to night dives as the most impressive to date. "I snorkeled one night with three giant manta rays that were 20 feet across. They're just gorgeous, but they kind of humble you. You see completely different animals at night than you do during the day. It's a complete change. You see octopus and a lot of different crabs, and a lot of different fish that hide during the day will come out at night and feed," describes Neely. "When the parrotfish go to sleep at night, they build an invisible cocoon around them with mucus. If anything touches it, it wakes them up."

Ralph Neely has touched bottom and returned to the top. He's not afraid of the descent because he knows what it takes to begin and finish the ascent. But through it all, even Neely isn't trained to deal with everything. "My wife doesn't even like to eat fish anymore. It really has an effect on you."

The Economist Guy

A musician dies in a plane crash. His fans mourn the loss of their favorite entertainer. Shortly thereafter, a wrongful death lawsuit has attorneys scrambling to determine the future worth of the deceased.

Enter the expert. "Typically their heirs, maybe a co-musician that lost a lot of future opportunities, because this is a suit against somebody that has to be found at fault in trial for this person's death and then a lot of people can sue for economic loss because of this person's death," explains Blaine Nye. "I'm asked often to evaluate the economic loss suffered by these different people over what would have been, for example, Mr. Stevie Ray Vaughn's lifetime."

It was one celebrity case of many the former Cowboys guard has been called on to evaluate as a financial economist. That is just one area his current career covers. "It's like the economics of investment," continues Nye. "An economist looks at demand and pricing for goods in a period of time, and a financial economist looks at the trade-off over different time periods—how much you consume and how much you save, maximize your lifetime utility as opposed to just your contemporaneous utility."

It may sound like brainy stuff for an offensive lineman, but Blaine Nye never fit the stereotype of a dumb jock. He received a Bachelor of Arts in Physics from Stanford and then continued his education while playing in the NFL, earning a Master of Science in Physics and an MBA in between his duties in Dallas. "You had a lot of spare time when you played football, what the hell," Nye claims with a dry wit that often humors an otherwise heady conversation. "In those days it was a six-month job. That was my complement to beating my brains out."

Nye, the football guy, complemented his career with the Cowboys with his most memorable moment in his last game played, the 1977

Pro Bowl. "I finally got to block Curly Culp without worrying about whether Tom (Landry) would worry if I missed him. In other words, it didn't matter if I missed him. So I peeled my ears back and drove him back about 7 or 8 yards, and Walter Payton went for about 35 yards on a dive play. I thought that was a great way to go out. Of course, if I'd known they were going to win a Super Bowl the next year I'd have stayed one more year. Besides, there aren't too many jobs where you get paid for drinking beer and sweating."

Nye should know, he considered them all, resulting in a decision to continue complementing his curriculum with graduate school, earning a Ph.D. It was part of a post–football career path that had more direction changes than any play diagramed in the complicated Cowboys playbook.

"I sort of moseyed at being a physics teacher until I found out the job market was just awful. I got to about the masters level and saw that people who spent ten years on elementary particle theory were getting nasty letters back from high schools," says Nye. "I realized I better switch gears and mosey into another direction. I basically read my apartment lease and decided I didn't like fine print, so I ruled out law school. I hate blood, so I ruled out med school. That left business school."

Even then, his future did not seem to fit. "I went back to get my Ph.D. to go down the teaching route, and then I got out and was too damn old and had too much overhead to be an assistant professor so I went into what we call consulting, basically, but working as a financial economist."

Along the way Nye, the celebrity guy, began to shed his star status. "I quit wearing my (Super Bowl) ring because I attracted too much attention. It's nice to be recognized, but it's also a pain in the ass," claims Nye, who went through different phases of popularity along with his career changes. "I used to be recognized a lot as Charlie Waters, which is kind of a compliment because he's kind of cute. I get recognized as Alex Karras a lot now. That pissed me off. When I first played against him, he was an overweight defensive tackle and I was slim and looked pretty good, I thought. He's lost 50 pounds, I've gained 100, and now we look alike."

Nye has finally found the future that fits. It may not be the job that combines beer and sweat, but it is the one that often provides him the challenge and feel of his football days. "The testifying is a little bit like game day. There's a lot of pressure on because you gotta get up and get what you have to say out, and it's sort of a defined context with examination and cross-examination, like a court. So, that's a little bit exciting."

It is also a career path that has become quite comfortable and that keeps Blaine Nye out of the public eye. "When they do know who I am, they want to see if I can get Roger Staubach's autograph. Nobody on the street recognizes me as Blaine Nye."

Now he's just plain Blaine Nye, the economist guy.

Out and Up

There were so many drives that ended with his heroics. One was even described as a miracle moment.

But the drive that still flashes into Drew Pearson's mind every time he takes a trip down a north Dallas freeway is the one that ended his NFL career and changed everything—forever. "My car accident in 1984, when I lost my brother and I had to retire (due to liver damage). I think about it all the time," shares Pearson. "When I go past that exit, it's always prevalent in my mind. It shudders me, makes me think, and sometimes it even brings me to tears.

"That was a real awakening for me because before then, getting into the NFL, missing just three games in 11 years, never having a major surgery—I was on a pretty good ride. For that to happen was a slap in the face," admits Pearson. "It made me realize how delicate life is and that nothing is promised to anybody. It gave me the mind-set to live each day to the fullest."

And Drew Pearson has. So full, he could use more than 24 hours a day.

"Coach Landry used to tell us always prepare for life after football, but he never told us how much life after football there was going to be," admits the owner of Drew Pearson Marketing, a headwear company that has averaged over 50 million dollars in sales over the past half dozen years. "We sell a lot of hats, over 20 million a year. DPM has really been successful in a very competitive sports licensing world where we see companies like Starter and Pro Player go bankrupt and companies like Logo Athletics struggling. We've been good at creating a vision and forecasting what the market wants and trying to build in that direction."

Not unlike the play in the 1975 playoffs that Pearson is most famous for, there have been adjustments necessary to the pattern set out for his company. At one point he even needed an investment version of the "Hail Mary."

"In the early days when we were struggling and floundering for money, we were able to come up with a creative way to piggy back with another company that pumped money into our company and kept us afloat," describes Drew of a desperate day in 1990. "That was like one week or two weeks away from having a situation where we pretty much had to close the doors on this business. The executives, me and my two partners, we hadn't taken a salary from the company for over a year. It's so ironic, the company that invested in us to help us get back on our feet, they're out of business now."

Another key to staying inbounds while other companies could not was Pearson's persuasiveness, key to procuring licensing agreements for the three different divisions of Drew Pearson Marketing: professional sports leagues ("entities like the NFL, the NBA, Major League Baseball, the NHL, NASCAR, WWF, XFL, and all colleges") entertainment organizations ("we're licensed with Disney, Warner Brothers, and Lucas Films. We had the exclusive rights a couple years ago for the Episode One Star Wars movie") and private labels ("we do all the headwear for Wrangler Jeans, Massimo, Cherokee Brands, Utility Brands, and people like that").

It was not always the recognition of Drew Pearson—No. 88 in a Dallas Cowboys uniform—that landed the big bombs in the boardroom. "What it guaranteed us was a meeting, an opportunity. In some cases, especially with the NFL as a matter of fact, it was more of a detriment than an asset, simply because other ex-NFL players had been granted licensing rights and they failed with those opportunities. The NFL turned us down five, six, seven, eight times. One thing I learned about business is that you gotta be able to persevere, number one, and you gotta be persistent in supporting that perseverance. I certainly learned a lot of that on the athletic field. But man, you might have to do that in certain situations here and there on the athletic field, but in business it's a daily thing. When somebody tells you no, it doesn't necessarily mean no. It means you go back and regroup and restructure and find out why you failed the first time and go back in there and try to get another meeting and another opportunity to present yourself and hopefully somebody is going to say yes this time around."

Pearson has gone back to places he never thought he would be welcome again. Sometimes it happened purely by accident. Like when his company merged with one of its distributors, forcing the man who single-handedly beat the Minnesota Vikings with the controversial catch to open an office in a suburb of—of all places—Minneapolis. "They're still a little upset with me, but they still take that paycheck every two weeks," quips Pearson as he reaches across the desk with that same right hand to retrieve a decorated photograph showing the contact with a cornerback just prior to the catch. "They have not forgotten that play. Here's a birthday card they gave me at my last birthday. It says, 'You pushed 43 (Vikings cornerback Nate Wright) and now you're pushing 50.' Needless to say this guy is no longer working for us. Just kidding."

Pearson is not kidding when he says the "Hail Mary" may be the most talked about play wherever he goes but is not his most memorable. "To me, the biggest moment in my career was in 1973, my first playoff game, when I caught an 83-yard touchdown from Roger (Staubach) in the fourth quarter to pretty much solidify that victory over the Rams," reveals Pearson of the third-longest playoff catch in Cowboys history. He was a rookie starting for the injured Otto Stowe. "It was just big for me because after making that play in that situation, it pretty much engrained me as the starter from then on with the Cowboys. The next ten years, that job was mine."

Which job is his today is nowhere near as defined as the career carved by the precise patterns Pearson was known to run. Along with his headwear company, Pearson performs as a radio and television broadcaster during the Cowboys season. He has an advertising business called Drew Pearson Impressions on Hold. "Say somebody calls the office here; instead of putting them on hold and hearing radio music or static, we offer a customized, specialized message for the customer." He is also owner of Drew Pearson Fine Lines. "We sell apparel merchandise to promote corporate identity."

But the identity Pearson preferred all along after his football playing days were over was the one that kept falling incomplete. The drive to direct a franchise stalled long before the score. "When I retired from the game, I wanted to work in the front office of a professional sports team. With the NFL, the opportunity wasn't there," points out Pearson, who finally caught the eye of a new league that emerged in the new millennium. Its founder, Vince McMahon, asked Pearson to take over the XFL's marquee entry, as vice president and general manager of the New York/New Jersey Hitmen. "I wanted to prove to the NFL people, baseball, hockey, whatever—sports people—that I've always had the capabilities of doing this and all I really needed was to be given an opportunity to do it. The XFL provided that opportunity." Even if it was for only one season.

Doomed by low television ratings, the league folded in May 2001. Despite the brevity, Pearson hopes his name will be back in the forefront of football minds everywhere. "I'm going to sit back and see if any professional opportunities come out of this."

Maybe even in the "old" NFL, where his name has not attracted enough attention to place Pearson where many believe he belongs: in the Pro Football Hall of Fame.

"I see how people who have their name out there get more recognition than people who really deserve it, a la Howie Long and Dan Dierdorf," shares Pearson. "I know a lot better defensive ends who have played the game and accomplished more than Howie Long who deserve to be in the Hall of Fame before Howie Long. But because he's on TV and everything, people know his name so he's in the Hall. Same thing with Dan Dierdorf; there's no better tackle that ever played the game than Rayfield Wright, and how's Dierdorf in the Hall of Fame before Wright? Well, who's on TV? I don't know what it's going to feel like if I ever do get that opportunity to be elected into the Hall of Fame. If I do, it'll probably be in the old-timers category the way things are going at this point."

It could be worse. Actually, from Pearson's perspective, it is worse that his name is not one of the ones that adorn the interior of Texas Stadium as part of the Cowboys Ring of Honor. It is a constant conversation among Cowboy fans who claim Pearson's big game grabs— the 83-yard rookie reception in the 1973 playoffs, the 1974 Thanksgiving gift from the Mad Bomber Clint Longley, the Hail Mary miracle in 1975, a Cowboys record eight playoff touchdown catches— are more than reason enough for enshrinement.

Yet, through the 2000 season, ten names appeared—not one was a wide receiver.

Bob Hayes finally broke through in May 2001, but not until beating the odds in a battle with prostate cancer that had him closer to death than the decoration. "It should have been done a long time ago," points out Pearson of the Hayes honor. "Because Bob is sick and going through his physical problems, it kind of waters down the offer, in my opinion." Pearson is obviously past being politically correct. "I've been out of the game now over seventeen years, and if that organization, whether it's the new owners or old owners, doesn't think that what I offered the Cowboys at that time was significant enough to be included in the local team's Ring of Honor, then that's fine. What I really feel is embarrassment for the players that are in there because those players know that they are not the only ones that made the success of the Dallas Cowboys," he shares with a sharp tone. "If it ever happens I don't even know if I would accept it at this point because I really don't care about it."

More likely, Drew Pearson will be too busy to notice.

Jack of All Trades

That's probably just my nature, to try to be able to at least know something about everything I'm involved in," says Preston Pearson when describing himself as a player and as a businessman. The third down specialist, known for his ability to do anything and everything on the football field, is carrying on with the same style in his life away from the game.

"Sometimes when you go to college you put down on your entrance papers what your major is, even though it may not end up being that way from one year to the other. I'm kind of like that in a sense that I'm still, even at this age, trying to find that one real thing that fits all the career goals that I've been looking for."

The Cowboys were pleased Pearson did not settle on one particular talent during their Super Bowl runs of the late 1970s, especially that particular January Sunday in 1976. "I was in 'The Zone,'" recalls Pearson of the NFC Championship victory over the Los Angeles Rams. "Any player who's been in that zone, hey, forget it. There is nothing you can do to them. You can't shake them up. You can't tackle them. They're gonna catch everything that comes their way. That's exactly what happened that day."

It happened three times for touchdowns. As Pearson remembers it, every pass caught by No. 26 went for a first down or a score, including the one that often illustrates his career—outstretched, parallel to the ground, inches from the turf, football in fingertips. "You can't duplicate games or plays or careers when it comes to being in that zone," adds Pearson.

So far, he has struggled to duplicate that effort off the field, in part because Pearson has carried the "jack of all trades" moniker he was known for in the NFL into his business life. "I didn't concentrate on any one thing—speed or strength, being a receiver or being just a running back, or whatever. I think it may have hurt me to some degree on the field and off," admits Pearson while reviewing his list of endeavors and realizing his shortcomings since his playing days in Dallas.

He has hosted radio programs but has not taken advantage of his degree in physical education and biology. "I haven't done the things in the area of sports that I'd thought maybe I'd like to get into, like coaching or owning my own fitness location."

He was involved in the restaurant business for several years. "I was the first Wendy's franchisee in the city of Dallas. Myself along with other former Cowboys including Ed Jones, Benny Barnes, and Butch Johnson, owned twelve Kentucky Fried Chicken franchises around the state of Texas." Again, Pearson was not comfortable enough to make it a career. "Those are tough businesses, and I had my fill of it. I had to move on."

In his final years as a player, Pearson came up with the concept of the designer do-rag. "The first bandana that was ever sold for the Cowboys at Texas Stadium and at Sears department stores was designed by me. I was the one that introduced it to NFL Properties." But it didn't always find its way onto his favorite forehead. "Thomas Henderson, if you recall, was one of those guys who wore it, had it with him. Thomas' problem was, he was such a crazy guy at that time, and he went overboard with it and unfortunately had it on his possession that game (the 1979 loss to Washington, Henderson's last game in a Cowboys uniform). It got a lot of play, wrong kind of play, on TV because he was acting like an idiot with it."

Another idea placed a Pearson project on the side of 7-Eleven drinking cups. "I'm the one that brought the caricature thing to the Southland Corporation, and they put it on their Big Gulp cups." But it was another artist who actually sketched the players' pictures that adorned the plastic pieces, despite Pearson's own artistic abilities. "Remember the old comic books, in the back page where you could sign up to be an artist, and it had 'Draw Me?' Well, I won that contest way back when I was like 10 or 11 years old."

He's also written a book and currently owns Pro Style Associates, a company that brokers athlete appearances. In true Pearson form, the range of athletes and appearances is never ending. "It could be a speaking engagement, a personal appearance, an autograph session, it could be a product endorser, it could be just to go to somebody's house and yak about football. It doesn't matter what sport the athlete's in or what gender—male, female, high school, college, or pro. We put those together."

Despite everything Preston has put together, he is still often referred to as the "other Pearson" in Cowboys lore. And his wide variety of interests has continued to keep him from specializing in something that may have ultimately increased his overall success. So far, it has kept him from entering the post–football zone. "I'm not dissatisfied with the things that I've done," says Pearson, "but I'm not sure if I could say that I've accomplished the things that I really, from a goal standpoint, want to do."

Probably better than anyone, Preston Pearson understands the blessings and the curse of being a "jack of all trades."

Airport Treasures

Thousands glance at the souvenir selection in the J. P. Dude Ranch every day. Many hurry past a kiosk filled with Beanie Babies as they rush to catch a flight. Others stop by the Ropin' and Ridin' shop to pick up gifts on their way home. In each case, travelers passing through DFW International Airport are crossing the post–football path of Jethro Pugh.

"I'm actually out at the airport a lot," says the former Cowboys defensive tackle of his business that includes five shops and various kiosks at DFW. "I like being out there. People are very nice."

Nice enough to stop and talk about a 14-year career that earned Pugh a pair of Super Bowl rings. Yet, it's Pugh who is nice enough to respond to the one topic that always stops airport traffic the most. "People talk to me about the Ice Bowl everyday. Everyday. I guarantee, everyday," explains the man who was blocked out of the hole that allowed Bart Starr's winning quarterback sneak in the 1967 Championship game. "I got used to it over the years. A lot of business people are my age. Most of us sort of grew up together and now they're executives in business and they do a lot of traveling. They remember those days and like to stop and talk about it."

Interest in the Cowboys and encouragement from the Dallas Black Chamber of Commerce convinced Pugh that travelers passing through DFW might put their money where their mouth is. And for a while, they did. "Initially I planned to just sell Dallas Cowboys memorabilia. The Cowboys are America's Team," says the soft-spoken man once called the best defensive lineman never to be named to the Pro Bowl.

Pugh has since been named to honors even more dear to his heart, inducted into the Elizabeth City College Hall of Fame, the Central Intercollegiate Athletic Association Hall of Fame, and the North Carolina Sports Hall of Fame. "I thought everybody would have forgotten about me because I'd been gone so long," Pugh quips.

Maybe it's the ability to talk to the man who made the memories, but sales of the memorabilia Pugh originally built his business around have long since faded. So, in true football fashion, Pugh changed the game plan and found a better way to defend his dollars. "I branched out and started selling a lot of Texas memorabilia," explains Pugh. "You know, the Western type stuff. We even have a gourmet section with Texas foods. In fact, now we sell very little sports memorabilia."

Instead, Pugh gives his memories away to anyone who can stop between gates to gab. And it is often an impressive airport audience. "Not only do I see some of my former teammates but a lot of other players in the NFL. I used to see Coach Landry a lot. He was quite a traveler," says Pugh of his list of visitors. "I met Colin Powell in the airport not too long ago. He remembered my football days, and we talked about it. He remembered the games against the Redskins. I guess he's a Redskins fan."

No matter the NFL team, during the 1960s and 1970s, Pugh probably played a part against them. So, while traveling through DFW Airport, the itinerary should include some time between flights. Whether it's memories or memorabilia, a stop at one of Jethro Pugh's shops will provide a souvenir to treasure forever.

Honored

The river flowed through some of the most beautiful country he had ever seen. People were speaking languages he recognized but did not understand. Mel Renfro sat back and took it all in with a grin. He had arrived.

"Things opened up to me, and I began to experience life," shares the Cowboys all-time interception leader about the turnover he encountered once awarded his rightful place in the Pro Football Hall of Fame. Doors that were closed suddenly sprung open. The world was now his playing field. Renfro was ready to steal the opportunity.

"I never thought I wanted to go to Europe, but when I got there, boy, I just loved it. Frankfurt and the German people, the autobahn. Man, I just went nuts. Going down the Rhine River and listening to the history of the French and the Germans and all that, stuff that I read about and learned about in school, and I'm right there where all of it took place."

It happened much later than expected for Renfro. As the Cowboys second-round draft pick in 1964, in his rookie season, he led the team with seven interceptions and led the league in punt and kickoff returns, earning the first of ten straight Pro Bowl selections. The 26.4 yards he averaged in kickoff returns still ranks at the top of the Cowboys record books, twelfth best in NFL history. His 14-season career included eight NFL/NFC Championship games, four Super Bowls, and two rings. Yet Mel Renfro felt like a forgotten rookie, defending himself for 19 years in a business world for which he was not as well equipped before the Hall of Fame selection committee was ready to induct him in the Hall and into the world in which he belonged.

"That probably led to my bankruptcy and ruin. I didn't have the expertise or the financial stability to hang, or the marketing skills or the administrative skills. I struggled a lot after I retired," admits Renfro of a variety of failed efforts including a fried chicken franchise in the Northwest. "I was frustrated and angry because of my business, some things that happened to me that I didn't quite understand. And I thought I deserved more, and then finally getting the call to go in. And the things that happened immediately after that—it's like, I suddenly became who I thought I was but just couldn't get there."

Along with his 52 career interceptions, the native Texan could have carried the frustration and anger with him to the 1996 ceremonies in Canton. In fact, he would have, if not for some sound advice from the Cowboys first Hall of Fame inductee. "He just said, 'When you get there, don't throw any stones because it won't do any good. Be humble and do all of the niceties,'" Renfro remembers Bob Lilly's words of wisdom before revealing the keen sense of timing that an All Pro defensive back could appreciate. "That kind of hit home because I was bitter before that and I was getting ready to throw some stones. As a matter of fact, I had pieced together a speech over 10 or 12 years, and each time something a little more brutal was added to what I was going to say in striking back. When he said that, I kind of released all of my hard feelings, animosity, frustrations and just let it go. That helped me in letting go a lot of other things that, I think, through the grace of God, allowed God to open the door for me to step into the whole thing. As soon as you find that grace, the doors open and your path straightens out."

It may be hard to believe Renfro's path was anything but perfect, considering his Cowboys credits. "The key play that I can cap off my entire career was in the Detroit game in 1970 in the Cotton Bowl. We were leading 5–0 and it was the last minute of the game and Detroit was threatening to score inside our 20-yard line. If they score, they beat us 6–5. Previous to that year we had lost four years in a row in play-off games, and that's when the books were written—next year's champions can't win the big one. I intercepted the ball with 20 seconds to go to preserve that victory. The next week we went into San Francisco and beat the 49ers and got into our first Super Bowl."

Renfro can rattle off plenty of other personal highlights. And he does—for a living. "The sports marketing business is a very good industry right now particularly for a football Hall of Famer," he admits of current successes thanks to a calendar filled by speaking engagements; corporate, league and charity events; card shows; and golf tournaments.

But Renfro has remained true to his honor, adopting the Starfish Foundation as his personal nonprofit parade, helping a cause that deals with drug prevention and continual care for kids. "I readily accepted mainly because of some of the things I had seen late in my career with some substance abuse and with the things that I've read lately that are going on throughout the league and the problems they're having with some of the athletes and their continuing problem with substance abuse. Doctors are trying to find a way to test and research to find out how the brain works as far as the chemical addiction is concerned. There is a way to clean the brain up where you won't have a lifetime of that addiction until you die from an overdose. It's medical research and it's also hands on with the families and the kids that are having the problem." In fact, it has not just been his football family influencing Renfro's reciprocity. "I have a niece that went through a bad experience and left the Northwest to come here to Dallas to stay with me for a year and a half to help her to transition from that experience, and she's done very well."

The transition from struggling businessman to successful Hall of Famer has been so sudden that Renfro has experienced his share of stumbles. "This time I went to Bosnia with Ben Davidson and Duane Thomas as ambassadors for the league to visit the military camps. We spent a week there flying in those helicopters. I gained an insight into our military." Renfro's voice carries an inflection of awe as he conveys the message of his mission. "I made a silly comment at one of the dinners with the troops when I said, 'We've been here four or five days and we're about to get out of here,' and this gal who had been living in tents and barracks and walking up and down paths where if you step off there are mines says, 'Well, I'm here protecting these people for our country, and I've been here a year.' I said, 'Oh, my God, that's what it's all about.'"

Finally, the eye-openers are happening for Mel Renfro as readily as he made them happen for football fans. He is as honored to take them in as we were.

Not So Golden

It is late afternoon on a sunny school day in Utah. A 1987 Honda Accord makes the turn onto a neighborhood street. As it rolls to a stop in front of the house that is not its own, a bright and happy boy quickly leaps out of the passenger seat with class work under his arm.

"I'll be back in a little bit to pick you up," hollers the driver.

"Okay, I love you," is the reply from the golden child as he scampers across the lawn.

"I love you, too, son."

There is a momentary pause as John Golden Richards feels a sudden strike of emotion. He takes a deep breath before the conversation can resume. "That's amazing."

Seven-year-old Jay Golden Richards, nicknamed "Goldie," has just made his dad's day. Little do he or his 4-year-old brother, Jordan, know that they may have also saved his life.

"I had no conception of love until I had children," admits the former Cowboys receiver who caught the game-clinching touchdown on a halfback pass from Robert Newhouse in Super Bowl XII and caught the eye of female fans with his golden locks and sparkling smile.

Little has sparkled in Golden's life since.

"I have been homeless. I have gone hungry. I spent seven days in jail. I am addicted to painkillers," reveals Richards of his life after football.

Less than a decade before he had boys to drive from school to their mother's home a few blocks away, Golden Richards stretched out across the backseat of a car parked in front of another house that was not his. There were no sunny days then. "I slept in my car in front of my dad and mom's house. And when I didn't have a car, I slept in my dad's car. I'm so embarrassed about that," says Richards of the nights he felt he had nowhere else to go. Writhing in pain. Broke. Hungry. Alone. "It's very humiliating because I wouldn't tell anybody. I have a wonderful family and I could have gone to them, said I don't have any food and it would have been no problem. But I was too embarrassed, too ashamed."

Shame was the furthest thing from Golden Richards' mind when he played out his fantasies as one of seven children in a Mormon family. His mother had named him Golden. There had to be a star shining over his future. "When I was in junior high I'd have my PE coach throw me a pass, and I said, 'One day I'm gonna be a Dallas Cowboy' because I fell in love with the star on the helmet, and I liked the word 'cowboy,'" claims Richards. "When I was at BYU, I wore No. 22 because Bob Hayes was my idol."

He now says it isn't the 63-yard punt return for a touchdown in the NFC Championship game his rookie year against Minnesota, still the second longest in Cowboys play-off history, or the Super Bowl score that is his favorite football highlight. "Making the team was number one," says Richards without delay.

He also doesn't have to think long to come up with his lowest career moment. He is still living it.

"Football is a violent sport. The most I think I ever weighed going into training camp was 172 pounds," remembers Richards. Whether it was his sore knee, cracked ribs, aching back, or the seven root canals that came courtesy of the pounding his body took over time that first found relief from the painkiller Percodan is not quite as clear. Neither was the understanding that the impact of the drug itself could take an even bigger toll. "You want to play so badly, it's anything you have to do to be ready at 1:00 every Sunday. It's what we called 'Showtime.' I wouldn't let them inject me, but as far as taking oral pain pills, well, I didn't consider that to be wrong."

Not even as Richards spent countless mornings forcing pills down his throat, often with the violent reaction from a stomach that would throw them right back up, or when his Cowboys career came to an end shortly after a 1978 overdose sent him to a Dallas hospital by ambulance, did Richards believe he was an addict.

"With all fairness, my concept of a drug addict was someone who is lying in an alley in New York City with a needle in his arm. I'd go get a legal prescription, fill it, and I wasn't a drug addict. That kept me in the terrible cycle of disease for a very long time."

In the early 1990s, it would get worse.

The cycle eventually took Richards down an illegal path that magnified his disease to the rest of the world. Stealing checks from his parents' house and using them to buy prescription pain pills resulted in an arrest on forgery charges. "Being arrested was an eye-opener. I was living at my mother and dad's at the time and I purposefully went in and got the bottom pad of their checks. I could go out and there was a doctor that got busted and sent to prison who would get me, for example, 40 pills. Then I'd go back tomorrow and get 40 more."

The arraignment took place on his forty-second birthday, December 31, 1992. "I was guilty on all accounts, and I never said I wasn't, but they plea-bargained it down to attempted forgery. I spent seven days in jail. I don't know how to put it into words. That was tough. It was just so humiliating, so embarrassing. It was certainly a place that I just don't want to return to."

Richards did return to a treatment center where he met his third wife, Amy, who is the mother of his kids. They have since divorced. "She was a psych tech," he quickly adds. "She wasn't a patient. I was."

To date, Richards has been through four rehabilitation programs, but according to a published report, suffered another overdose during the winter of 1994. Richards calls the story "a slaughter job." He then explains that on November 15, 2000, he slipped and fell in a bathtub, was knocked unconscious, and injured his back. "I woke up to my son saying, 'Dad, wake up, wake up, you're bleeding.'"

Now Richards says he is taking new anti-inflammatory medications that "really help a great deal, and they are non-narcotic" for the pain caused by three compression fractures in his lower back. He also claims to be checking into a pain clinic for some alternative relief.

But there has been no relief from Richards' financial fall. Now 50 years old, he lives on $583 a month from his NFL pension and picks up occasional odd jobs working on a friend's lawn. He is one of the most difficult former Cowboys to locate and has often had to go without a phone. But Richards says he is satisfied with this lifestyle because it gives him time with his kids, and he is committed to keeping it that way until his youngest son begins school.

His lifestyle has also forced him to face the reality of sharing his past with his future. "Goldie was watching 'Cops' on TV one night, and he said, 'Dad have you ever been arrested?' 'Ah, yes, son.' There was that still quiet, and before I let it get uncomfortable I said, 'let me turn this off, son, and let me explain to you what happened.' I simplified it. He doesn't know it's forgery. He doesn't understand that concept. I just said I did something inappropriate, wrong, against the law."

As for his addiction, Richards explains, "They know that a medicine you can get from a drug store is still a drug. When the boys get older and they can comprehend more, I will explain more in detail all that kind of stuff."

Other family members who have watched Richards rebound and fall so many times before still wonder if he understands all that kind of stuff himself. One of his five brothers says he hopes someone will motivate Golden because the family has done all it can. Another, who is an assistant attorney general for the state of Utah, says they have all seen that fatherhood has given Golden a responsibility he has wrapped his arms around as tightly as he did so many catches for the Cowboys.

Early in 2001, Richards accepted an invitation by teammate Tony Hill to speak to high school kids in McAllen, Texas. It was the first time he had heard from any of the Cowboys in several years. "I had an absolutely wonderful experience down there," says Richards as the spark returns to his voice. It is a moment of realization that No. 83 is once again at least one step ahead of his addiction.

"It doesn't haunt me, but I'm not past, beyond, or over it. I'm not, as recovering people call it, living my addiction."

Life has been anything but golden since Richards' early days in Dallas. But as he drives back to the house to pick up his boys, Golden Richards truly believes, thanks to them, he still has a chance to once again live up to that name.

"It is my real name, you know. It still fits. Not that I'm a golden boy or God's gift, but that's my name and I'm very proud of it. I'm still Golden Richards—a lot wiser and a lot more content with life and certainly a lot happier than I've ever been. That's nothing against the wonderful career of football. It came all from my boys. Having been so addicted on pain medication I know what hell on earth is like, but I assure you there is such a thing as heaven on earth—and that's being in the birthing room and seeing those two young spirits come into this world. Bar none, that is the absolute, without a doubt, highlight of post–football and would have been the highlight of my life prefootball."

Blue Collared

The drive to the airport starts out like any other trip. Time alone to think about the business at hand. He has presented hundreds of his incentive plans to company vice presidents. They are designed to increase productivity with travel incentives.

But this drive turns out like too many lately. The solitude forces the thoughts away from business and back to the memories that have made the new millennium so painful for Jay Saldi. "Coach Landry passing away and then a couple months later my dad passed away," says Saldi as his voice begins to crack. There is an uncomfortable pause as tears well up in his eyes. The emotion has come in waves before and will again. "Just losing two men like that in one year has been a real challenge."

A man who fought through five surgeries to stay on the battlefield for the Cowboys now tries to fight back feelings, but he can't. Saldi apologizes even though there is no need. "Between the two of them it's, ah, who I am."

Rough and tough, he was a tight end with a linebacker's mentality who could catch but would rather throw a vicious block. Jay Saldi was the Cowboys blue-collar kid. "My dad had a construction business up in New York that his dad started in 1908," he explains. "Their motto was, 'Columbus may have discovered America, but we helped build it.'" Saldi helped the Cowboys build a Super Bowl season in 1977.

While Roger Staubach, Tony Dorsett, Drew Pearson, Randy White, "Too Tall" Jones, and so many other superstar names were hogging the headlines, Saldi was quietly going about his job as captain of special teams. It was a duty he considered a career highlight. "My second year Coach Landry and Bob Ward, our conditioning coach, recognized me as the most improved player during the off-season program. Coach Landry rewarded me by making me captain. I'll never forget the first regular season game, walking out for the coin toss, you had Pat Summerall (in the television booth) probably saying, 'There's Roger Stau-

bach, Harvey Martin, Bob Bruenig, and . . . Jay Saldi? What the freakin'
. . . he must have won something, somebody is sick, what the hell is
he doing out there for the coin toss?'" jokes Saldi.

He suddenly becomes serious again as another wave rolls in. "I
was one out of 100 free agents that made it in 1976. Coach Landry
telling me I could be a captain of anything with him, put me at probably my most proudest moment. It was in an environment that my life
was committed to excelling, and here I am with the almighty coach of
all times, telling me that I could be one of his five captains." Saldi
stops to sniff between sobs. "It just gave me the certification that the
blue-collar stuff that my dad instilled in me was the right stuff."

Saldi has the right stuff with his kids. "Life after football began
when my three boys showed up," admits the proud papa. All three are
talented football players, from a major college linebacker prospect to a
Super Bowl champion child on a team coached by Dad. "If you've got
kids, go coach their teams and go win a couple of Super Bowls. There's
nothing like it."

They are new memories that Saldi is storing away, but in the back
of his mind he will always wonder if one day they will fade. "I had to
take care of my father for a year because he had Alzheimer's," reveals
Saldi as the emotion creeps back into his throat. "He never forgot who
I was, but it's merciless. It has no prejudice. It takes all colors, all
walks of life. The only thing is, it's painless to the patient, it's just
painful to everybody else." The tears have returned. Silence says more
than any words could convey.

Jay Saldi still feels the pain of playing football in the NFL. "I'm
kind of limited now in basketball because the hardwood floor bothers
my left ankle too much and cold weather still reminds me of the frost-
bite I got up there in Philadelphia when it was something below. And
my neck, well, when you have to make a living being in collisions."

But he would take that toll over and over if he could just make the
next trip down memory lane without all the hurt in his heart.

Perfect Harmony

Music is playing in the background. He begins to hum along with the tune. The lyrics bring a smile to his face. "I'd like to teach the world to sing, in perfect harmony. . . . " One of the world's most recognized commercial jingles has just produced a hint of the Herb Scott story.

"I've been working for Coca-Cola for over 11 years," explains Scott, who quickly adds, "I'm still a singer."

Harmony began for the former Cowboys offensive guard while he was earning All Pro status. First he would flatten a defender, and then sharpen his skills on another as he finished the score. "We started a little gospel group when I was playing, and we've been singing together for over 15 years," says the second tenor and baritone. "We still go around to churches and schools and prisons."

Scott's group performs spiritual songs like "Heaven Is Falling on You," rather than corporate jingles, but he has been personally uplifted by the way his performance in the company has been rewarded. Scott began by driving delivery trucks for Coke in 1989. He is now training and managing those employees for the company.

So far Scott has not been singled out to join in any of the Coca-Cola jingles, probably because he rarely sings his own praises at the office. It was that way with the boisterous boys in the locker room as well. "They say I was quiet. I didn't make as much chatter as some of the others, I'll put it that way."

Spoken like a true lineman. Always overlooked and under-appreciated. Always passing the praise on to one of the skill position players, like during Scott's favorite Super Bowl moment, which turned from an apparent disaster in the huddle to a success on the scoreboard. "The fullback pass for Robert Newhouse," remembers Scott of the play brought in from the sidelines during Super Bowl XII. "(Newhouse) had stickum all over his hands and the panic he was going through trying to get it off of his hands before the play was snapped. It started soon as the play was called. We couldn't wait until he got it off. He was in the process during the whole time we were going to the line. I knew he was successful from the reaction from the crowd and the jubilation of the players that actually saw him (Butch Johnson) catch it."

It would be fitting for Herb Scott to strike up the band at this point and start singing "It's the Real Thing."

Not in the Cards

I don't think I qualify as a Cowboy."
The words come from a man over 20 years removed from a play many of his teammates say should not have branded Jackie Smith the way it did.

"It was a play we had practiced only for goal line situations," admits Roger Staubach, who recalls signaling a time-out to question Tom Landry's decision to run the play during Super Bowl XIII. "Jackie just did what the play told him to do. He ran to the end zone. But it was designed as a timing play on the goal line, not from where we were on the field, so by the time he ran about 15 yards to get into the end zone all of the timing was off. It was not his fault that the play did not work. It should never have been called. Jackie didn't deserve what he got."

"Jackie Smith got credit cause he dropped that pass," adds Randy White. "It was a big pass play, but he got blamed for losing that football game and there were a lot of other plays in that game that could have changed the outcome of that football game to where it didn't come down to that one catch. I had one of 'em."

In his only season as a Dallas Cowboys tight end, after 15 Hall of Fame years with the St. Louis Cardinals, Smith finally reached the Super Bowl stage. It was a moment that would haunt Smith forever. The third-down play with the Cowboys trailing the Pittsburgh Steelers 21–14 late in the third quarter of Super Bowl XIII is constantly replayed as a lowlight of Super Bowl lore. The shot of Smith alone in the end zone rocking back with a frightful look of frustration after dropping an apparent touchdown pass flashes on the screen. Jackie Smith is reminded with every replay.

He is back in the comfort of St. Louis working marketing and customer relations with the Casino Queen and Crowne Hotel. With his 1994 enshrinement into the Pro Football Hall of Fame, Smith separated his career with the Cardinals from his final days with Dallas.

"Let's just say you've got plenty of material down there with a lot of fine guys and a lot of fine history, and you certainly don't need me involved in it," explains Smith of his desire to disassociate himself from any Cowboys connection.

In other words, just drop it.

All Hail the Chief

As he walks down the hall, conversation stops and adoring eyes follow his every move. He addresses each with the confidence and charisma carried by very few. A man who has witnessed his arrival leans to another and says, "He is presidential, isn't he?" Roger Staubach has just entered the room.

As he sits at a conference table, overlooking a North Dallas development stamped with his company name, the sincerity of a man revered by more than just the fans who followed his football heroics begins to shine. The conversation quickly conveys the core of a philosophy that has earned Staubach the status of royalty. "What we achieve ourselves is important, but just as important is how you can help someone else be successful also."

They are the words of wisdom that helped Staubach and his teammates rewrite the Cowboys standard of success, as it was when "Roger the Dodger" weaved in and out of the San Francisco 49ers defense to score 17 late fourth quarter points in one of the first of his record 23 come-from-behind victories. "That was one comeback that shouldn't have happened," admits Staubach. "That made our team believe we could always come back."

Or the consistent creativity of "Captain Comeback," who first came up with a Hall of Fame play, then followed it with an equally famous phrase. "When we beat the (Minnesota) Vikings it was a big upset with the 'Hail Mary' pass, which really was named 'Hail Mary' after the game when I said I had closed my eyes and said a 'Hail Mary' and Drew (Pearson) caught a pass that I underthrew," recalls Staubach, who settled a stir of controversy over the phrase's origin in an article written for the twenty-fifth anniversary of the game-winning wonder. "That play gave us confidence. We were in three Super Bowls then in four years." Or the Super Bowl VI play that Staubach surprisingly ranks as his most memorable Cowboys moment. "The first touchdown pass to (Lance) Alworth (against the Miami Dolphins)," says the Heisman Trophy winner whose name also adorns the Texas Stadium Ring of Honor. "Even though it wasn't a big deal, it was just a 7-yard pass, I probably threw it as hard as any pass I've ever thrown in my life because I didn't want to get it intercepted down at the goal line. It was the beginning of knowing that we're not gonna blow this game. Overcoming that 'can't win the big game' syndrome was really important to Dallas and its history." All hail the Hall of Famer.

Roger Staubach has become equally as important to the history of the Dallas landscape. Working with and learning the real estate business from Henry S. Miller during the off-seasons of his early NFL days, Staubach decided on a direction that would take those around him on another championship drive. "I always was one that would try to focus on something and try to do it the best, so we picked a part of the business that I was comfortable with," explains the founder and chairman of The Staubach Company, which specializes in tenant representation. "We're helping the user locate facilities, manage their facilities, do whatever it takes to oversee their real estate. When we decided we were going to just represent tenants and grow a business in that direction, people at that time didn't look at that as, it didn't make sense. We stuck with it, and we've learned from it. We knew if we are successful with satisfying the customer, the money will follow, whereas a brokerage, it's, 'Hey, what's in it for me?' I didn't know where it was going, but I knew that we could build it and maybe become a good-sized Dallas real estate firm."

What an understatement. Under the leadership of the Naval Academy graduate, The Staubach Company is now an enormous international real estate firm. "We have about 1,000 people, about a 200 million dollar a year company in revenues that's grown about 30 percent a year for the last number of years, and we still have a lot of growth coming because we have such a large infrastructure. There are a lot of customers out there that we don't have yet that we hope we can get someday." All hail the chief executive officer.

The presidential persona appears again as the discussion develops into a more personal nature. Former teammates regularly reveal Roger Staubach as the source of support they have received throughout the years on a variety of needs. One player's post–football financial status suffers when his company collapses, and a job offer arrives. Another player has a bout with booze, and assistance for rehab appears. Yet another player loses a family member and feels lost himself, and the invitation of a secure home helps.

The eye contact that has continuously connected throughout the conversation suddenly softens. Staubach refuses to take credit for specific examples. His response is general but genuine. "My teammates, as have my college teammates, have meant a lot to me. Some of my closest friends are guys I played high school football with. It's a fraternity, it's an appreciation of what you can do for each other, and I've always appreciated what I had with the Cowboys," shares Staubach. "I gave back, but I probably got more in return from teammates and Coach Landry. I think you sometimes have to appreciate the value of yourself, but even more so you gotta appreciate the value of somebody else other than just yourself. To get that balance is difficult. I don't know if I've touched them more than somebody else has, but I've always appreciated the relationships I had with former teammates. Some are very successful. Some have struggled. You want to be involved any way you can to help those that might need some help or associate with those that are doing fine themselves."

Staubach admits he has given too much at times and has had to learn the lesson of the enabler, a person who actually worsens the problem by providing assistance. They are lessons he shares with the success of his associates. "We try to preach giving back to the community as a company. Those are basics of life. The more you have in life, you can't take it with you, but you also don't want to become an enabler and have people take advantage of you. Each situation is different, and there's no set formula. A lot of it is private."

Staubach credits the private life of Dallas's first family as the foundation of his success before, during, and after football. "I guess I married my second wife first," jokes Marianne Staubach's husband of 36 years and father of five children. "A lot of people go through challenges at home or they have divorces. Dealing with that at the same time as trying to build a business to me would be pretty tough." Spoken like a true leader who understands how important it is to rely on the support around him. It goes back to the basics of Staubach's success spelled out at the beginning of the briefing. "For an athlete to make a great run, it takes a lot of blocking to make it happen. There are a lot of people in the trenches sometimes that don't get the credit. A lot of the things we do for the customer, there are people that are not the higher profile people but they're just as important to the success we have with the customer, and making sure they're part of that team and getting the credit they deserve is the challenge."

Staubach has always received the credit he deserved. Despite having most of his Cowboys records erased by Danny White and then

Troy Aikman, Staubach is still considered by most the greatest quarterback to wear the silver and blue. He talks the game as well as he played it but turns down more speaking requests than he accepts. "I could probably exist today on just being an old former quarterback by going to autograph shows," admits the six-time Pro Bowler who owns two Super Bowl rings. "Those things are kind of fun, I'm just not depending on that as a livelihood. Athletics taught me a lot of hard work, and you want to be creative and make things happen. At the early age of 38 (when Staubach retired), I didn't want to play golf every day. Life is more than that. It's getting up every morning and facing the challenge, I think. Every day was a competitive day to try to be better than you were and business is the same way."

Politics can also be that way. Staubach's name has often been thrown around when public office is discussed, most recently when President George W. Bush, a family friend, was searching for a secretary of the navy. So far, he says, he is not interested in a political path, and while Staubach does not live anywhere near the White House—yet—the kind of gatherings he has had on the basketball court outside his home in Dallas might suggest a coronation is in order. "We've had all the great NBA players on my basketball court. We had Michael Jordan and Grant Hill, Dominique Wilkins, Charles Barkley, all those guys," says the proud host. "Jordan was just there for dinner one night and went out and played. I can say some of the greatest NBA players have played basketball on my basketball court." Not even President Bush can say that.

Everyone's attention turns to the presence that appears as the conference room door opens. The greetings begin again. Roger Staubach has left the room. All hail Captain America.

Out Wide

Birds are chirping in the background. The image of an incense-filled California beach house comes to mind as Otto Stowe begins to tell his daily routine.

"I guess you could call it my career, but I just call it a love for the knowledge that it gives me and trying to share it with others," explains Stowe, pausing frequently to gather his thoughts. He has just returned home from a park in Goleta, California, where the former Cowboys, Dolphins, and Broncos receiver has contorted his body into some of the many postures of yoga. "It has something like 184,000 different postures. It's to work to control the mind by putting your body into that particular posture and telling you that you can stimulate different organs or different ways of feeling by putting yourself in that position. A lot of people like for some reason, as they exist, to treat themselves like dirt almost. It's just giving yourself the best possible blood that you can and hopefully not having to use a medical doctor."

Stowe spent only one year as a wide out with the Cowboys, bridging the careers of Bob Hayes and Drew Pearson. Some may think he is way out wide in the lifestyle he now leads. Stowe considers it "a more natural life existence. I have been fortunate enough to come up with something that has enabled me to live a life free of pain and something that has given me a lot of enjoyment."

Stowe admits it has not given him a lot of income. Yet, despite earning a health studies degree from the University of California–Santa Barbara shortly after retiring from football, he considers learning and teaching yoga his true calling.

"Everybody has their reason for how they live and who they live with and who they are. I think I've grown to have a fondness. I can say to myself that I haven't felt better in my whole life."

Bitter Back

I'm at a standstill right now," says the man who never seemed to be able to stand still with a football in his hands. A microphone was another story.

Duane Thomas rushed onto the Dallas scene as a first-round draft pick and quickly dashed to NFL Offensive Rookie of the Year honors in 1970. He scored the historical first touchdown, a 56-yard run, when Texas Stadium opened the following year. He helped lead the Cowboys to their first Super Bowl win at season's end. Thomas played the game between the sidelines as well as anyone could. But, that's where he drew the line.

"The '70s was the beginning of the media player. I stopped doing those things at the beginning of my playing years," admits Thomas of his refusal to talk in public forums of any kind, "because the white guys, Charlie Waters, would go out and get $500 or $1,000 for a speaking engagement. They want to pay me $150, and I got to pay my expenses." To this day, Thomas claims it was a conscious decision to deny interviews and public appearances to make his point, even though he knew it could cost him his Cowboys career. "Dallas gave Roger (Staubach) all of the opportunities. I mean every last one of them. They say it's a team sport, yet I didn't see Tom (Landry) try to make any concessions in terms of providing something for a team concept. That was one reason that Dallas really didn't dominate the '70s. They weren't a team. They had talent and great players but what wins championships is a team concept, and I think I brought that on. That was the subtext behind the Duane Thomas controversy, more or less. I was a player just trying to better himself just like any other person. My whole thing was the betterment of one person was the betterment of the other. The reason those things backfired is because I wasn't a white boy. If I'd a been a white boy, I would have been a Lance Rentzel or a Lance Alworth. I just would have been a rebel."

Thomas has always been a rebel. The misunderstandings usually surround the confusion over his cause, which is clearer now than ever before. "I have seven kids. I used to be the fastest gun in Texas. I hung my gun up and said forget this stuff. They're all doing as well as can be expected," says Thomas, who adds that his current wife works as a lymphologist. "A lot of my time has been dealing with raising my family the best way I can under my circumstances, and money has been an issue. Everyone was concerned with me about selling my Super Bowl ring. I sold the ring when my family needed money."

It was a moment after football that Thomas does not regret. It is, however, a topic like so many others, according to Thomas, that had more of a story surrounding it than anyone cared to know. Not that he was particularly interested in assisting with an explanation. "I went to this radio station there in Dallas. There was a sales job for $25,000, and I told them, 'I could increase your business.' The worst thing you could do is to tell somebody in Dallas that you could increase their business. It's like, 'Who do you think you are?' 'What do you mean who do I think I am? I'm the motherfucker that's gonna deliver your ass.' They told me that I couldn't live off of $25,000 a year. I said, 'Goddamn, I'm living off of nothing now, don't you think $25,000 would be a great increase?' So, we needed money," excuses Thomas of the need to consider his next step.

It was the solution that shocked Cowboys fans everywhere. "I look at championships the way I look at war. Wars are to improve you. Why go to war if you can't improve yourself, so why win a championship and you can't improve yourself? Anything you get from the war or championship should be able to be used to your benefit. That's the way I looked at the ring. I went to a pawnshop. I sold it for $5,000. To be going around talking about my ring when my kids need food, no, I couldn't see that."

Since that time, Thomas's life has taken him on a path more misdirected than the one he used so successfully on the field. "I've tried the insurance world out, sales, I've dealt with a lot of sales." But, each time the talk begins to take him down a positive road, the bitterness brings it back where Thomas seems to believe everything begins and ends.

"Every time I'm trying to make money, Dallas set up there and try to figure out some way of blocking it. People always say let bygones be bygones and all that, but they're sitting up there in their ivory tower making that statement. If I was making a million dollars a year, I could make that statement, too. Dallas made sure the stigma stayed with me. I done a book with Warner, and Tex Schramm, with his connection with CBS and all the media people, stopped that book because they were selling the team."

Thomas and his family spent five years in Hawaii while his wife helped put together a clinic there. He says he spent many of his days directly influencing his boys. "They were able to be exposed to different cultures. It was time well spent helping them psychologically develop themselves, and it isolated us where we weren't really concerned with things going on on the mainland. It was very healing." As was the project Thomas took on when he returned to California. "The thing that's really helped me out was more like a ministry than anything, was raising money for the Children's Miracle Network with the Wal-Mart stores and meeting fans one-on-one on my own. That was very healing because you hear all sorts of things."

But many of those things included conversations about his conflicts with the Cowboys organization. Another road back to bitterness, this one the roughest of all.

Despite the passing of Tom Landry, Thomas makes it continuously clear that when it comes to his former head coach, the healing has yet to begin. "No one was concerned with what I was going through and what I was dealing with one-on-one." Thomas takes the handoff. "It was all about, well, you're supposed to do what the coach tells you to do. That's bullshit. I didn't do everything my father told me to do, so let's be realistic about it. Just because someone has a head position doesn't mean that they're right or what they're saying is right for me."

Breaking outside, Thomas readies himself to cut upfield. "How can Tom Landry tell me what's right for me as a, quote-unquote, black man in this society, and he doesn't have a clue what it's like being black because he was white all of his life? That's like me trying to tell a pregnant woman like I know what it's like being pregnant because I've seen it."

He jukes left, then right, down the sideline. "Tom was not a very honest person with players. People don't want to admit that because they want to sit up there and say, 'Well, he was a Christian man' and so forth. I'm quite sure Jack the Ripper was a Christian."

A spin move has Thomas facing one last defender, ready to deliver the final blow. "He was one of the most ruthless and coldhearted son of a guns I ever met in my life in terms of a coach and just a human being."

The offensive explosion finally over, time for the solitude of the locker room, where Thomas could remain quiet even if questions are fired his way.

Duane Thomas admits that even in the early days, he wanted his mouth to work as well as his feet. But he could never get past the racial rage inside him to say the three words that might have made a difference then. They are words he uses now when asked about his financial future after football.

"I need help."

Is anyone listening?

This Particular Sunday

H e stood on the sideline as he had so many times before, but this time something was drastically different. Instead of wearing a Dallas Cowboys uniform, he looked more like a coach. The man standing next to him donning a fedora had only a slight resemblance to Tom Landry. The plays on the field were being started and stopped not by referees but by a man with a megaphone.

This was Oliver Stone's game, *Any Given Sunday*. Pat Toomay was more than an interested bystander.

"The title of the film was almost the same title of a novel I had written," explains the former Cowboys defensive lineman, who has published several books and stories since stepping away from the playing field, including a book titled *On Any Given Sunday*. "People started calling me from around the country congratulating me on hitting the big time, but there had been no sale of literary rights. That started an interesting sequence of events in which I ended up acting in the movie, sort of, alongside Y. A. Tittle. We were the opposing coaches for the second game (in the movie), the Chicago Rhinos, and we're over there waving and gesturing, but he (Stone) does a lot of flash cuts."

In all, Toomay's time on the big screen lasted less than a minute. But the experience had a lasting impression in one of Toomay's subsequent short stories. It is one of the published pieces in a series entitled "Best American Sports Writing 2000."

"What the piece is about is the collision of the sort of, in certain ways, sentimental vision of the game and the reality of the game and the reality of the competitive attitudes that exist within the players and how those collided with Oliver Stone's sentimentalized notion of coaches and what they're about," says Toomay of his literary work. "What Stone was trying to get he had difficulty communicating.

There was one moment where he wanted (Al) Pacino and Tittle to meet eyes across the field, you know, he wanted these two warriors to acknowledge each other, which is sentimental. True warriors don't acknowledge the opposition at all, lest they admit their existence. He had Pacino prompting him. All of this goes by in the film in about a tenth of a second, but the behind the scenes drama was just as interesting."

The film was being shot in Miami's Orange Bowl. Toomay felt the drama of a day 20 years earlier inside the same stadium walls. He had experienced a Super Bowl here his rookie year. On a finger dangling at his side now was the ring he won a year later against Miami in Super Bowl VI. There was a momentary reminder that the sixth-round draft pick out of Vanderbilt had his own sentimental start to professional football.

"My first two years we were in Super Bowls. I thought that's how it worked. Only in retrospect did I begin to appreciate how difficult and tough that task was."

Toomay is quick to point out that his book and Stone's movie share a resemblance only in title. His other published novel, *The Crunch*, was written in the mid 1970s and is based on the Cowboys, a team he left after five seasons to play in Buffalo and Oakland.

There are other recognizable results of Toomay's efforts. "I worked on a number of films in the writing end of the process assisting as what they call an A-list writer. I'm not a credited writer. I'm sort of help for hire on these things to do research and all that. The first was *Casualties of War*, and I was involved in the first pass at John Grisham's *The Firm*, which my employer got credit for when it finally found its way to the screen."

That Toomay goes about his passion in the shadow of big-name stars is reflective of his days in Dallas. He proved a solid starter despite Landry's law that, as Toomay tells, "for every rookie you field that's a loss generally during the season. Somebody will cost you a game. He went to great lengths, rather than play a rookie, that was me. He shuffled the line around, which was a disaster." Yet, the Cowboys continued to draft high-profile personnel for the defensive line, and when Ed "Too Tall" Jones and Harvey Martin made the list, Toomay's time was up. It is all part of what makes the manuscript.

"I've been confused for a good part of my life. I'm not ashamed of that. I'm interested in people's motivation and deeper structural issues and why people do what they do," admits Toomay. "I've never written for market. I've always written to sort of help myself try to figure out what's happening. It's a sort of personal endeavor but fortunate in that people found the issue interesting enough to print."

Especially when Pat Toomay is talking about those issues that happen on any given Sunday.

Improvising

The interview was going well enough. Verne Lundquist had asked the Cowboys newest acquisition all the standard questions he had expected to hear. Then came the one that caught Billy Truax by surprise. "He said, 'How do you feel about competing with Mike Ditka for the (starting tight end) job?' He had been there. He was the guy," recalls Truax. It was time to improvise and take the heat off of his arrival. "My answer was that it was up to the coaches."

The answer was right on. Ditka broke his hand during the preseason, and Truax became the starter for the first nine games of the 1971 season. When Ditka returned, because of Tom Landry's philosophy that a starter could not lose his job because of injury, Mike was the starter again. "By then my knee had really gotten bad, and I was just gimpy," says Truax. "I couldn't hardly practice, and I had to have it drained before every game." But the controversy over the starting position had already been established—thanks to the question months before.

One play at the end of that season, during Super Bowl VI, proved at least that those involved knew there was no bitter battle between the two. "We had a play in the game plan called a tight end reverse. The reverse was called to go from right to left, meaning I'd have to run from the right side to the left side and cut upfield with my left leg," Truax tells of a sacrifice in his only Super Bowl appearance. "Tom called the play and sent me out on the field and I remembered my left knee was my bad knee and I didn't want to take a chance on falling down or breaking down. Mike (Ditka) was coming off the field, and I had a head-on collision with him to stop him and say, 'You need to go back in there and run this play.' He turned around and went back in, and he damn near scored on the play. I don't think anybody knew except me that I turned around and came off the field." Truax earned a Super Bowl ring for his quick decision.

Fifteen years later, business was going well. The Dallas area was growing rapidly, and Billy Truax was enjoying success in land syndication. But in 1986, the federal tax laws changed. "The tax benefits that accrued with that investment vehicle were totally eliminated," explains Truax, "so basically it put us out of business." It was time to improvise again. "I moved back home to Mississippi and got on the other side."

Just like his decision to turn back from running the tight end reverse play, the turnaround in business has also been to his benefit. Truax took over his family's shopping center, in Gulfport, became the food stamp agent for Harrison County, and added a Bell South agency and check cashing business along the way. "We've had a major tenant turnover here at the shopping center and the income has tripled from what it was when I came here with a little bit of redevelopment and remodeling and tenant lease negotiations," adds Truax.

Further improvising is necessary for the knee that still bothers Truax. "It needs to be replaced." And it has kept him from picking up some of the usual post–football hobbies. "I don't have a shotgun, I don't have a rod and reel, I don't have an outboard motor, I don't have any golf clubs. I don't play golf, I don't play tennis, I don't hunt and fish, I don't play cards, I don't gamble. I'm just a regular, normal, average 57-year-old guy, I guess."

Throw something unusual Billy Truax's way. Then it would be a different story.

Better Not Forgotten

Lynn Swann remembers it. Cowboys fans remember it. NFL historians remember it. Mark Washington would kind of like to forget it. "I've had to comment on that thing forever," says the former Cowboys cornerback. "It's not the most positive thing to talk about."

"It" was the super catch by Swann in Super Bowl X. "It" helped the Pittsburgh Steelers beat the Cowboys 21–17. "It" was voted No. 2 on a list of most highlighted Super Bowl plays of the twentieth century. But, according to the defender on the play, most people do not understand that "It" was a super play on his part as well.

"There were certain things we were doing as a defense on that play that the average fan could care less about," Washington explains. "With the max blitz that was called, they (the Pittsburgh Steelers offense) shouldn't have had time to throw. But they did. I was there to make the play, but he (Swann) just made a better play."

Maybe it was because of that play, or maybe it was why that play happened at all. But since that day in 1976, Mark Washington has spent his lifetime helping those closest to him make better plays.

A chemistry degree from Morgan State helped Washington settle into a post–football career in the chemical industry. Living and working as a retired Cowboys player afforded a comfortable lifestyle in Dallas. But another member of the Washington family, Mark's daughter Lisa, was reaching the kind of athletic heights that disrupt even the most comfortable lifestyle. It was time for Dad to make a play so his daughter could make a better one.

Lisa was a 13-year-old gymnast with an Olympic dream. Bela Karoyli was the Olympic coach. For the two to work together, Lisa had to move to Houston, Texas. It did not take long for Mark to move his career so the family could join her. "Thirteen-year-old daughters should be with their mothers," explains Washington. "I made the decision to change positions and find something in Houston."

Eventually, Lisa decided the Olympic dream was just that, a dream. Again Dad was there with blanket coverage. "Kids see the bright lights, and they all want to go for it," says Washington about the experience. "I'm realistic about stuff. I know the odds. You can't plan for these things, just like you couldn't plan for what happened in football. There are just too many things that can go wrong." Yet, like her dad, Lisa Washington beat the odds more often than not, earning the title as Pac-10 vault champion while a senior at Cal–Berkeley.

Washington was not about to backpedal after his daughter's experience. He was ready for another change in pattern. He did not have to wait long. This time Mark Washington made the ultimate play as a former Cowboy so his wife could make a better one. The Washingtons moved to—Washington, D.C.!

"I did not realize how vehement these people are," says Washington about his new home in the middle of Redskins country. "People get fanatical about this Cowboys stuff."

Washington now works with an Internet recruiting company. He is again choosing to take a secondary role while his wife, Linda, enjoys a much more high-profile career as a director at the Library of Congress. But there is always a Cowboys story to be told. Current Cowboys owner Jerry Jones is a member of the Library's management council. And Mark still seems to have the knack for the bump and run. "I did go to the White House and I ran into (former Cowboys defensive assistant) Gene Stallings, of all people," Washington remembers. "It was bizarre. We were there for different reasons. When we came out of different rooms, we literally ran into each other."

No, Stallings did not talk about the play that everyone else wants to talk about when Washington is recognized. He knew better. But it will come up again. And again. And again. But that's okay. Washington knows he will be around to make the play. As long as someone else is there to make a better one.

"That's what, in my mind, Super Bowls are supposed to be about—super plays."

Sometimes it's best not forgotten.

A Safe Haven

I was on the fast track," says Charlie Waters of the coaching career, following his retirement from the Cowboys, that included seven years with the Denver Broncos and a Cotton Bowl season as defensive coordinator at the University of Oregon. As a player he was an overachiever, worked his way to Pro Bowl status, and earned a Super Bowl ring under the tutelage of Tom Landry. As an assistant coach, he worked alongside Super Bowl player and coach Dan Reeves. Waters had every right to expect that a head coaching job would be on the horizon.

No one could ever expect what met the Waters family instead.

"I lost my son. My oldest son died," says Waters of the one thing every parent fears most. It is a fear heightened by the circumstances surrounding Cody Waters' death. A healthy, athletic 17-year-old soccer and football player, just two weeks short of his eighteenth birthday, Cody never woke from his sleep on December 3, 1995. Doctors have never been able to deliver an official cause of death. Unexpected. Unbelievable. Unreal. "There are many, many nights I wake up in the middle of the night and go, 'Ah crap, it's not a nightmare, it's real.' For years, that was the way it was every morning. I'd wake up and just slap my face and say, 'Uh, it did happen, it wasn't a dream.'"

Just as suddenly, Waters was slapped with the realization that his dream of becoming a head coach was over. He resigned from Oregon to spend time simply trying to survive. "It's the ultimate tragedy. The pain, the grieving is so real you just can't breathe. I was just thankful to make it one day at a time there for a while," admits Waters. "I'm improving."

The improvement began when Waters realized that his family, wife Rosie and two younger sons, needed help. It was something they had to come up with themselves. "When he died, it sent me and my family reeling," Waters shared openly. "Grieving is a different cat. It's a different animal. There are no formulas. The books are just words, I promise you."

Waters knew exactly where to look. "I moved back to Texas to heal. I needed to be back in Dallas. My family needed to be back," says Waters with an emotional pause in his voice. "They embraced me. The city is wonderful. They hold us in high regard, those of us that turned the fortunes of the Cowboys around in the '70s. They remember that. Believe me, I don't look at what we accomplished as any magical feat. It was just a game. It's just pro football. It doesn't give us carte blanche because we were successful at football. But, those that are real good friends of mine knew how important it was for me to be successful and conduct myself like a professional. Those are the people that you end up gravitating to in times of crisis. Most of them were right here in Texas."

Friends like Roger Staubach, who offered Charlie a job in real estate, which he took during the toughest of times, the first six months. Rosie is now the executive director of the Staubach Foundation. And friends like his on-field partner, Cliff Harris, a brotherlike member of his Cowboys family, whose Energy Transfer Company provided Waters a more permanent home moving wholesale electricity.

There have been offers to return to coaching, but the desire of that dream has faded, or at least changed, since the death of his son. "It's forever," says Waters of the thoughts about his future. "There's no such thing as closure. It's affected how I look at things an awful lot. When I got those coaching job offers, I really reflected on how much time I spent at home when I was coaching, and I wasn't spending very much time here. I didn't want to do that anymore. I wanted to go to baseball games and I wanted to go to the PTA meetings and I just wanted to maybe leave work in the middle of the day and pick the kids up from school or something. You can't do that as a coach, ever."

What Charlie Waters did as a player may have as much to do with his ability to deal with the despair caused by Cody's death as anything he has done since. Breaking an arm and frequently being burned at cornerback by the Washington Redskins early in his career, then moving to strong safety and returning an interception for a touchdown that helped the Cowboys win at RFK Stadium later in his career. "That was a big moment for me," remembers Waters. "I thought, 'Okay, I went through all this hell for all these years and now, by gosh, I'm on top and we're on top again.' and I played a role on getting on top instead of playing a role in them beating us."

There were other moments that may seem trivial in comparison, but have collectively built the inner strength that brings Waters some comfort. "I figured out how to lose. I figured out how to just eventually face the music. You get beat for a touchdown pass, what are you gonna do—run, hide? You stand right there and you face it. You're better for it. You got through the pain. You don't make light of it. You're disappointed in yourself, you're disappointed in what you did and then you try to learn from it and go on. The same thing holds true on the tragedy I went through. It's real."

So are Waters' feelings about his adopted hometown. As a safety for the Cowboys, he helped bring Dallas a Super Bowl title and the label America's Team. Dallas returned the favor with a safe haven when he and his family needed it most.

"I won't leave Texas. I'm not a Texan, but I love it here."

The feeling is mutual.

Milder Manster

Ever since I stepped off the plane to come to Dallas, Texas, in 1975, it's been like a dream come true for me. My worst day was not a bad day."

Randy White uses that phrase as a general description of any day during the past 25 years. The specific examples are as good as ever; they're just different than they've been before.

"I've never found anything, business or hobbies or anything that has given me the thrill that I had right before a football game. When things go right for you in business or you get a certain deal and it works out, you know, that's pretty satisfying—but nothing like playing football," admits the man known as the Manster—half man, half monster—on the field during his NFL days. "When you retire from football, you can't go out in the real world and act like that or they'll put you in jail."

So White has had to figure out another way to satisfy the physical, emotional, and mental urge to attack without working himself into a football frenzy. His off-field release used to come in the form of his favorite hobby and the source of so many stories during his Cowboys career—fishing.

"When I retired I said, 'All I'm gonna do is fish,'" says the one-time spokesperson for Skeeter, Ranger, and Nitro boats. "I did that for about two months and thought there's gotta be something else to do. You feel like you're not accomplishing anything. You don't feel like you're being productive."

White was a guy whose glory came from being a productive pro. The Cowboys second leading tackler of all time, he harassed quarterbacks, offended offensive lineman, chased down running backs and receivers, earning Super Bowl XII co-MVP honors in the process. But the moments that make up the Manster's memory may best belong on a football follies reel rather than the Hall of Fame highlights that honor his career.

"The play that really sticks out in my mind more than anything else is when I fumbled the kickoff in the Super Bowl (X) against Pittsburgh, when I had a broken thumb. (Roy) Gerella squib kicked the ball, he missed the ball, and I picked it up and thought I was back in my high school days running the football. The guy that hit me and made me fumble that football was Tony Dungy (later the Tampa Bay Buccaneers head coach)," adds White, who enjoys entertaining with that tidbit of trivia. "Jackie Smith, 'cause he dropped that pass, got blamed for losing that football game, but there were a lot of other plays that could have changed the outcome to where it didn't come down to that one catch. I had one of them when I fumbled that football on the kickoff and Pittsburgh recovered."

White pauses to think about other highlights he knows he should share, but those images have not left the same lasting impression. "I can't sit here and tell you one play in the (Super Bowl XII) game where I won the Most Valuable Player. I can replay that fumble on that kickoff to the tee."

Maybe it is the sense of humor and humility that he has turned on during his post–football days, as opposed to the pure power he displayed as a defensive tackle, that now has White thinking back to times that tickled his funny bone rather than his ego. He is a master storyteller who captivates an audience at a local tavern as easily as he corralled quarterbacks in stadiums around the NFL.

"This guy named Greg Couch played for Green Bay when that stuff started getting publicized about me bringing martial arts into football," begins White of another tale he tells of a humorous highlight. "I got into it with this guy, and he just looked at me and goes, 'What are you gonna do, Kung Fu me, Mr. Kung Fu man?' It kind of tickled me, really. The next year he was playing for Minnesota, and I got into it with him again. This time he goes, 'You're not a Manster, you're a manhole.' I looked at him, and I said, 'Manhole?' He said, 'ya—half man, half asshole.' It cracked me up. I never laughed on a football field. I was always wired, intense, and pissed off. This guy made me laugh."

It must be about time for the Manster to manhandle a bigmouth bass to set himself straight again. "I still go fishing, but I'm not as mad at those fish anymore, either." An evolution really is underway.

White's lighthearted nature may not have been useful on the playing field, but it has become the endearing quality that continues to attract autograph seekers and sponsors. He has appeared on Chevrolet, Miller beer, and Justin Boot commercials and is a long-time spokesperson for Smokey Mountain Chew. White is constantly in demand on the speaking circuit, as an infomercial host, for personal engagements, and occasionally during dinner.

"The Manster was on the field; off the field I enjoy people. I never had a problem with people wanting to talk to me, people wanting an autograph. That part of it I've always felt like was an honor," says White of an attitude that is rare among current high-profile athletes. "Today when people say, you know when you're eating dinner somewhere or you're out somewhere and they say, 'I know you hate this, but can I have your autograph?' I always tell them, 'Look, at this point in my life I'm glad somebody still wants my autograph.'"

Calling on his fans has also become a new professional proposition for White, who is part owner of Randy White Telecommunications, a long distance telephone company. "It's a tough business, a very competitive business," explains White. "When you have the right products and you have the backing that we have, it's a good deal. I just wish I'd gotten in on it when it first got deregulated."

The first hint of executive stress begins to creep into his voice. It must be time for White to throw a line into the lake to settle the nerves and humor himself with a new fish story. "I really don't fish as much as I used to. I got too busy. Heck, I'm having to work for a living."

Not that White would allow himself to get too far from physical fun. Football is gone, except for some talk time on a television show, "The Edge," cohosted by former archrival running back John Riggins (Washington Redskins) and another former NFC East foe, Phil McConkey (New York Giants). "It's made me pay attention to football more than I did in the past." And now that he's not paying attention to the tackle box as much anymore, White is wrangling with another amateur activity.

"I started team roping, and that's something I really enjoy because it's physical and it's a challenge. Now I'm mad at those steers." Excitement and exuberance return to White's voice as he describes the depth of his new passion. "I built an arena out here at my house. I have lights and I've got my own steers. I've got horses. Roping is the most humbling sport that you've ever played. You can go out there one day, you can catch 20 in a row, and you can go out the next day and miss 10 in a row."

The storytelling is about to begin anew.

"I cut the tip of my thumb off," reveals White of a recent ride.

"You get your thumb caught in the dally when you got a four- or five-hundred-pound steer behind your horse and your thumb gets between the rope and the saddle horn, that thumb comes off."

But enough about the tough tales of his new sport. Remember, White would rather reflect on the lighter side of legend.

"I rode in a celebrity team roping for charity," he continues. "They had Christie Brinkley, they had Johnny Rutherford, there was a bunch of celebrity-type people over there and we were practicing. I got my Western shirt and my cowboy hat and my sunglasses, I was duded up there. And I got on this horse and rode out to cut a cow, and this horse pitched a fit. It bucked me off. I went over the top of her head and went nose first into the dirt. My hat came off, my face was full of mud, my sunglasses were all dirty, my shirt, everything was full of sand. That was one of the most embarrassing things that has ever happened to me. I had to get myself up, dust myself off and let (the trainer) ride the horse around for a little bit to make sure it wasn't gonna buck me off again."

All is right with Randy White. He is having another good day.

The Lean Years

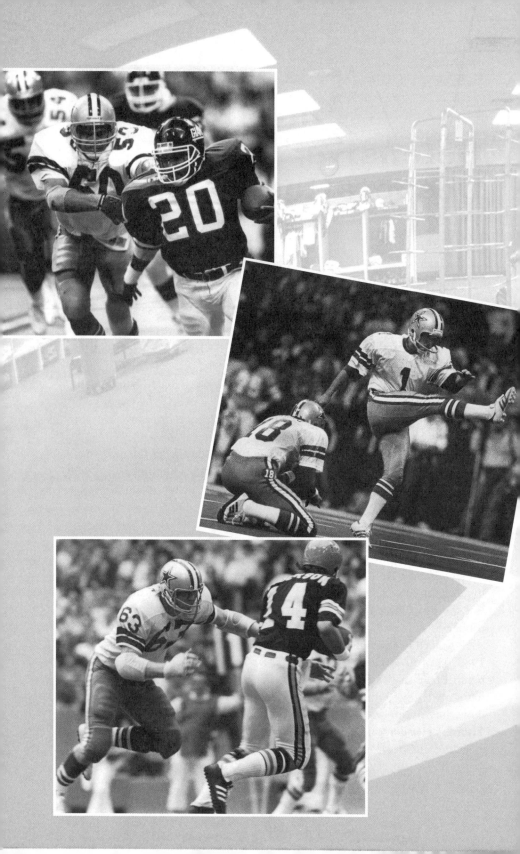

Defensive Desperation

With their first-round pick, the Dallas Cowboys select defensive end Larry Bethea from Michigan State.
                        Pete Rozelle, NFL Commissioner, 1978 NFL Draft

They are the words most football players live to hear. But for Larry Bethea, they may have been the words that ultimately caused his death.

For six seasons, Bethea battled himself as he tried to become the force expected of a first-round draft pick. It was a battle he never won. Despite the experience of a Super Bowl appearance in his rookie season, the lack of personal success, his never being able to crack the full-time starting lineup in a defensive line loaded with talent, apparently was an experience Bethea was ill equipped to handle.

Leaving the Cowboys for the USFL did not prove to unleash the potential, which Bethea took as his final football failure.

In the few years that followed, Bethea took out his frustrations off the field. A cocaine investigation in Dallas, a guilty plea to setting fires in Mount Rainier Park, an arrest in Dallas for allegedly accosting his estranged wife, a suspended prison term for stealing his mother's life savings, identification by witnesses as the gunman in two armed robberies . . .

Bethea's best training camp was his last one with the Cowboys in 1983. He told a *Dallas Morning News* reporter he had his "personal perspective in life together." He went on to say, "As a Cowboy, you have all things coming to you. There's a whole lot going on. If you don't have your perspective together, you can get swallowed up like Thomas Henderson."

That perspective changed dramatically in 1987. Just hours after the robberies, Bethea used the same gun to kill himself. He was 30 years old.

For Larry Bethea, being a first-round selection in the NFL draft was both a blessing and a curse.

Protection Guy

His helmet was strapped and secure. Staring through the bars that crossed in front of his face, Guy Brown looked into the eyes of a man he had watched intently for years. "Franco Harris was my favorite player before I came to the Cowboys."

And now Brown faced the scenario a linebacker lives for. Guarding the goal line at all costs, knowing the opponent would send the irresistible force to meet the immovable object, mano-a-mano, the idol against the idolizer, future Hall of Famer Harris of the Steelers versus Cowboy Brown. "We had the opportunity to face him in a really direct sense in a base goal line defense."

The power of the play would require all the protection Brown's armor could provide. "The contact I made with Franco in that defense was one of the best hits as far as form that you could make. It wasn't the crown of the head, it was just facemask straight on and it flattened my facemask."

Brown stood astonished after the contact created the deformed dent. Harris was even more morose. The goal line still striped before him. "We held him out and someone I respected as I did Franco as a player and to sustain that position and keep him out of the end zone in that situation was a real highlight for me."

Not lost from that highlight was the need for the safety device that kept Brown from being disfigured during the collision. Safety concerns continue to grab his attention as owner and general manager of Great Southwest Fire and Safety, a company that provides such fire protection devices as alarms, suppressant systems, extinguishers, and life safety systems for the commercial, industrial, and institutional market.

"After the 1981 season we ended up in the Championship game against San Francisco and the next day a friend of mine called and was excited," remembers Brown. "This friend demonstrated a Halon fire extinguisher for me. I was really fascinated with that. So much so, I looked into the market further." What he found during his off-season from football sent him in a new direction. "Ninety percent of all fire-related deaths occurred in the home and more than 90 percent of the residential market didn't have fire equipment, which meant there was a tremendous need in the residential market. We initially set out to try to sell that market. I discovered along the way that market is one that is not regulated, and that's one of the reasons it doesn't have fire equipment in place, particularly fire extinguishers."

The fire caused by the NFL players strike of 1982 actually helped Brown extinguish his burning desire to attack a market that did not require his service and redirect the flame towards one that did. "That nine-week strike actually allowed me to make some direction towards evolving the business towards commercial and industrial markets. Little did I know that would also be my last year with the Cowboys."

A neck injury ended his football future but helped him focus on his future in business.

Similar to the goal line stand, the intensity of his focus took a hit when he was blindsided by news that his wife was stricken with Parkinson's disease. "That's been something that has affected us in a very significant way," shares Brown, whose two debutante daughters are developing futures in the legal and medical professions. "The scheduling change and different consideration that we have to adjust to in our family life, of course, with two daughters in school, makes it difficult. You have the financial obligation that pushes you in terms of meeting those obligations."

Brown often finds himself reaching back to his football foundation to gain the strength and experience required to meet the challenges head-on.

"The whole scenario of professional sports actually serves to teach us life in a concentrated fashion over the course of a game," theorizes Brown. "You experience the very experience that you have in life, the ups and downs, the highs and the lows. You can go from a hero to a goat and back to a hero again in the course of that three hours. Perseverance is something I gained from that and believing and knowing not to give up."

Guy Brown knows that protection is an important part of the equation.

Roll of the Dice

He stared into the eyes of the fiercest competitor he had ever seen. A man known to have spent time in jail charged with a violent crime. A man who only months after his release from jail stepped into a boxing ring and violently removed a piece of his opponent's ear—with his teeth. And now that man was just a few feet away, ready for action. Glenn Carano did not blink. The odds were in his favor.

For seven years Carano stood alongside some of the greatest players to ever wear a Dallas Cowboys uniform. He was drafted the same year as, and just one round after, Hall of Fame running back Tony Dorsett. It did not take Carano long to realize he was in for the fight of his life. "I remember what Roger Staubach said to me the first time I met him during a meeting at quarterback school," Carano recalls a generation later. "I was a No. 2 draft pick, pretty high in those days, and right in the middle of the meeting, while Tom Landry was talking, Roger passes me a note that says, 'Yeah . . . but did you win the Heisman?'"

He did win a Super Bowl ring along with the rest of his rookie class. As Staubach reached the end of his illustrious career and handed the leadership of America's Team to Danny White, Carano was the backup quarterback for both. Watching and waiting for his turn. "People say to me not everyone gets to be a Super Bowl quarterback, but I went to Dallas to be a starting quarterback, and I didn't reach that level."

Carano's most memorable moments on the field included his first NFL completion on Thanksgiving Day of 1980 against the Seattle Seahawks. It was a touchdown throw to Billy Joe Dupree. The following Thanksgiving, with the Chicago Bears in town, Carano got the call again. A rib injury to White allowed Carano to stage the kind of come-from-behind win that has helped vault many to legendary status. But that wasn't in the cards for Carano. He would get his only start as a

Cowboys quarterback a week later in a win over the Baltimore Colts. "Did I achieve my goal as a football player? Absolutely not," Carano now admits. A better hand would be dealt in the years after he left the NFL following the 1983 season.

Raised in Reno, Nevada, Carano always knew where the chips would fall after football. He had heard them rattle on the table many times before. His family owns and operates casino properties in their hometown. Glenn would become the executive director of marketing for one of those casinos. "I've been fortunate and blessed, getting the chance to work for a common goal with my family." It was a job that seemed to be the safest gamble of his life. With his background as a pro athlete and the Dallas Cowboys name behind him, an appointment to the Nevada Athletic Commission did not appear to be much of a crapshoot either—until Mike Tyson walked through the door.

The former heavyweight boxing champion was slapped with a lifetime ban from the sport after biting the ear of Evander Holyfield while losing a title bout. Only a reinstatement process that brought Tyson before the Nevada Athletic Commission could get his boxing life back. Glenn Carano watched again, while a superstar athlete put on his best show. He recognized the look. "The NFL has some pretty ferocious-looking people," Carano explains. "When you see a linebacker across the line of scrimmage, you may not see him without his shirt on, all pumped up, but you see the eyes and the frothing at the mouth."

As he had prepared himself to do so many times before as a backup quarterback in the NFL, Carano drew upon a cold and calculating calm to make a decision under the pressure of a watchful world. He also knew what it was like to have someone else stand in the way of your ultimate chance at success on the playing field. "A lot of the experience I had in football did give me light into what Tyson was going through. I tried to take the name Mike Tyson away and put John Doe there to make a fair decision."

Carano finally had his chance to make the call. His vote was yes. Tyson was allowed back in the ring. The trump card had been played.

For the Love of the Game

I t was late in the fourth quarter. The Cowboys appeared to be on their way to another Super Bowl when Doug Cosbie pulled in the touchdown catch that put Dallas ahead of the San Francisco 49ers. But Cosbie and his efforts would be forever forgotten. Thanks to "The Catch."

"Most don't remember that I had scored the touchdown about five minutes before to give us the lead to kind of make 'The Catch' necessary," admits Cosbie, who has added to his own anonymity by living his post-NFL life in the San Francisco Bay area. There, only the heroics of the hometown 49ers remain in the memory bank.

"I had the opportunity to work with Bill Walsh for two years at Stanford. Keena Turner and Mike Wilson played for Bill with the 49ers and were on our staff also, so a lot of people would come up to me and go, 'Now, what position did you play for the 49ers?' And I'd say, 'No, no, no. I was on the other team. I was with the Cowboys.' That kind of hurt."

Maybe the pain has something to do with Cosbie's desire to remain lost in anonymity. Instead of striving for a big-time coaching position after stints at his alma mater Santa Clara, Stanford, Cal, and the World League's Sacramento Surge, Cosbie is content walking the sidelines at little Menlo College, an NCAA Division III school in the Bay Area. "It's really just a lifestyle choice," says the Californian of his decision to coach at a non-scholarship school of about 700 students, despite offers to play ball with the big boys of the collegiate and professional coaching ranks. "You're basically married to football when you're at that level. At a smaller school you can have more time to spend at home with your family." And that may be about the only place Cosbie is known as the former Cowboys tight end.

Like the 49ers fans who failed to recognize him as the player who made "The Catch" necessary, there are few in the stands at Menlo home games who even recognize Cosbie as a former NFL player. Of course, there are rarely many in the stands at Menlo College at all! "There's just two or three thousand watching instead of 80,000." Yet, Cosbie gives his Menlo Oaks the same Pro Bowl effort he gave for ten seasons with the Cowboys.

"You do all the same things," explains Cosbie of his coaching style. "But, the kids at this level appreciate it so much more, they're a lot more coachable. There's no athletic scholarship. They're taking loans or getting financial aid to be able to play. They're playing because they want to play."

They're Cosbie's kids . . . humble, eager to learn, ready to sacrifice . . . to a point. "I think a lot of people coach at a high level, the NFL, the major college level, for themselves, for their egos. What difference does it make if you're coaching a non-scholarship, 6-foot 1-inch, 250-pound lineman, or you're coaching an All Pro in the NFL? You're doing the same thing. The strategy and all that stuff is the same. Just for love of the game and teaching the game, it doesn't matter the level you're doing it at."

It also helps that Cosbie can afford to coach at a lower level. "You do have to probably have money from somewhere else to coach at this level on a full-time basis," admits Menlo's head coach. "I'm fortunate enough to parlay football money into something that'll take care of myself and my family for the rest of our lives." Thanks to some good investments of his NFL earnings and the help of another former athlete, whose name further shadows Cosbie's lack of recognition.

"I'm not paying bills coaching. I'm paying bills partnered in a sportswear company with Kurt Rambis (Los Angeles Lakers) and a couple other guys I went to college with at Santa Clara," explains Cosbie, whose business expanded into the surfing industry just as the sport was enjoying its own high tide. "We're the domestic licensee for the surfwear division of O'Neill, whose family invented the wet suit in about 1952. We're also the worldwide licensee of sportswear for the Lost surfboard company."

Cosbie admits he will not be mistaken as a surf bum on the West Coast any more than he will be properly identified as a former Cowboys great. "I'll boogey board or body surf but I'm not brave enough to get up on a board—yet. I haven't even tried it," points out Cosbie. "A lot of people tease me about it and I say, 'Well, I need a board about as big as a dock.'"

Maybe that's what it will take for Cosbie to catch the wave of attention he deserves.

Lightning Strike

For as little as I played, people seem to still remember," says a surprised Doug Donley.

The former Cowboys receiver played at a time when Dallas was struggling to get back to the Super Bowl level enjoyed during the 1970s. And, in his own words, Donley came to the Cowboys as damaged goods. "I had a pretty good shoulder injury when I came into the league, so I knew as I started to play more, that kind of sped up the retirement process."

So the Ohio State graduate, who played for the volatile Woody Hayes while with the Buckeyes, tried to secure his future even as he was catching passes from Danny White in a Cowboys uniform. "While I was playing, I bought a tennis and health club," says Donley. When homeowners in the area balked at Donley's attempt to market the club to outside membership, he realized it wouldn't benefit him to pull a "Woody Hayes" on the association, so he cashed in his investment instead.

Now the creator and owner of Advantage Golf, a golf tournament coordinating company with a number of franchises throughout the country, Donley still finds his short stint with America's Team has staying power.

"I was kind of a fast white guy, which was a commodity," admits Donley now. "I used to be White Lightning. Now they just call me White!"

But they still call him.

A Safe Career

I was part of a start-up business with a couple of friends. We actually wanted to be agents to help professional athletes. That turned out to be kind of a treacherous business to be in. None of us really had the taste for it."

Having been a long-shot free agent who made it in the NFL, when Michael Downs found himself telling a young free agent candidate that he probably did not have the stuff to make it, it was enough to send Downs himself back to the safety of a more comfortable career.

Downs was back at his alma mater, Rice University, talking to a prospective client, a linebacker who had played sparingly in college but appeared to have some of the qualities that are attractive for NFL free agents—until the scouting reports began to filter in. "I had gotten some information on him about his speed, and I shared it with him. He just couldn't believe it," recalls the mild-mannered Downs. "He was hurt that that's what the (scouting) combine had him at. I tried to explain to him that his chances of making or just getting into camp would be tough because of that. That was hard, as an older guy who has played in the league and was able to fulfill some of my dreams, to be telling a guy that his chances just don't look very good. He was an emotional guy, so he didn't take it very well."

Neither did Downs. Instead of the relating to the famous line "show me the money" from the agent movie *Jerry Maguire*, Downs was screaming, "Show me the door!"

"Because I had been a player, I understood how players thought about agents. It's kind of a necessary evil," Downs now admits. "The part I didn't know was that you really had to, over a period of time, sell yourself to the player and be his buddy, his father, whatever he needed at the time. You have to do a lot of babysitting."

Instead, Downs has moved back to the business in which he began his post–football career—as a Dallas-area insurance agent. It makes sense. As a safety, Michael Downs spent a football career providing insurance on the field. It's only fitting that he spend the rest of his career providing insurance off the field.

A Quiet Thunder

He was part of the defensive line creating the turbulence that set up the storm. Alongside Randy White, John Dutton was the "Thunder" that helped unleash the "Lightning" of "Too Tall" Jones and Harvey Martin. Yet, despite the promotional campaigns of the Doomsday II Defense, Dutton has forever been in the shadows of his more decorated teammates. "A lot of times people don't realize I was All Pro and Pro Bowl. It's not mentioned much around here, but I was," explains Dutton from his home in the Dallas suburb of Plano, Texas.

Constantly battling, constantly defending his territory and his name has translated well from the football field to the business world for Dutton. Yet, he realizes his lack of attention as an NFL star may have something to do with his defensive demeanor. "I can't say that people would say I'm a nice guy. A lot of times when I was playing they didn't see that side. I was a Jekyll and Hyde on the field."

Long before his football career ended, it appeared Dutton was receiving that same treatment off the field. "I worked for Miller beer here (Dallas) for years when I played ball. Supposedly they were going to help me find and finance a beer distributorship when I was done, in exchange for me working for them for nine years," Dutton recalls. "They turned around and didn't do anything when I retired. They never lived up to their agreement, their part of it at least."

But Sparkletts Water poured its resources into Dutton's hands. He spent the next couple of years selling product in the West Texas towns of Amarillo and Lubbock, until the company reorganized and again Dutton was the odd man out.

"In football you had your ups and downs, and in the business life and in family life you have your ups and downs. I learned a lot of that in football, that not everything is gonna be roses all the time. They haven't been since football, either," says the philosophical Dutton. "I've been able to come out of 'em just being mentally strong. When you're playing football you have to be mentally strong. There's a lot of good athletes out there. The good players are the ones that have the mental capability of doing it. I played against guys that were probably better athletes and stronger and faster, but I beat them because mentally I knew I could do it and I'd just keep going. That's basically the same thing in business life."

Believing the best offense is a good defense, Dutton has used his style to resurrect a successful after-football business. He currently owns and operates a modest company that provides signage for homebuilders and real estate agencies.

The thunder still rumbles inside Dutton and when it does, he reaches back to another football favorite to settle the storm—fishing with Randy White. The pair had legendary fish stories during their playing days. "It's a little mellower, put it that way," admits Dutton today. "We had some wild times." Times Dutton is not quite ready to share.

"Maybe when Randy dies I'll write a book or something." Let the "Thunder" roar.

Covering Kids

H is greatest day as a Dallas Cowboy was the first day he stepped foot into the team's Valley Ranch meeting room.

"I remember Coach Landry walking into the room. He walked around to all the rookies and free agents and said, 'I'm Coach Landry. A lot of you guys may not make this team, but there are three things I want you to know about Coach Landry. Number one is that God is first in my life. Number two is my family and number three, the Cowboys,'" recalls a rookie whose eyes were glued to the legend standing before him. "He then said, 'Good luck,' and left. I had a lot of great plays and great moments, but I think that was probably the one profound thing that I have taken with me."

Not only did Manny Hendrix take it with him, he uses that message in his daily duties as director of athletic relations at the University of Utah. "One of my jobs is to monitor and track athletes in making that transition from high school to college and also from college into the real world," explains Hendrix. The list of athletes who have come through and benefited from his counseling include many who have become stars in the professional game—Jamal Anderson (Atlanta Falcons), Keith Van Horn (New Jersey Nets), Kevin Dyson (Tennessee Titans), among others.

"The best example of what I am trying to accomplish is Andre Miller. He was a kid who came in as a prop 4A, which means that at the time he had to come in and prove himself academically. He couldn't play with the team. He couldn't practice with the team. It was a tough time for him. There were many nights where he thought about leaving and going home, many nights in tears. This kid came in and not only did he become an All America his junior and senior years, but he graduated in four years, which is unheard of. He stayed here every summer and went to summer school. He and I are very close."

Miller moved on to the Cleveland Cavaliers. Hendrix hopes one day to move on to an athletic director's position at a major university after earning his masters in education and sports administration. He can then step into the room his first day and introduce the three things his student athletes need to know about Manny Hendrix.

Carrying a Load

He never really got the chance to carry much of anything for the Cowboys, even though he was the only running back drafted by Dallas in 1988. So little Mark Higgs is making up for it by carrying a load every day.

"I'm driving now, I've got a customer," says Higgs as he talks while arriving at his last scheduled stop of the day in Fort Lauderdale, Florida. The owner and operator of M & T Transportation, Inc., Higgs has the welfare contract for Brier County, driving elderly and handicapped persons to and from work, job training, and medical appointments and kids to day care. "When we first started (in 1996), we bought two vans and I drove one every day. I thought, you know, I didn't retire from football to drive a van every day. But, I drove for about two months, until somebody tried to sue me. This old lady fell trying to get in the van. The next thing you know—lawsuit. It happens a lot in this business."

With a fleet of more than 50 vans, and plenty of insurance, his business has grown enough that Higgs rarely takes the wheel anymore. He's a manager now, a coach in the office. "My football experience helped out a lot in business because of some of the speeches I got from Coach Landry, Coach (Don) Shula, and Buddy Ryan—I played for him, too. I still use some of those speeches with my employees."

But the Cowboys experience the 5-foot 7-inch former running back shares most is one of waiting, watching, and learning. Even if it seems the wait will never end. "My first year, Coach Landry told me to just sit and watch Herschel Walker. He said, 'It's gonna be like you're a redshirt freshman, so just sit back and learn.' I never played, not one offensive play, because Herschel did not come out the entire year, which is incredible," says Higgs with an excited voice that got faster as the story continued. "I never seen a running back go through a whole season and not come out—not one play, not the whole year. Every offensive snap, he took. I played eight years, with four different teams, and I never seen that. It was amazing. He was like a robot. Basically, all I did was follow Coach Landry around on the sideline all season."

Mark Higgs has been carrying the load ever since.

A Little Too Greedy

I have a need for 'Greed'" were the words used to hype his decision. Spotlights began dancing around the studio. Dramatic theme music was blaring from loudspeakers. The audience cheered. Tony Hill was center stage again.

"I didn't know crapola about cars," admits the captain of a team of contestants on the network television game show "Greed." Hill had the closest response of six competitors asked 'How many registered Elvis Presley fan clubs are there worldwide' to earn his title as leader of the pack. He said 602. The correct answer was 612. Now, as the game progressed, he was facing the only members of his team remaining with a half million dollars on the line. "The question was 'What are the top global car companies in the world today?' I had (two) partners and at the time we were all together. I knew I didn't know anything about cars but (they) gave me the indication, the inclination that they wanted to go on."

It was not the pressure that got to Hill. He had experienced the eyes of the world on his stage before as a four-time Pro Bowl receiver for America's Team. His name is prominent in the Cowboys record book including his status as the second all-time leading receiver in career yardage. Many of "Thrill" Hill's catches were dramatic attention grabbers. "Danny White threw me one pass, about a 75-yard bomb down the sideline, that I didn't really think I could catch. I put my hand out there with an attempt to catch, and the ball just stuck. It went for a 75-yard touchdown. If we were to throw that play maybe 100 times, I probably wouldn't be able to catch that ball but that one time."

Certainly the odds were better for Hill even as his game show group answered the questions necessary to reach the $50,000 level. "Fourth down and 80 to go," was their captain's response. On to the $75,000 mark where Hill harkened, "We've got a first down, but we're not in the end zone." The $100,000 decision was a bit tougher to decipher. "We had a holding penalty, so we need more yardage." Quickly past the $200,000 level, with the plum of two million dollars dangling ahead, they faced the category "Best Selling Cars" for $500,000.

Hill seemed secure with the gamble ahead. Since retiring from football he put together Legend Sports Promotions to help himself and fellow teammates attract this type of appearance. "I came to the conclusion that here's a market that these guys at one point in time in their careers were untouchable and really didn't have a desire to make themselves accessible who are now willing to become humbled, and I'm that vehicle for those guys. It's turned out really well."

With the spotlights and music signaling the climactic moment, a selection of four correct answers out of seven selections were necessary to continue the climb. Honda, Toyota, BMW, and General Motors were chosen. Volkswagen and Ford were not. The captain made a change, adding VW and removing GM. Show host Chuck Woolery reread the question, "Which four of the following seven automobile companies and their affiliates have the highest global market share?" It was one of the few times Tony Hill had bobbled the catch. Two of the four were wrong. The audience moaned. Frustration showed on the contestants' faces. For the captain, the worst was yet to come.

"My dad had called me up. He said, 'If you get to 250, quit.' And I told my kids when I get to 250, I'd quit," says Hill, who went for broke instead, forfeiting the $200,000 gain in the process. "When I got home, I told them I lost, and my son, who was nine years old at the time, said, 'How far did you get?' and I said we were at 500. He said, 'YOU DIDN'T QUIT?' No compassion. The first words out of his mouth, 'YOU MEAN YOU DIDN'T QUIT?' It was unbelievable. The funniest thing is that when everyone goes 'Didn't you know General Motors and Ford were the largest companies?' No, I just wanted to lose the contest! Of course not, but that's the most typical question I get."

For a guy who was used to going for the big-yardage catch, if given another chance, this time Tony Hill would probably heed the greed.

A Kid at Heart

He set a completions record during his first NFL start on a Monday night in 1984 against the Los Angeles Rams. "I remember Doug Donley running a slant pattern and catching it with one arm and Doug Cosbie making a great catch for a touchdown."

His name was often mispronounced by Tom Landry, whose news conference video clips announcing "Hogenbloom" or even "Pozderac" as starting quarterback were the subject of jokes long after he moved on.

But the moment Gary Hogeboom cherishes most from his playing days as quarterback of the Dallas Cowboys is one that helped lay the foundation for his life after football. "I would say it probably started out with Bob Breunig giving me my first Bible when I was with the Cowboys," remembers Hogeboom, who now dedicates his days calling signals in a Youth for Christ ministry. "It just grew along the way through all the ups and downs and the injuries and everything else in my career."

Hogeboom was thrown into one of the team's infamous quarterback controversies during much of his career with the Cowboys. Danny White was the fan favorite, but Gary Hogeboom had the rifle release. Hogeboom occasionally won the battle, but White won the war. When traded to the Indianapolis Colts, Hogeboom suffered three serious injuries in three seasons, enough to shake the faith of many followers. "It was the biggest character-building time of my life," says Hogeboom, who would soon see the need to share his character and his faith.

He saw it in the eyes of a failing youth. "With the breakup of the family unit, you see a lot of kids in school that are searching for all kinds of different things, whether it be discipline or love or whatever," explains Hogeboom of those his ministry meets. One particular student blindsided the former quarterback harder than any linebacker coming on a blitz. "Seeing a kid come into high school hung over, flunking out, not making right decisions and sitting down and talking with him and saying, 'What's going on in your life? You're hung over this morning in school,' and he says, 'Hey, I was up until 3 o'clock drinking, and that's just the way it is.' It kind of put a new shed on my life about alcohol and the different things in our society that are swaying kids," remembers Hogeboom. "I think at that moment I made a decision that, hey, my life had to change as far as a role model and the things you do on and off the field. I was one of the worst. I was a beer drinker in the pros."

Hogeboom quickly realized the need to call an audible on the mixed signals going from professional athletes to kids in the form of advertising and public lifestyles. "You never realize what type of effect it has on kids in our high schools and junior highs when they see somebody in the NFL or NBA, or whatever, doing a beer commercial. They say, 'If that's all right, then I can do it.'"

It really hit home for Hogeboom—at home—one night with his seven-year-old son. "I'd have an occasional beer, maybe one or two a month, and he said, 'Hey, Dad, how come you can do that and I can't?' It just kind of struck me as funny," admits Hogeboom. "I wasn't abusing it or anything, but if it's wrong for somebody under 18 why is it right for somebody over 18 just because the law says it is? That kind of woke me up."

Hogeboom was always a quarterback who preferred the comfort and protection of the pocket to a free-spirited scramble. Not that he shied away from an occasional joust. Neither has changed. His current conservative, low-profile lifestyle is reflected in the real estate transactions that share his career in ministry.

And his fiery competitiveness is fulfilled with reining horses, an arena-style event similar to cutting horses. "I own four or five horses," says Hogeboom, who just happened to be both a Cowboy and a Colt during his NFL career. "I enjoy riding every once in a while."

It should not be difficult for Hogeboom to find a new lesson for his youth ministry. He can lead a horse to water, but he can't make it drink.

Aches and Gains

He was on his way. Three turnovers and several tackles as a backup safety and special teamer in Super Bowl XII had Randy Hughes headed for stardom.

"The one year I started the full year Tom Landry said in numerous publications I was the best strong safety in the league," remembers Hughes. Unfortunately his shoulder was not the strongest in the league. "I was prepared mentally and physically more than I had ever been any other time in my life. I felt like I was really prepared to meet the challenge, but I had an injury that doctors couldn't get well."

While Hughes was unable to recover from the shots his shoulder took on the field, he was certainly prepared to shoulder the responsibility of life after football. It just came quicker than he had hoped. "I had been working long enough to have a profession to fall right back into," says Hughes of his off-season experiences with an apartment builder and developer in his hometown of Tulsa, Oklahoma, ironically named Never Fail. Hughes understood "never" to mean even when the timing isn't right. "When I got out, I think prime interest rates were 21 percent. It wasn't a good time to get out. I would have rather stayed in football for another six or seven years, but we don't always get what we want."

Or do we? Since retiring from football, Hughes has been building high-end homes in the Dallas area, with annual sales totaling 15 to 30 million dollars. "The market here has been good for about the last ten years. It's been a pretty good run for housing," admits Hughes.

Even if this run does not last any longer than the run he prepared for in football, the lesson he learned will. Hughes has put his children on his shoulders many times to share the story. "A lot of times in life great opportunities only come your way one time. That's why I think being prepared is very important for the opportunity that you want in life, because when it comes, if you're not ready for it, then it will surely pass you by and you can't go back and get it, just like football," Hughes explains, adding his own personal reality. "Adversity makes us all a better person. It's just no fun to go through."

Randy Hughes should know. He's lived the cliché "no pain, no gain."

Don't Drink the Water

I think it would be real shocking for you to find out what is actually going back into the water systems that are being used for drinking water somewhere downstream."

That comment coming from a football player may not create much concern, until it is learned that former Dallas Cowboys linebacker Bruce Huther is doing the talking. "I am an aquatic toxicologist."

Actually, Huther received his zoology degree from the University of New Hampshire with every intention of becoming a marine biologist. Those plans dried up when his football career stream flowed into North Texas. "The opportunity to come down with the Cowboys as a free agent came up, and I took that opportunity and made the team," explains Huther. "I guess, geographically, I got landlocked here in Dallas, not very close to any marine life, and went to the closest thing I could find, which was a fresh-water biology approach."

At his lab in Dallas, Huther occasionally finds himself locked into the thought of a hit he delivered Washington Redskins running back John Riggins during a game in the early 1980s. "It was one of the best hits I ever had in my life," recalls Huther. "He fumbled the ball at the goal line, and I thought John Dutton recovered it. I have seen that play quite a bit." But every time it ends the same. "They called it a (Redskins) touchdown. That one I wish I could have back again. I think it would be a coin toss on how many times they called it a fumble and how many times they called it a touchdown."

Huther peers through a microscope knowing his daily decisions must be more precise than the flip of a coin. "I have a company that does environmental work," describes Huther of a specific aquatic toxicology example. "We work for all of the Texas utility power plants. They use a large volume of water in the generation of electricity. They discharge that water back into a creek or back into a lake—that lake water is used somewhere down the line as drinking water. Most Texas waters are water reuse. As such, they have very stringent requirements in terms of what level of water they can discharge back into the lake. In their permits they require the facilities to do a test on water called a toxicology test—an aquatic toxicology test. We get samples of that discharge water going back into whatever body it may be, and we expose some very, very sensitive aquatic organisms (grown in Huther's lab) to that water for a period of time and look for adverse effects. There can be mortality, obviously, as an adverse effect, but it can be a sublethal effect. We look at reproduction, we look at growth, and if there is inhibition of some sort of sub-lethal point, then we are hired to go in and identify what is causing the problem," continues Huther.

So far his company has not uncovered the kind of covert disregard for public safety that attracts Hollywood to movies like *Erin Brockovich*. "For the most part, when we do find a problem, it is an accident, not a consistent thing or something they are intentionally doing."

Huther admits his post–football future did take some intentional preplanning. "I was always somewhat on the edge of making the team or not making the team, so I prepared myself a little bit each year with the thought that I may not be here next year." Yet, Huther hung around for five seasons in Dallas. He is still not quite comfortable with the smell of fresh-cut grass, which reminds him of the practice and playing fields of his football days.

Not to mention the drinking water that was used to replenish and refresh during workouts and games. Bruce Huther, the aquatic toxicologist, knows now what Bruce Huther, the NFL linebacker, did not know then. "I have bottled water here (in the office), and I have carbon cartridges at the house, if that is any indication of what I think of the water quality."

Support Staff

Deion Sanders doesn't own it. Bob Hayes can't claim it. Butch Johnson and Kelvin Martin were close but no cigar. The name that leads the list of the Cowboys all-time single-season punt return records is James Jones.

"That is my trivia question that no one would get right," admits the third-round draft pick from Mississippi State. As a rookie in 1980, Jones had more returns for more yards than anyone before or since. It was his moment to shine before being buried in the backup running back role behind Tony Dorsett, where he learned the importance of patience and discipline as part of the team's support staff.

"It's one of the things I use with my management team all the time," says Jones, who now runs a support center for a computer networking software company. "If I can trust the guys to execute the little things then the big things will take care of themselves. That translates throughout whatever you are trying to accomplish."

Jones cannot claim that the return records translate into his most admirable accomplishment with the Cowboys. "From a personal standpoint it would be a touchdown catch against the St. Louis Cardinals in 1984," reveals Jones. "It was a personal highlight because the year before I was injured with a serious knee injury and at that time I didn't think I would play again and the trainer and doctor didn't think that I would play again, either."

Where Jones needed his own support was not in the belief that he could come back to the Cowboys, but that he could succeed after his career was complete. "As an athlete growing up back in the 1970s you would read about the horror stories of individuals that played professional sports and hear that once they finished, they weren't that successful after football," Jones remembers. "So, in essence you start off not real confident, and you feel somewhat scared. You go from making six figures to making maybe $20,000 a year. Uh, kind of a culture shock."

Eleven years in the network software industry has eased the shock and eliminated the fear. It probably helped that Jones had already backed up the best. "Just like with football, I don't get overexcited about the good things, and I don't get bummed off at the bad things. When you're running a support organization, you had better get used to that because you can do a hundred good things and talk to a hundred of your customers who are happy with the way your organization performs their jobs. You're not gonna hear about that most of the time. You will hear about the time that you screw up really bad."

James Jones would probably take those odds on the answer to a certain trivia question.

Spreading His Wings

Every week he faced some of the biggest and fiercest the NFL had to offer. At one point, Crawford Ker was the highest paid offensive lineman the Cowboys had ever had.

Yet, a moment that might seem small and insignificant to some was priceless to Ker. It was just before a regular season game in Tampa, Florida, near his hometown. "I was the captain of the Dallas Cowboys going out for the coin toss with Mom and Dad watching," remembers a proud Ker. "I don't know if we won the coin toss, but we won the game."

Flipping a coin had not always come up heads for Ker. Despite financial success on the field, his first attempt at his next career failed. "I did a restaurant when I was playing," says Ker. "I lost a lot of money in it." He was finding out what many professional athletes discover much later in the game. "What do you know about? You know football and you know your education but that's about it. So, you really come out of athletics as a 30-year-old with an 18-year-old of experience. It's kind of sad. But no one is going to feel sorry because they see all the millions you make. Then what are you going to do, get on the golf tour at 30? You play golf like a 65-year-old."

With his lesson learned, Ker took another swing at business after football by spreading his wings—literally—as the creator and owner of Ker's Winghouse, a group of restaurants that mirror the highly successful Hooter's chain. It was no coincidence that Ker grew up in the same area where the Hooter's concept was born. "They're not real happy with me," admits Ker of the competition. "I took some money out of their pocket."

With half a dozen restaurants sprinkled throughout northern Florida, Ker's Winghouse has earned an average of $2 million per store. "It's been good, but it could have been the other way, I could have lost a lot of money. Luck was on my side, and I made the right calls at the right time."

Including that day in Tampa. The Cowboys won the toss. Ker elected to receive and has been collecting coins the rest of the way.

The Hits Keep Coming

As a player, he was Eugene "the Hittin' Machine," setting an NFL record with 222 tackles in one season. Eugene Lockhart was a workingman's middle linebacker. It is no wonder he's become a workingman's man.

"You know how intense I played the football game," explains Lockhart of his need for competition outside of the game. "If I didn't have something to fall back on after football, I just don't know if I could have made it."

True to form, Lockhart began hitting his business ventures head-on, even before his football days were over. "I started my photo lab my second year with the Cowboys," describes Lockhart. "It just started out being something where we were just going out and taking pictures of these little league football games on Saturdays and processing and developing them and taking them back to the field. You know how them mommas like to see their little boys."

But without their own photo lab, the cost of processing the film became too large an overhead cost. So Lockhart and his partners bought their own lab and added retail and commercial business to the little league activity, growing the business to almost 200 commercial accounts. "Then technology started to change and everything became digital." It was time for Lockhart to tackle something else.

A swimming pool business and a restaurant co-owned by fellow teammates Tony Dorsett, Everson Walls, and Alfredo Roberts followed similar patterns. Eventually the constant battle of business without the benefit of shoulder pads and a helmet took its toll. "You just get tired of the headaches after a while."

Lockhart still longed for the competition that has always oiled the machine but without having to throw a wrench into his family life. "I just wanted to get out of the several businesses where I had all the headaches. I wanted to spend more time with my four boys. So now I just got a regular job where I do sales." In fact, selling for a telecommunications company seems to be the spark that has all his gears running at the right speed again. "Once you're a Cowboy, man, it's great for business. It gets me in doors where naturally I wouldn't be able to get into," admits Lockhart. "There's a lot of competition out there, and I just welcome it. That's my high now is closing deals."

"I'll always be 'the Hittin' Machine.' I'm just hitting in different areas now."

Forever Free Agent

Hours before the fans filled the stands, long before the team buses arrived at the stadium, even as the television crews were assembling their gear to broadcast the game later that day, Aaron Mitchell and teammate Steve Wilson wandered the Oakland Alameda field. Their feet felt something strange.

"Al Davis (Raiders owner) had watered the field down," Mitchell remembers. "We were there early enough that when the equipment managers and people came there, we alerted them and, by doing that, guys went on the field—Tony Hill, Butch (Johnson), Drew (Pearson), (Tony) Dorsett—and they were able to see what it was like before putting on the shoes that had the lower cleats, so we went to longer cleats. That helped the footing out because it hadn't rained there all night, they just left the sprinkler systems on all night."

Mitchell made the most of his discovery with a career day for Dallas. "I had an interception and, I think, six pass deflections with people like Cliff Branch and some pretty good burners up there."

But it was the attention to detail and his skill in selling the Cowboys on the curious field conditions that gave Mitchell a hint of his post–football plans. "I started out in the insurance business in 1983 when I retired," explains the former Cowboys cornerback who continued playing with the Tampa Bay Buccaneers and the USFL's Los Angeles Express before his return to the working world in Dallas. Mitchell handles insurance and investment sales for his clients while consulting in the professional employer organization (PEO) industry.

It is blanket coverage that an NFL cornerback can appreciate. Mitchell is never far from his football foundation.

"Today, if I'm sitting down with somebody, I might share some of Coach Landry's wisdom in a sales call, because running a business is a lot like running a football team. Why wouldn't you have an employee handbook and have policies and procedures?" adds Mitchell of the consistent characteristics. "I remember when I played with the Cowboys, we had in our playbook fine schedules, when to show up for meetings, policies and procedures, how to handle yourself on the road and dress code on the road. That's no different than business."

Unfortunately some of the similarities in Mitchell's sales life are also the ones that had forced him to play for three different teams, in two different leagues, during his six years of pro ball. "I'm in a free agent marketplace," he admits. "It used to be the time where if you didn't move that much you were looked at as a stable employee. Now we're in an era where, with all these dot-coms and techies that are out there, the more times you move the more favorable they look at you. It is a true free agent environment. Being in sales for so long, I'm not the complete pessimist, but I'm the type that plans for the worst and then hopes for the best. I don't know if it just comes from being a defensive back, people trying to beat you all the time, but things change. Nothing is ever etched in stone."

Sometimes it may even be watered down.

Ground Strokes

He spent most of his time in a Dallas uniform bouncing off one opponent or another, clearing the way for Tony Dorsett to pile up more yardage than any Cowboys running back had before. He served his fullback duties quietly and consistently. But Timmy Newsome's swing through the NFL did not include much of a chance to show off his own ground strokes carrying the football.

He is making up for it now, bouncing a different ball and serving up a new set of skills. "I play a lot of tennis," says Newsome. "It's actually replaced football in that regard."

To replace football in the financial regard, Newsome attacked a career that he volleyed with during the off-seasons while playing for the Cowboys. "I always worked in computers. I was a programmer for a number of years in the off-season," explains Newsome of the background that made his transition into a post–football career smoother than most. "I'm very grateful for Coach Landry and the administration of the Cowboys for giving me the opportunity in the off-season to do what I enjoyed doing, which was computers." Newsome now serves his own style of computer systems as owner of Newtech Business Solutions. "The best move I think I've ever made was owning my own business."

That includes the move Newsome made against Tampa Bay in 1983, the one he considers his best in a Cowboys uniform. "It was just a basic out route and Danny (White) threw me the ball. It's the kind of play that you get maybe 5 or 10 on, maybe pick up a first down and go out of bounds because we were under 2 minutes at the time. I thought I had an outside chance of outrunning the defender because I had somewhat of an angle on him. I ran down the sidelines and scored a touchdown to take the game into overtime." A game the Cowboys eventually won, on their way to the play-offs for the ninth straight season.

Now the sidelines have become baselines and fit well with his current career of coming up with the right combinations for his clients' computer needs. "It's very much a strategy game," Newsome says of his tennis game. "It lends itself to trying to figure out what shots to make when."

Timmy Newsome's tennis ability has been tested in many league tournaments, and most of the time he is the one hoisting the trophy overhead. It makes up for a lot of things he could not accomplish during his football days. Except for one.

"The biggest void in my life is the fact that we never won a title and that will haunt me for the rest of my life. Nothing can ever replace that void. Nothing. I could win 20 tennis titles and it would not be the same."

Extreme Measures

He's still not quite sure what hit him. "I stood up and then kind of just fell down right away, so I must have been out for a little bit."

Frankly, Steve Pelluer would just as soon not be reminded of that October day in Chicago. But just over a decade later, at a stadium in his hometown Pelluer thought was a safe haven, there it was again, blindsiding the Cowboys quarterback. "I went to a Seattle Seahawks play-off game. It was the last play-off game in the Kingdome," explains Pelluer of a 1999 outing with his family. "We were sitting there and they were showing hits on the big screen. Sure enough, I was the last one, the finale. My wife and brother-in-law were like, 'Hey, that was you.'"

This time Pelluer was more prepared for the blow. He barely flinched. A career of shots from NFL linebackers (he once suffered 47 sacks in a season, 1986), fans, and front offices were only part of what numbed his senses. "When I was released in Denver, I kind of had a bad taste of football in my mouth. The moving around and the pressure that I had to deal with was kind of like I needed a break from it," shares Pelluer of his unsettled career after five seasons in Dallas. "So, I just renovated a cabin in the foothills outside Denver and learned how to snowboard."

From one extreme to another, Pelluer left the life of football Sundays to study biblical counseling in the Rocky Mountains. He earned his masters from Colorado Christian University and has since returned to his home state of Washington, where he works commercial real estate in downtown Seattle and is on the state board of the Fellowship of Christian Athletes. "My biggest goal is to be a good husband and dad," says Pelluer. "Part of that is not getting caught up in the rat race of being a huge success at work. I want to do well, but I don't want that to be my focus."

Of course, Pelluer has had to refocus a time or two. He just seems to go at it from complete opposite ends of the spectrum. "I actually used to own a snowmobile, and I'd go up to the Collegiate Peaks near Buena Vista, Colorado," describes Pelluer of his after-football flare for fun. "We'd snowmobile up and jump off cornices and do a little bit of extreme snowboarding, which was quite a thrill. It was pretty dangerous, too. We went off some stuff that we found out later that people had died in avalanches previously, but we never started any."

Fortunately Pelluer survived his own personal avalanche during the 1988 season. Now he knows to take extreme measures whenever he sees Bears linebacker Mike Singletary about to lower the boom.

Secure

Magnum P.I. never had to do it. Neither did Barnaby Jones. Jesse Penn, private eye, found himself in some unusually sticky situations. "Once you put your garbage out on a curb, you know it's no longer ours and it's free if somebody wants to come pick it up," explains the former Cowboys linebacker of a case he faced shortly after retiring from football. "A business partner thought a guy was trying to knife him out of the business, and he wanted us to check up on him. We went by and took his garbage and replaced it with some dummy garbage and put on masks, big gloves, and a bunch of clothes and went through the garbage. You know, they didn't show Magnum doing stuff like that."

Apparently television tainted Penn's expectations. The overdramatized lifestyle of a private investigator played out every week during prime time. He quickly discovered it was not that way in real life. "A lot of it is deception and things like that," said a disappointed Penn of a career that lasted less than a year. "It's more stakeouts, drinking stale coffee, waiting for people to do things, trying to pry information out of little old ladies in the neighborhood about somebody who's trying to beat workman's comp. Or you're telling somebody's husband or wife what they're up to. A whole bunch of crap like that, and I just would rather do something else than kind of putting on stories to get information out of people, which is called a white lie or a little deception—but it's still a lie."

Another frustration for Penn was not finding his usual history of immediate success. It is what he remembers most about his days in a Dallas uniform. "The first game I ever played at Texas Stadium was a preseason game against Green Bay. I intercepted a ball and ran it back about 77 yards," remembers Penn. "It's revered as the Cowboys temple so to do something like that in your first game, it was a highlight, and things kind of blossomed from there."

Things are blossoming again for Penn in the Dallas area. After spending eight years with a security company in Denver, Colorado, rising to the level of general manager, Penn moved his family back to Texas to take on a similar role. This time he knows what he is in for. "It's not brain surgery. It's basically customer service. Anybody can unlock and lock doors, and that's not the kind of security we do. We're on the higher end," explains Penn. "We specialize in high-rise office buildings, and that's our main focus."

Actually, this time Penn has a bit of excitement and is looking forward to more. "I've had managers steal master keys and go on their own little shopping sprees and had to do an investigation. Now I'm working on getting my personal protection officers license. It's a fancy word for a bodyguard. You have to get your concealed handgun license for that." Not that he is expecting or even hoping for the television version he has seen many times before. "I've got a young family. I don't know if I'm going to be jumping in front of a bullet."

Probably a good idea considering Jesse Penn is no Magnum P.I.

Getting a Grip

Holding, No. 75. It was a call that rang through the public address system more times than Phil Pozderac would like to remember. But it is not the opponent Pozderac is hanging on to in a public reminder that keeps calling his name.

"Seems like the image everyone has of me is from a photograph looking down on Danny White, holding his broken arm," Pozderac ponders.

It was November 2, 1986. The Cowboys were in a division battle with the rival New York Giants when Carl Banks sacked the Cowboys quarterback, ending his season. Unfortunately for the offensive tackle who appeared to get beat on the play, the misery has yet to end. "I made a call at the line of scrimmage, and the guy next to me said 'No, no,'" says Pozderac of his linemate Crawford Ker. "The linebacker broke through and broke White's arm. It was my call, my fault."

Pozderac has had his share of broken plays since leaving the game. "It's been mighty painful," Pozderac admits. Now working for a telecommunications company in Dallas, the Notre Dame graduate has often found it more difficult getting a handle on business than on an NFL linebacker.

"I haven't found there to be much crossover from football to business," admits Pozderac. "Football is a straightforward game—business is not. No matter what is written on a piece of paper, it comes down to the person that wrote it. The biggest problem I've faced since football is naiveté and trusting people. When you are inexperienced in business, people take advantage of you."

Somehow, Phil Pozderac will figure out a way to hang on. He always has.

A Centered Self

When Tony Dorsett took off on his NFL record 99-yard touchdown run against the Vikings in front of a national "Monday Night Football" audience, it could not have happened without the snap, and block, of Tom Rafferty. In fact, EVERY offensive play during the 1984 season got its start because of Rafferty. "I didn't miss a down. I played every play, every snap."

Yet, it may have been one of the quietest 13-year careers in league history. So quiet, apparently few knew it was over. "There were some opportunities," Rafferty remembers about the months that followed his retirement from football, "but there weren't as many as I thought there might be out there."

As a center in the NFL, Rafferty obviously knew how to get things started. He went back to school to earn his MBA and took a job as a stockbroker. Unfortunately, it turned out to be one of those rare mistakes by a man in his position, a false start. "I hated that job. It wasn't me," explains Rafferty of his year and a half staring at a computer screen and making cold calls. "I felt like everyone had a dollar sign tattooed on their forehead."

It was time for an audible, and this time Rafferty began the play he expects will go the distance. He is now a regional sales manager for a sports equipment manufacturer, back in his element, delivering a product into the hands of people who need it. High school coaches and athletic directors are his quarterbacks now. Of course, once a center, always a center.

"Let's face it, probably the best story I've got is when I went to visit a coach in San Benito and he was in a hurry to go somewhere. I said, 'Let me give you my two-minute speech.' So, I gave him my two-minute speech, and he goes, 'Well, your name will be easy to remember since you've got the same name as the old Cowboys center.' I said, 'That used to be me.' About thirty minutes later, I left his office. He wasn't in a big hurry anymore."

Neither is Rafferty.

"I kid my wife, going, 'Hell, I've had the best years of my life.' I don't know what I expect now, I enjoy what I do, but I don't think I'll ever have the same highs doing what I do now that I used to have playing football. It's just two different things."

Kind of like being known as the center or the running back on a record-setting play.

Still Fast Enough

I could outrun everybody until about the time I went to TCU (college), so about half of my career I thought I was fast. And then, by the time I got to be about 18, I realized there was people other than in my neighborhood that I had to run against, and it came a little tougher."

Mike Renfro can joke about being born without the blazing speed of his pro football father. He has plenty of it now. "I do enjoy speed," says Renfro.

Ironically, the guy who spent four seasons as the Cowboys possession receiver has his pair of less than lively legs to thank for the thoroughbreds that run around him in his post–football passion—horse racing.

"My last year was Michael Irvin's rookie year, and I was on injured reserve," explains Renfro. "The good Lord above was saying, 'Renfro your legs are done.' I think I pulled my first muscle of that training camp about the second day in '88. I get it well and here came another muscle pull, and my legs were gone. I was trying to steal that last year. You play that long, you're supposed to steal one—that's what all the old veterans say. By gosh, by then—by 33—I was believing them."

Realizing the end was near, Renfro wasn't wasting his time watching from the sidelines. He was spending his time—literally—preparing for the future. "On the weekends, since I wasn't gonna be part of the game, I would journey over to the horse races, which I'd been going to off and on at Louisiana Downs. I saw a horse that we put a couple dollars down on a wager, and he won, and it was fun. His name was Dr. Death."

Within a few weeks, Dr. Death would breathe new life, after football, into Mike Renfro. An offer to buy into the horse on the eve of a $100,000 stake race, in which Dr. Death was the favorite, was too good to pass on. "If he did win, I would get all my investment back," Renfro remembers. "It was a one-day, kinda big investment for me at the time. If he does what he's supposed to do, I'll get it all back. So, it sounds like it's not very risky. But we've all been around gambling, or we've certainly seen a horse race. If they all ran true to form, we'd all be rich."

Renfro knew a thing or two about running true to form. His precision routes often placed the receiver in a favorable position to make a catch even when the opposing cornerback was known to be much swifter afoot. "We opened (the 1986 season) with the Redskins at home, and I still get to describe this—they say, 'How did you beat Darrell Green?'" It was one of Renfro's finest moments on the football field. "It was third and 9 with about 20 seconds left in the half. No way I shoulda got behind anybody. I ran a button hook and go on Green, and Danny threw a perfect pass. I had broken clear of him (Green) at least by 6 yards. When Danny lets the ball go, I'm 6 yards behind him (Green). By the time I catch it, Darrell is parallel to the ground, his hand is extended, and he missed knocking the ball down by like 2 inches. That's how much ground he covered just in the flight of the ball, when Danny threw it. I'm not exaggerating; I burned him as bad as anybody could be burned. He almost tore his ankle trying to turn around and recover. We scored on like a 70-yarder."

So it should have come as no surprise to Renfro that the legs he would invest in on the race track would run true to form as well. The surprise would come with Renfro's reaction. "It was the biggest thrill I ever had," he says with the giddiness of a rookie playing his first game. "He turns for home, and there's about four horses, and they all duel down the stretch. At the finish line Dr. Death sticks his nose out in front and wins by an inch. The exhilaration and the feelings that went through me was just as high as any touchdown I caught in the NFL."

Renfro would have plenty of those feelings. Dr. Death took the rookie horse owner on an 18-month ride that earned the horse Turf of the Year honors and almost a half a million dollars worth of prize money.

"I fell in love with the sport after that," admits Renfro.

So much so, he has become a member of the staff at Lone Star Park, a class-one racetrack in the Dallas–Fort Worth area. It is his new team, with a very similar game plan. "Before the game, or the race in our sport today, my adrenaline flows just like it's a pregame preparation. We get the horses out of the barns and bring 'em to the saddling paddock. We're strategizing with the trainer, which in our sport, he's our coach and conditioner of the athlete. Then, the pilot, or quarterback, if you will—in our sport, we call him the jockey, of course. We all sit there and strategize for a few moments prior to the race. Every horse has a different running style. We've prepared and analyzed those styles just like we study game film in a football locker room. We study what their tendencies are and how they like to do it."

And although he has not had another winner as successful as Dr. Death, Renfro continues to buy into the sport. In fact, his experience and exuberance has encouraged some unlikely partners to climb into the investment horse saddle. "I had two guys get in on a small venture in horse racing that were pretty good rivals on our football team. Gary Hogeboom and Danny White were both partners in a two-horse syndication with me. We didn't do real good. We didn't lose the shirt off our back, but we didn't make any money off that one."

Renfro has made enough of his new career that it is beginning to nose out his previous career when it comes to recognition. "I'll be in a restaurant and a gentleman will walk up that's an old football fan, and sometimes it'll be like, 'Hey, you're a Dallas Cowboy,'" Renfro says about being approached in public. "But sometimes, believe it or not it's 'I know your name, I know your name, I used to remember all that fun y'all had when you owned that horse in Louisiana named Dr. Death. You're that old Cowboy but I can't think of your name, but I remember your horse was Dr. Death.' I'd rather talk to that guy than the die-hard football fan, really."

Maybe it is because the conversation always seems to be about speed, instead of the lack of speed.

The Tiger Rohrers

Watching the world's greatest golfer tap a ball on the face of his club and then strike it in midair 180 yards on a rope—he had an idea.

Flying into an uninhabited jungle to witness a base jumper leap off a 900-meter cliff—he had a vision.

Viewing a priceless painting in a California museum—he had a plan.

Water-skiing on a river full of anacondas—he had a screw loose.

Jeff Rohrer's freelance world is as wild and wacky as his memories as a former Cowboys linebacker. "We were playing the Redskins in RFK. That was when Riggo (John Riggins) and (Joe) Theismann and all those guys were there," recalls Rohrer of a moment in the early 1980s. "It was a big game. It was like a fourth-and-1 deal, and for some reason Theismann came up and called a time-out and the place just started going absolutely insane. I remember just taking my helmet off for a minute and I screamed as loud as I could and I couldn't hear my own voice. I just went, 'This is what it's all about.' Everybody else was in the huddle, but I was, for some reason, tripping in that very moment, in my own little world trying a discovery. It was insane."

Rohrer's discoveries were just beginning. Stepping away from football after six seasons without the experience of a Super Bowl berth, he finally earned his title almost 15 years later in his career in commercial production. "At Cannes, they have a film festival for commercials just like they do for films. We won the Gold Lion, which is THE commercial, and the Silver Lion," explains the proud producer. "In our business, it's that (Super Bowl) big."

The stories surrounding Rohrer's accomplishments are even bigger. "I started out goofing around with TV. I did some really cheesy cheap shows, like this one show called 'Party in Progress,' which is basically a bikini contest at a big party that we made into 13 one-hour shows," admits the Californian of his early days away from Dallas.

"We didn't have any money so I, basically, directed it and hosted it and produced it."

But Rohrer was home, where he felt comfortable, fresh off a career with the Cowboys that prepared him for any tough times ahead. "Dedication, loyalty, trust—it was great to be around such a diverse bunch of people and gain that, just learn about people from all walks of life, from all backgrounds, all income groups, all racial groups. Me being one of those racial groups, being a surfer boy, I was probably THE minority on the team."

The idea was to get his feet wet and learn his new business as quickly but thoroughly as possible so he would feel like he belonged. Diversity would be the key in his new world. But Rohrer had no idea he was about to take a Tiger by the tail.

It has become a legendary story with as many versions as a tiger has stripes, or in this case, as a Tiger has championships. Tiger Woods, the world's most celebrated and talented professional golfer, shooting a Nike commercial on a driving range where admiring golfers begin to copy his every move. One of the producers on that particular day was—Jeff Rohrer.

"I had a crew of like 70 or 80, and we're filming the driving range spot. (During a break) they're all over eating lunch," describes Rohrer of the "rest" of the story. "I'm sitting there with an ad agency guy named Hal Curtis, and Tiger was right behind us. He was chipping the ball and hitting it." Rohrer, the athlete, was amazed at what he was seeing. Woods, tapping a golf ball 20 to 30 times on the face of his golf club, between his legs, around his back, finally popping it up a little higher, and with a full swing, hitting the ball out of midair straighter and longer than most can while it is sitting still on the ground.

Rohrer, the producer, knew he was seeing something special. "We're sitting there and we kind of, almost at the same time, look at each other, and we go, 'Why don't we get this?' So, I went over and I wrangled up a camera and a director real quick," continues Rohrer, who then asked Woods if he would duplicate the trick on film. "Tiger said, 'As soon as I'm done with my cheeseburger.' He was waiting on his burger; so instantly I'm on the walkie-talkie going, 'Get the hamburger over here, right now.' I had 70 people eating lunch, and we shot that commercial with a crew of three—the director operating the camera, me holding a big piece of white card bouncing light onto Tiger, and a girl on the stopwatch."

This is where Rohrer clears up the myth of what happened next. It was not a one-take trick. Timing Tiger to begin and end within the 30-second timeframe of the commercial created some complicated coordination. The first three times they try, Tiger fails. "He screws up again and again and again. Now, there's like 50 people gathered around us. So, the director puts down the camera, walks up to Tiger and goes, 'Ah, Tiger, I don't know how to put this, but you don't seem the kind of guy that would, how do I put this—choke.' The whole crowd goes, 'Whoaaa.' It was like a big deal, and then Tiger got it on the next take, and the next thing you know, we won the Silver Lion at Cannes."

In fact, the film crew finished both commercial spots that day, "We got that spot for like three grand, and we spent a half a million on the other one," adds an astonished Rohrer. Both paid off with critical acclaim—the Gold Lion was "Tiger Woods: Driving Range," and the Silver Lion was "Tiger Woods: Bouncing the Ball." Winning gave Rohrer the one thing he missed most during his career with the Cowboys. "I gotta keep going, man, now that I've got one I'm kind of thirsty. I've got the taste."And he's got the touch.

Rohrer's next project was even bigger and better. The Energizer Titanium commercial released in the fall of 2000 was certainly more extreme. "We were in Canaima, Venezuela. We were going down there to film a guy base jump off Angel Falls," Rohrer begins the story. "Here's how you get there—first you fly to Caracas, then you get in a Czechoslovakian Let and you fly three hours into the jungle, so far that there are no more roads in there. You land in Canaima. You take a Jeep up over a waterfall, and then you get in a log boat and go up to the jungle camp, and then from the jungle camp you're a half hour in a Russian Mi-8, it's a Russian military helicopter, to the top of this waterfall way back in the jungle. It's 900 meters tall and the only way you can imagine that is take the World Trade Center, the Empire State Building, and Sears Tower and stack them up and dump the Hudson River over the top of it. That's Angel Falls." And this is the rest of the Rohrer description as only he can come up with. "It's fucking insane. It's pretty gnarly stuff."

Rohrer's film crew spent several days in the Venezuelan jungle at the mercy of Mother Nature. Some days were more productive than others. "There were days when we literally had to wait for a hole in the clouds to go by and we'd call down to the base camp and the helicopter would be down there just running and we'd go, 'Okay, let's go. Get it up,' and it would be like, 'Go, go, go,' and we'd just be like running under these five, rotating, 500-pound meat cleavers right above your head, just trying to get in and get the hell out of there," describes Rohrer as he recaptures the image from the camera within his mind. "The water was so intense coming off the top, but when it hit the bottom, our landing area was out like a quarter mile into the jungle, and the winds a quarter mile from the water hitting the ground were like 60 miles an hour. We couldn't land our base jumpers because the winds were blowing so hard."

Finally, everything comes together and the shoot begins. Again, more than one take is planned and more than one is necessary. "He jumps off (Angel Falls) and deploys the chute. The guy did land in the jungle a couple times, and we had some rescue crews, some Indians from Venezuela that were really good guides, went up there and grabbed him." The finished product is another amazing example of commercial film making, another spectacularly successful story.

"Everybody came home safely," adds Rohrer as an afterthought. Considering his spare time tales, it should have been the first thought that came to mind. "We were water skiing in a river with anacondas behind a log boat, 40-foot logs hollowed out with Evinrudes on the back. But they (the anacondas) didn't get us."

Not yet, but Rohrer is not ready to rest. The few years away from football have been filled with the flair and flavor that would be a lifetime of legend for most. Not Rohrer.

"I'm a freelance producer. One of the reasons I like it is the pressure, because it's a lot like football. You're as good as your last job, so you're always under the gun to perform," explains Rohrer of the drama that draws him to the next project—a PT Cruiser commercial at a Swiss Army Knife factory, or a trip to Barcelona, Spain, to do "Heineken for the Holidays," or Vancouver, Canada, for Hershey's. Soon, Rohrer hopes the projects will be his own creations. "I want to start directing and get my vision out there."

Actually, Rohrer has already freewheeled his way into figuring out a forum to get a head start showing off his vision. It is another one of those stories that is so extreme even Rohrer sometimes wonders if he is just California dreaming. "When me and my wife were so poor we couldn't afford a painting, we just went to the museum and I copied one and it came out killer," claims the football player turned producer turned painter. "I'm serious. I am not bullshitting you. I did a Monet, like a water lily thing. After a couple of those kinds of things, I got enough courage to go after some portraits and now we do it all the time." He had a painting of Tom Landry sent to hang in a Dallas medical facility named for his former coach, and another portrait of the ancient Hawaiian Kahanamoku that Rohrer says is a hit among surfers on the West Coast. He describes his work as a mix between a Warhol and a Van Gogh.

"They're killer. They're abstract. You get into the painting and it looks pretty cool but then at the late part of the night, I'll be sitting there with a bottle of wine and a cigarette going, 'Okay, here I go,' and you go for the face and it's like really fucking scary. You can't go back on this oil. I only go one time. I paint them all in one day, usually about five hours."

Then Jeff Rohrer is off to whatever he comes up with next.

Not Much of a Vacation

Looking out over the ocean, he sees what most people would call a vacation paradise. He calls it home. The view Rafael Septien has spent over a decade straining to see is the paradise of a playground he used to call home.

"I think people deserve another opportunity, and the United States is the best place at giving people opportunities," explains Septien from his office in Cancun, Mexico. "But why did I not get one yet? Why one of these days can't I get one? So, I would like to have that opportunity, and if that happens I'm still ready to do it."

The opportunity is a return to the States where Septien has already seen his star rise for nine seasons kicking a football in the NFL only to fall in one night with the wrong kind of kicks. He owns Cowboys records for field goals as well as a criminal record for pleading guilty to indecency with a 10-year-old girl. Septien says he has been ready to resume his kicking career but continues being kicked around instead. His team scoring record was broken by Emmitt Smith in 1999, but he claims to never get a break from his criminal record of 1987.

"I've more than paid my dues," says Septien with a strong Spanish accent. "A lot of people have gone down, and I'm the opposite. I have a great family now again, and I'm ready to be excellent also particularly in the community in many positive ways. A lot of people like have a bad taste sometimes. That's gone. It's been ten years."

Septien has been spending most of his day the past few years as president of the Crystal Vacation Club and is hoping to expand his real estate efforts to include former teammate Roger Staubach's company. "We have our own resorts in Puerto Vallarta, Ixtapa, Mexico City, and Cancun."

But a portion of each day is also spent playing soccer, racquetball, or beach volleyball or working out in the gym. All are designed to assist in his return.

Septien has kept in communication with a number of NFL teams, including the Cowboys. "I would like to go back to play, but they won't want to give me the monies yet. So, if next year we could come to an agreement, then I could be back to play somewhere," claims the Cowboys career leader in field goal percentage, attempts, and field goals made.

He led the team in scoring for nine straight seasons until his final kick in 1986. Septien has more long-distance field goals than any other in a Cowboys uniform, but he is just a few years short of his fiftieth birthday. "I'm ready. I'm in great shape. Eddie Murray is always coming back and also Gary Anderson from Minnesota; age without beauty. I have the mental capacity and my body is okay because I didn't get hurt, then I can do it."

He was Dallas's all-time play-off points producer. "I never missed an extra point or a field goal—15 straight games." And his league totals were climbing the charts before his conduct kicked him out. "That hurt because I was taken out of an opportunity that I could have still done. At one point I was the 13th all-time leading scorer in the NFL, and I knew I could have broken that. I was in great shape, and I could already have played more than anybody else."

To remind Rafael Septien that the opportunity was taken away by Septien alone reinforces his point that the punishment has lasted longer than the ten-year probationary sentence suggests. "There's always life after death. I was dead, mentally and spiritually and all that," admits Septien. "But fortunately I never got drugs or alcohol. The winner makes it happen, and we have to keep on doing it. But you need opportunity."

He is still thousands of miles away from the land of opportunity. His home may be paradise to some, but Rafael Septien wants the vacation to end.

Helping Hands

He always had the hands to make it in the NFL. It was one of the reasons Mike Sherrard was the first receiver taken in the 1986 draft, a Cowboys first rounder. But, early on, he didn't have the legs.

"From what I remember, my legs were real fatigued from just running a lot of routes," Sherrard remembers of the day during his second training camp that was the beginning of the end of his days with Dallas. "They actually had a lot of stuff planned for me, which was nice. I just remember running a route, and I felt like the defensive back kicked my heel, which happens all the time, legs get tangled up. My right leg hit the back of my left leg, and I heard a loud snap. I immediately went down to the ground and I grabbed my shin and I could feel the bone protruding through the skin. It was just a weird thing. I could feel my foot in a certain angle below my calf bent at a 90-degree angle and just feeling the bone. But it didn't really hurt. It was kind of weird. Maybe my body was in shock."

Fortunately for Sherrard, the shock quickly turned into a dose of reality. Another break while running on the beach during an off-season workout forced the Cowboys to give up on their receiver of the future. Sherrard did not give up, playing for eight more NFL seasons and preparing for a day he learned could come much sooner than expected.

"I started thinking about life after football," says Sherrard of the Cowboys experience. "You always think it's going to happen to somebody else. Especially being a top pick, you think, 'I'm a first-round pick, I'm going to definitely stay at least ten years.' But injuries can wipe out a career real quick. It made me think about things. It helped me invest my money. I was real conservative because I didn't know when it was going to end and I didn't want to play and break bones and have nothing to show for it when it was over."

Sherrard has plenty to show. Not only a 73-yard touchdown while being interfered with against the San Diego Chargers, in front of hometown friends and fans, a play he still cherishes as his career high-light, but also a weekly show on college football every Saturday. It's the part of his post–football days that keeps him close to the action and not too far from different dangers of the game.

"We were broadcasting a game and usually you do a lot of studying but you can't study everything," admits Sherrard. "UCLA was kicking to Cal and they kicked to this guy number 68 and my play-by-play guy said, 'Oh, it goes to number 68.' We both look at our list and we see the guy's name and it's a Samoan name and neither one of us wanted to butcher it. We just started laughing and said, 'Ya, number 68 doesn't get the ball too many times.'"

The hands that once earned Sherrard stardom in football are now helping others on the field become successful off the field. Not every-one learned the lesson Sherrard was afforded by accident. His com-pany, Athletes Business Network, is a sports marketing group that focuses on business development for pro athletes. "A third of the guys in all of professional sports, the four major sports, are making a mil-lion bucks a year. A vast majority of the guys aren't going to make enough to live forever," explains Sherrard of the need for his service. "So, we go to corporations and work out a deal where, not necessarily guys get paid to sign autographs but a guy can do something for a com-pany and maybe get paid some money. But, more importantly, own equity in a business and just learn about running a business. Maybe, actually have a future and a career with that business."

Sherrard's client list began with an impressive group that included former teammates Ken Norton Jr., Merton Hanks, and O. J. Anderson. Once again Sherrard's helping hands are a gift for others.

An OffSpring Has Sprung

That made me say, 'I finally have arrived.'"

Ron Springs was not talking about making the team as a fifth-round draft pick out of Ohio State in 1979 when the Cowboys already had Heisman Trophy winner Tony Dorsett in the backfield. "I enjoyed it because I took a back seat, but if I had it to do over again, I would love to have been where I was the featured back."

He was not talking about the 1983 season, the best statistically of his career with the Cowboys. "When they finally figured out I could do a variety of things," adds Springs, "I led the NFC in receiving, and I rushed for like 600 yards. I had like 12 touchdowns, and I threw touchdown passes."

He was not talking about moving back to Ohio after retiring to begin a career in commercial real estate development, or even about the abrupt end to his flag football future in Cleveland. "It was the most embarrassing thing that ever happened to me," Springs admits. "I got kicked out of the flag football league for fighting. I was playing quarterback, and these little bitty guys was out there. They were being aggressive, trying to prove that they could do something to the former Dallas Cowboy Ron Springs. A guy sacked me too hard, so then I went to defense and I ended up sacking him. The next thing you know I end up fighting. I had to beat up the whole team. About nine of them jumped me. I was throwing them around like pieces of pretzel. Come to find out, man, the police escorted me off the premises, and I got kicked out of the league."

Nor was Springs talking about his five years coaching alongside former teammate Steve Wilson at Howard University.

And he was not remembering a story that still makes him laugh today. "The night Tony Dorsett thought he was having a heart attack," Springs begins. "It was like 1981. Tony had a new wife, Julie.

About 7:00 P.M., I got a call; they said it was an emergency. His wife told me to meet her at the hospital because she thought Tony was having a heart attack. We go out there and she's crying and feeling bad and I said, 'What the hell, he done party too much? How could he have a heart attack at 28 years old?' Come to find out she had cooked tacos that night, and he ate about six of them and had heartburn."

What caused Ron Springs to feel like he had "finally arrived" was a spring day in 1997 when Ron and his offspring heard NFL Commissioner Paul Tagliabue say these words during the first round of the league draft: "The Seattle Seahawks select cornerback Shawn Springs from Ohio State." "He was drafted the highest defensive back ever been drafted," says proud Papa. "After football the highlight for me was being able to compete with my son from the ages of 12 to 18 and physically kick his butt at everything. When I would come home from the office, he would be waiting for me dribbling a basketball and we would play a thousand times or he would want to race one day or he would want to swim. I tried to physically beat him at everything to make him a very serious competitor. I finally retired when he started dunking and I saw his genitals in my face. I said, 'Well, it's time for me to quit!'"

Now the competitors are partners in a small land development company in the Dallas area. Ron would just as soon keep it small, once again taking a back seat to some of his former teammates. "Randy Hughes is a big homebuilder here, Larry Cole is a homebuilder and developer, Staubach is doing it, Breunig is doing more retail, and Robert Shaw is big in it, too. These guys are big time. I really don't want to be big time."

Besides, Ron Springs knows from experience, there's only room for one superstar at each position on any team. "Shawn makes ten times the money I made. He's probably going to make 100 million dollars in his career. I made three million. As a parent, you always want your offspring to do that."

It lets you know you've arrived.

It Takes a Thief

The radio voice reverberating throughout his car had an edge of urgency. It sounded like the play-by-play call of a Hall of Fame running back's route through a rival's defense. But the descriptive locators being used to analyze one of the NFL's greatest players during this broadcast were highway markers instead of yardage markers.

He's now coming off the 57, and he's on the 405 headed north with the cops in close pursuit.

"It was one of the weirdest things because I was on the 405 freeway going the opposite direction and all the traffic was stopped," recalls Dennis Thurman of an afternoon in Los Angeles. Bumper-to-bumper traffic at that time was certainly nothing unusual but the commotion being caused by the radio report was borderline highway hysteria. "People were on top of cars, on top of overpasses and people were chanting 'Go, O. J., go. Go, Juice, go. Don't give up. Don't give in."

The nation witnessed the white Bronco taking its tour of the L.A. freeway system with O. J. Simpson inside. As bizarre as the scene seemed to a television audience, to Dennis Thurman it was surreal. "It was really a strange deal to know that there was a man that you know who was now a wanted fugitive," admits the former Cowboys cornerback who played his college football at the University of Southern California, Simpson's alma mater. "It was very, very difficult because he was such a hero to many of us who went to USC. A lot of us went there because of O. J."

Dennis Thurman had come back home to help develop the Trojan's future heroes. As USC's defensive backs coach for almost a decade, Thurman has had his share of success stories from Sammy Knight to Jason Sehorn. "A lot of people didn't think Jason Sehorn, being a white cornerback, could play that position. I only had one year to work with him, but Jason said some very nice things about me and very complimentary of me as far as helping him become the player that he's become in that league," says Thurman, who was also mentioned as a mentor by former USC teammate Ronnie Lott during his Hall of Fame induction speech. "The reward comes from the compliments and the kind words and the nice things that people say about you in terms of having helped them further their careers."

Thurman resembled that remark during his playing days in Dallas. An eleventh-round draft pick by a team coming off a Super Bowl championship, the smallish cornerback developed into a leader in the secondary. He still owns the Cowboys career record for interception touchdowns and can be found near the top of the record books in a variety of categories, enough to warrant a felony theft charge. "We were opening the season (1985), and everybody was talking about the defensive backs not being the strength of the team but being a concern area. We didn't have high draft picks back there. Most of us were free agents, late-round draft picks, and pretty much castoffs who a lot of people didn't think could play," remembers Thurman. "We went out against Joe Theismann and it was his birthday. We ended up with six interceptions that day, all by the secondary. Somebody asked Danny White a question after the game, and he said, 'Oh, that was just Thurman's Thieves.' When the year ended and the smoke cleared, we led the league in interceptions and played a pivotal role in helping to win the NFC East."

Thurman's thievery also played a pivotal role in his future as a football coach. It was recognized by Tom Landry as an ability that came not from physical talent, but from mental mastery of the game.

"I got the itch to get into coaching from Coach Landry. He called me in one day and asked if I had ever thought about coaching, and I was very honest with him. I said no. He said to me in that conversation, 'I feel like you have been preparing yourself to be a coach, but you don't even know it.' I said, 'What do you mean?' He said, 'Well, you think like one.'" Thurman adds part of that thought process came from Landry's legacy. "Landry's ability to talk in terms of preparation. He believed in being thorough, first of all learning what you do, understanding what happens to you, where your help is, where the weakness is in the defense, where the strength is in the defense and being able to play to your strength and understand and minimize the weakness in it. I didn't like the word 'weak' associated with football, so I changed the word from 'weakness' to 'vulnerability.' Play to your strength and understand where you're vulnerable."

Being a coach has its own level of vulnerability. Thurman began as an assistant for his former defensive coach Gene Stallings, who took over the sideline for the St. Louis Cardinals after leaving Dallas. "I ended up playing that year for Gene in St. Louis. We finished first in the league in pass defense, and then I retired and the Cardinals went from first to twenty-eighth in pass defense. I think that had something to do with Coach Stallings calling me the next year and asking me if I wanted to come back to coach."

When Stallings was let go from the Cardinals and moved on to the University of Alabama, Thurman decided not to tag along, stealing some time away from football until the phone rang again two years later for a chance to become defensive coordinator of the World Football League's Ohio Glory. "I was excited because it was my first opportunity with running my own show. We were 1–9 that year, but we finished third in the league in total defense." The league was finished as well, although Thurman was not. A call from John Robinson brought him back home to Southern Cal where he lasted through the reigns of Robinson and Paul Hackett but had to watch the Trojan horse take a hit to its Heisman stature.

"When he was acquitted it was like in anticipation of a game-winning field goal where it was the last play in a game that meant everything," describes Dennis of the day the verdict was handed down in the Simpson trial. "We were all up in the office in Heritage Hall watching it on television, and when they announced it there wasn't a lot of hand clapping. There wasn't a lot of yelling and screaming. It was more like a big exhale by a lot of people. Did he do it? Did he not do it? Did he get away with something? Was he there and he knows who did it but he was told not to talk? Was he set up? There's still a lot of unanswered questions that he himself will carry to his grave, but it was a very strange feeling for those of us who are and were associated with this school at the time."

Dennis Thurman had a piece of USC pride stolen from his heart. Maybe a new version of Thurman's Thieves will pull off a Hall of Fame heist to get it back.

The Lesson Tee

Y ou better be at your best every time you come to the line of scrimmage or every time you come to the business world." It is a lesson Glen Titensor learned the very first time he put on a Dallas Cowboys uniform, lining up as a rookie against his idol, Randy White.

"When I was in college we used to get highlight films of Randy White, and our coach would coach us showing these highlights of Randy White," says Titensor, who played defensive end at Brigham Young University. "I was in awe by this guy Randy White. When I got drafted by the Cowboys, my first concern was how am I going to make this team with Randy White, Harvey Martin, John Dutton, and 'Too Tall' Jones on the starting lineup for the defense?" Titensor got his answer when he talked with Tom Landry. The Cowboys drafted Titensor to play offensive line.

Relieved, thinking the learning curve would give him time to adjust, Titensor got another lesson he would not soon forget. "The biggest eye-opener for me was when I then had to line up against Randy White," remembers Titensor. "It didn't go too good. First of all, not playing much offense at all and not understanding the technique involved and going against an All Pro, you know, my college idol. Mainly it was on-the-job training."

Training that served Titensor well enough to stick around the NFL for seven seasons. And training that continues to serve him as a business owner. After a brief stint doing lab work for his brother's dental practice, Titensor switched positions again, purchasing land in Lewisville, Texas, where he owns and operates the Timbercreek Golf Center.

"I wasn't one of the superstar players that made the high salaries that, as soon as they retired, could live off the money they made during their football days," admits Titensor. "I knew it was going to be coming to an end so I never did live beyond my means and what I did make I saved and put to use for the future. I always enjoyed golf, and everybody kept telling me to get into something I enjoy doing. So I got in the golf business," adds Titensor. "The reason I enjoy golf so much is the competition you have in golf. It's one of the main things I miss from my playing days with the Cowboys."

Standing on the practice tee, hitting golf ball after golf ball, Titensor looks out over the landing area and sees something else he experienced during his playing days—an eye-opener. "I bought this piece of property that we're sitting on right now, and it's appreciated around this area big time. We're looking in the future to sell the property, develop it, and then go on from there."

Glen Titensor will no doubt step to the line of scrimmage ready to go up against the best with his best.

The Walls Keep Spinning

He learned early on how to spin his story. At times it was as if he was his own public relations firm. First he pitched his playing abilities to Eddie Robinson shortly after arriving on campus at Grambling. It eventually earned him a scholarship. Then he told his tale to the Cowboys and got a shot as a free agent cornerback with his hometown NFL team.

Little did Everson Walls know his PR practice would be put to the ultimate test immediately following the play that ended his rookie season and has been a constant challenge long after his last interception.

"It's like my career really stopped right there as far as historians were concerned, and I think that's a shame because I went on to do a lot of other things," says Walls as the spin begins surrounding the play that forever frames his Cowboys career. It made the cover of *Sports Illustrated*. It is one of the most replayed highlights in NFL history. The outstretched arms of Dwight Clark grabbing what appeared to be an overthrown pass from Joe Montana in the back of the end zone to win the NFC Championship game. It all happened in front of a Cowboys cornerback wearing No. 24. It is simply known as "The Catch." "My thoughts of that game have always been mixed feelings because I was on my way to an MVP game and no one ever mentions that part of it. I had three turnovers that game. I had like nine tackles. I don't know how many pass deflections. I was having a great game and then, of course, you just go up against great players. It's who's got the last bullet is the one that won the game. I got 47 interceptions after that game, and no one wants to remember those. "

Students everywhere probably remember the adage from PR 101 class—any publicity is good publicity. Walls has found his fame to be a focal point of many meetings. Yet again, the spin must begin.

"It can be a hindrance at times because some of these people look at you and they're thinking, 'Man, this guy Everson Walls has been talking to me about something other than football' and you can see it in their eyes. They can't wait for the business to finish so they can start asking me about football, and that's just not what I want to do. I want to talk about business," says the Cowboys rookie record holder for interceptions and second all time on the Cowboys career interception charts. Oops, Walls was talking business, not football. "When they're looking at you they're not even really listening to you. They're just looking at you, and you can tell their mind is like, 'Why doesn't he just shut up so he can start talking about what was it like to play with Roger Staubach?' I didn't play with Roger Staubach."

Somehow Walls could make you believe he did, if he needed the spin to win support for his cause, which now includes a real estate deal he hopes will help develop a low-income sector in South Dallas. The All Star Fitness Complex concept started out slow but is getting one-on-one coverage from the three-time All Pro.

"I've been working on it for three, going on four years, and I've had so many people tell me that it can't be done. Just in those three years I've attained certain certifications and papers and documents that were not supposed to be attainable if I were to listen to the naysayers. That just keeps me going, keeps me fueled," admits Walls, who describes the vision for his project as more than a gym, with complete health facilities including physical therapy, cardio rehab, and scholastic help for high school kids. "That's the wave of the health industry now, and I'm trying to parlay on the health consciousness of America. Everybody nowadays realizes that in order for us to stay a thriving nation, then we have to be a healthy nation. Health has really taken a front seat with corporate America."

Like his football fortunes, Walls has had to define his direction and refine his resources. "I started off with vitamins, and I started thinking if I want to talk about the wellness for my people, then vitamins are not the way to do it," he explains. "Prevention and exercise is the way to do it. It just kind of snowballed into instead of trying to get a vitamin stand we needed an arena where a vitamin stand could also be a part of it. From there, we were like, 'Okay, what area of Dallas is really in need of it?' Of course, you think of African-Americans because everybody knows we're No. 1 in heart disease and stress and high blood pressure, so why not attack that head-on? When you start to attack something like that, then you realize that as a minority you are privy to federal dollars and certain set-asides that are obviously well deserved. That's when you start entering the politics of it, dealing with city council people and mayors, administrators. Man, I've been kissing so much butt it's ridiculous. I've signed so many pictures and handed out so many pictures."

Often it is the magazine cover that still makes him cringe. Sometimes it is the one that makes him smile. For every reminder of "The Catch" comes word from Walls of the one that showed him as a Super Bowl champion nine years later. "That's why I was so emotional when I went to New York and ended up winning the Super Bowl there. The Giants, man, it was my finest moment, the best team I've ever been on and guys that really trusted me. They took my leadership, my experience, and they parlayed it into a championship for the Giants," boasts Walls. Suddenly, the spin is gone. "It's a shame I had to go all the way to New York just to get the notoriety other than one particular play."

Notoriety is another way to parlay the publicity generated by a career that covered almost a decade in Dallas and included four Pro Bowl appearances. Walls spends his Sundays as a game-day analyst on a local television station. It may be the one place the former free agent forgets the public relations rules.

"That's really my first love but the politics of it all is just really so disheartening to see some of these guys on TV who can't hold a candle to me as far as when it comes to talking and my knowledge of sports, but that's not important to them. They want a certain face on there," claims Walls, who has a face for television and the gift of gab. "The people they want to give the try are the people that have done something real stupid in their career, somebody that's going to bring some controversy. Why can't I just bring knowledge? Why do I have to talk like an idiot? Why do I have to say something shocking for you to know that I know what I'm talking about? That got kind of frustrating."

Not that Walls would shy away from frustration. His first taste of the business world, as a partner with former teammates in the Cowboys Sports Café near the team's Valley Ranch headquarters, was ruined by a tasteless moment that still leaves him with a bitter breath towards the Cowboys current regime. "Jerry Jones for some reason came up to Tony Dorsett and Eugene Lockhart, and he told them, 'Hey, man, you guys are doing a good job over at the Sports Café.' And he patted Tony on the back, and he said, 'If there's anything I can do to help you, just let me know.' We found out the next day that Jerry had banned the players from coming into the Sports Café and that it was repercussions of Mike (Irvin) getting in trouble and (Alvin) Harper and Alfredo Roberts and all that kind of stuff going on," says Walls. "It's an extremely seasonal endeavor, and he just happened to ban the players during the high part of the season, and from then on we just couldn't recover. So, after a lot of griping and fussing and hiring the worst managers in the history of business, we ended up having to just sell. That was extremely disappointing. We just couldn't understand how somebody representing the Cowboys wouldn't want former Cowboys to do well, because it only enhances the Cowboys name. We were the only ones that weren't getting in trouble associated with the Cowboys. For some reason, he thought that strip joints were okay for them to go to."

Walls was not about to let that strip his confidence. He had been up against the wall before. Not offered a scholarship in college, he earned one. Walls was inducted into the Louisiana Hall of Fame in 1998. "That was one of the few times that a tear almost came to my eye when I was giving a speech." Not drafted in the NFL, he became All Pro. Challenge him and the spin will begin again.

"Once I saw that hard work and prayer and belief in yourself worked for you in some of the most pressure-packed situations that anyone could think of, then there is nothing, I feel, that bothers me. There's nothing else that I'm afraid of. I'm afraid of no man. I'm afraid of no man-made situations," describes the free agent turned free enterprise system stalwart. "Like this real estate development I'm trying to get into. Anybody that tries to tell me it won't work, then I tell them nothing is gonna stop me. Your words are not gonna stop me. You may try and block me, and it's not gonna happen. I'm gonna stick with this and I'm gonna make it happen because it's a dream of mine and I guess because of sports I realize that once you do stick with something and you believe in yourself it has strong possibility of coming into fruition.

"Things that I've accomplished and how I've accomplished them from such a long shot, in such a long-shot manner. It makes me realize, okay, it looks like it's a tall mountain to climb right now, but I've done this before and I know it's attainable. You are no better than I am. I am no better than you are. We are on equal ground no matter how much money you make, no matter who you are, no matter what you've accomplished, I realize you are the same type of person that has the same doubts, the same inconsistencies just like anybody else."

If the Walls keep spinning, before long we may all believe there was someone else wearing No. 24 when Dwight Clark made "The Catch."

Forget Me Not

He broke many of the Cowboys passing records after taking over when Roger Staubach retired. Just don't ask Danny White to replay any of the throws that allowed him to put up those numbers.

"I don't remember very many specifics. I can't remember games that I played. I can't remember even playing at Texas Stadium. I can't remember anything clearly. It's kind of a strange thing, but I know I did it. I know I was there. I know it wasn't a dream," admits White. "I don't know if it was the concussions or what."

White wasn't hit enough during his career to forget that despite leading the Cowboys to three straight NFC Championship games in the early 1980s, he never had the opportunity to quarterback a Super Bowl team. He left Dallas with that albatross hanging from his neck.

Now White is not so sure it wasn't a blessing instead. "I would like to have taken a team to the Super Bowl and won it, but I don't know if that would have been a good thing for me or a bad thing. I know what success in pro sports can do to you—the pressure, maintaining a level head, having a good strong family life," says White, who returned to his hometown of Phoenix, Arizona, after his playing days with the Cowboys.

"To be successful in professional sports, you have to be involved in activities that put pressure on a marriage and family life. The football player in me, and the competitive person that I am, would have loved to have gone to and won a Super Bowl, two or three. Maybe it's better that I didn't go to or win a Super Bowl."

Flashback to January 10, 1982. The NFC Championship game in San Francisco produced one of the most memorable endings in NFL history—unless you're Danny White. He's reminded about "The Catch" by Dwight Clark that brought the 49ers back late in the fourth quarter. But what about the touchdown scored by the Cowboys just a few minutes earlier that forced the 49ers to come up with "The

Catch"? "The touchdown that we scored? I have no idea," says White after a long pause to peruse his memory bank. Seconds of silence go by as he continues to query his mind. "You don't mean Dwight Clark's catch. Before that one? I have no idea. I can remember throwing a touchdown pass to Tony (Hill) down the left sideline. I don't even know if it was in that game. I know it was against the 49ers and I know it was in Candlestick Park. Was that it?"

Actually . . . no. It was a 21-yard pass to tight end Doug Cosbie, although White did seem to regain a little remembrance. There was a touchdown throw to Hill in the first quarter that day.

Fortunately, White has had total recall when it comes to coaching. The philosophies learned from the legendary Tom Landry have been used by White with the Arizona Rattlers, an arena football team that has more league championships than any other professional franchise in Arizona. "Most of it is the Landry influence. You won't read about this in any books, but Landry had a theory of critical mass, and he didn't talk about it a lot," explains White of the approach that has earned him two Arena Bowl titles in a career that has spanned a decade as coach and general manager. "If you could get enough players to buy off on your philosophy, you could create the kind of environment where people could actually exceed their own potential. That's what we had in the late '70s and even in the early '80s. We had very, very average athletes. I think we've been able to do that here."

Time out. If White remembers the game plan that built America's Team, certainly he can recall the games. Besides, as the son of Wilson "Whizzer" White, Danny inherited the talents that now have him enshrined alongside his dad in the Arizona Sports Hall of Fame and in the Arizona State University Sports Hall of Fame and that have led to both their jerseys being retired at ASU. Like father, like son. "My dad is photographic. He's in his 70's, and he remembers plays in high school that he ran and things that happened in high school. It's incredible to me," says a bewildered son. "I have great talent to forget." Which White now believes he developed as a characteristic necessary to play out the game plan in Dallas. "It was actually a great talent with the Cowboys. One of the hardest things you had to do playing for Coach Landry was forget. If you played a game on Sunday, by Wednesday you got the new game plan with 150 new plays and new formations. It was all sent in with hand signals. He would send in 15, and you had to know, based on the down and distance and the situation that the play was spread-orange-right-tight-fullback-short-divide-ray-15-x-cutout-fullback-out. That whole thing would change the next week. It would be maybe spread-purple-halfback-motion. You had to do a lot of forgetting. You had to quickly blank it out and get on to the next one."

Sometimes he forgot a little too fast. It's a Sunday afternoon at Texas Stadium. The Cowboys face a critical play against the Washington Redskins. What did you do, quarterback White? "The fourth down audible after he had just told me not to snap the ball, just to try to get them to jump offside?" Yes, Danny, yes. "Then no, Danny, no! I remember the picture of him (Landry) jumping on the sidelines and the quote and everything."

White is not particularly interested in jumping anywhere. Opportunities to coach in college, the XFL, and even the NFL have come across his desk. "I don't have an agenda. I'm not working towards a particular position or goal. I fortunately am in a position where I love what I'm doing," explains White. "I've been around too many coaches that get greedy and maybe too aggressive and think maybe the grass is greener on the other side and they want more. They only come to find out that as a head coach in the NFL, they're not having any fun. They're a puppet for somebody, working, having to coach players that they don't respect and they don't like."

White did not think he would like or even respect the arena game after setting records for the top league's top team. But he quickly discovered football is football and there is always more to the game than what you see on the field. "It really has become my passion to take young, obscure players who are eager to learn the game and help them become professional football players. That's both on and off the field. That's real important to me." Important enough to put his own financial investment in the team.

"Jerry Colangelo (original owner of the Rattlers) took a big chance on me ten years ago. I had never coached at any level before, and he literally turned the franchise over to me," White adds with an appreciative tone to his voice. "The prestige may not be there and the money's not what it is in the NFL, but if I didn't learn anything else in 13 years in the NFL, it's that fame and fortune doesn't always lead to happiness. I'm happy now."

So happy, he's building his getaway home—a log cabin on a ten-acre tract in the White Mountains of eastern Arizona. It's where he grew up fishing and hunting with his dad and can now share with his wife, sons, daughter, and grandchildren. Danny is doing much of the building himself. He knows the blueprint. If his past is any indication, someone may have to help him remember where he placed the logs.

"It's almost like that was a different person," says White of his days in Dallas. "I look at it almost as another person looking at someone else having done that."

Danny White did it all. He has the records to prove it and to remind him whenever he forgets.

How 'Bout Them Cowboys!

Blessed Back

Tommy Agee has been truly blessed his entire life. He started off a small little kid from Maplesville, Alabama, a town nobody knows about. God was able to put him in places, big cities, and play football in front of millions of folks."

That Tommy Agee tells his story in third person is testament to his humble heritage. It also tells the story of how a backup running back for the Cowboys has taken on a starting role for kids.

"At this point in my life, blessings that came down from God allow me to look back at everything that I've done and try to steer kids away from destructive lifestyles."

Agee is manager of the Covington Recreation Center in Opelika, Alabama. It was a run-down, beaten-down building with little future until Agee saw enough promise to leave the Alabama juvenile court system and foster a rebirth both for the building and for himself. "I enjoyed working with the juvenile court," admits the criminal justice major from Auburn, "but I just didn't like the idea of locking kids up."

Instead, Agee has renovated the Covington Center and added programs that build kids up rather than breaking them down. "One of my pet projects was being directly able to influence kids on the positive side and what better way to do that than at a community center, a recreational center, where kids come all the time?" explains Agee. "I'm bombarded with an array of different kids every quarter, and it just gave me an opportunity to have a face-to-face, hands-on approach to dealing with kids."

Opportunity for hands-on experience with the football escaped Agee during much of his playing days in Dallas. There were superstars in the backfield on a Super Bowl run. Yet, rather than pushing for playing time, Agee adopted an apprentice attitude. Watching and learning as Daryl Johnston displayed a work ethic that made "The Moose" an NFL fan favorite, and embracing Emmitt Smith as he provided the perseverance and heart of a champion. Another blessing had been thrown Agee's way.

"One of the highlights of my career was seeing Emmitt perform against the Giants in New York when we won the division on our way to the Super Bowl," recalls a proud Agee. "Emmitt got injured with cracked ribs and he was in excruciating pain but he gave up all of that just so we could win that football game. He went out there and he continued to run the ball harder and harder and harder. He was in the game sucking wind and trying to give that little bit of energy that he had left. When we got on the plane most people don't know about the pain that he was in. Seeing that man in tears and can't get his breath, I'm thinking we was gonna have to land the plane before we got to Dallas. I learned a lot from my little brother (Smith) that game that he will go far beyond the duty and he really did love Dallas and the players that played with him."

It's a story Agee always shares with troubled kids in need of direction. He can see in the softening and twinkle of their eyes that it always works. "I think that one of the reasons that I played football and was successful at it, God wanted me to use that as a tool to open doors to kids."

Tommy's tools may not have helped the Cowboys on the field as much as he would have hoped, but Agee would never ask for more than to keep opening those doors in communities all over the country.

Heart and Soul

The prayer had barely begun. *Dear God . . .* They were at his bedside. *. . . Please be with us, dear God. . . .* It was their nightly ritual since his name had appeared on the list. *. . . God, strengthen his heart. . . .*

A phone ringing in the neonatal ward interrupted their moment of meditation. Immediately Frank and Robin Cornish knew what it meant. "Our prayers were answered."

Eight years earlier, Frank Cornish felt his heart nearly skip a beat in the final moments of the NFC Championship game at Candlestick Park. "When Alvin Harper caught that pass that gave us the field position to win against the 49ers and go to the first Super Bowl," recalls the Cowboys backup center in his first season since playing with the San Diego Chargers. "Even though I wasn't out on the field at that particular time, I hadn't had a lot of success, and here we were in the play-offs and clinching an opportunity to go to the Super Bowl." Cornish quickly caught his breath on the sidelines in San Francisco.

Two Super Bowl rings and what seems like a lifetime later, he was back on the sidelines. Only this time the game was life.

Lying in the bed before Frank and Robin at Loma Linda University Memorial Hospital was their son Blake. He had been born with hypoplastic left-heart syndrome, a condition where the left ventricle, normally the strongest part of the heart, is barely developed. Most babies born with the defect die shortly after birth. Two weeks had passed since Blake's first breath. "We have a transplant coordinator on the phone," were the words that broke the silence.

"It was almost an eerie situation, like a tingle went through my body," Cornish candidly admits. "They called and said, 'Well, we've got what we feel to be a good match and we're flying to go get it and we'll be back in the morning. Be ready.' Obviously we didn't get much sleep that night knowing that our child was about to go into a major surgery and have his bad ticker pulled out of his body and a brand-new heart put in."

They were as prepared as possible. Frank feels much of the character and inner strength needed to take on the trauma´that faced the family was found in the trenches of the NFL. "I think it's directly related. It challenges you emotionally. It challenges your marriage because there's stress, being worried about your kids. It's challenging because you have to go out there and make a living and be focused in your business," says the financial advisor with Prudential Securities. "While people are doing their business, they don't want to hear me talking about managing their money and about their family situation. Their concern is their retirement. You have to be able to separate the two. That goes back to sports is kind of a Jekyll-and-Hyde situation where you get paid for a living to go out and run into 300-pound guys and try to knock somebody's head off and when the day is over you don't take the same attitude home with you."

But home is also where the Cornish family had fought part of this process before.

"I think we were a little bit more prepared in the sense that my wife and I have five kids, the oldest is six, and the four others had been premature and had spent time in the hospital. My twins were ten weeks early and my oldest daughter, who is a surviving twin, believe it or not was delivered at 22 weeks, 6 days into the pregnancy. That's barely half way. She's a living testimony to how great God is. They generally don't even give a percentage chance to survive, and she's living and is a bright young lady and probably is the toughest kid I got."

It is no doubt an inherited trait. Imagine the difficulty of the decision facing Frank and Robin when their son's condition was detected during prenatal exams. Doctors determined that three options were available for the Cornishes to contemplate: 1. Compassionate care— "It was not an option for us at all. That's just basically let the baby live as long as it'll live." 2. The Norwood procedure—"Three surgeries over the course of the first two years of life. I just couldn't see myself putting my child through three major surgeries, having his chest cracked open three times." 3. The transplant—"We made our decision that we wanted to offer him the best quality of life."

Fortunately Frank was helped by Robin's research, which found the best quality care available for neonatal transplants. Dr. Leonard Bailey, who pioneered the procedure at the Loma Linda International Heart Institute when "Baby Fae" received a baboon's heart in 1984, performed Blake's surgery. The transplant and recovery went remarkably well with Blake returning to the Cornish home in Dallas before his first Christmas. "It's been an uphill battle but the little guy is doing well," says his proud parent. "To see him today you would never even imagine that he has been through what he has been through so far in five months of life. He's a precious part of our family. I'm convinced this guy is destined to do some great things."

He already has. A foundation called the Blake Cornish Organ and Tissue Donors Foundation has been established in the hopes that others will learn about the need for early detection and donation.

In the meantime, the nightly prayer can continue. . . . *Thank you, dear God, for the blessings of your heart and soul. . . . Amen.*

The Helpful Hardware Man

Whether he was wrenching his opponent out of position or hammering him to the ground, John Gesek used his physical tools as part of the blueprint that rebuilt the Cowboys into Super Bowl champions. Now he's selling tools for the everyday projects of others.

"I've always heard that business is better in Texas when the Cowboys are winning, but I don't know if that has anything to do with us," says the former Cowboys offensive guard, now running, among other businesses, his own Ace Hardware business just down the street from the team's headquarters. "Obviously, friends and former teammates come in that are hanging around, but I made it a point not to use the Cowboys name. None of my trucks have stars on it. People told me I was crazy, but I wanted to do it separately."

It's not that Gesek isn't proud of his connection with the Cowboys. His two Super Bowl rings fit rather nicely. Besides, when it comes to business, Gesek has plenty of tools in the shed, thanks in part to the neighbors from whom they were borrowed.

"I've been able to carry over some of the things we learned in sports," Gesek explains, listing the characteristics he learned in football like an inventory list from his store. "Planning, finding people that fit, utilizing people to the best of their abilities, and then trying to get it out of them. Putting people in winning situations and not setting people up to fail. Attracting and retaining the best possible people for the job. Motivation. And being able to keep in mind what the goal is."

Of course, it doesn't hurt that the Cowboys are some of his best customers. "We sell them all kinds of stuff. Nothing big, it's mostly just stuff to keep Valley Ranch (the team headquarters) running."

Gesek has his hands full keeping his own businesses running.

Along with the hardware store, Gesek has ownership in a commercial floor maintenance company and is a partner in an investment group that builds office buildings. As a former offensive lineman, he knows how to get his arms around his projects and hang on to what works, always looking for a chance to knock down the next opportunity.

"I once heard a farmer being interviewed," says Gesek of a cliché that hammers home how he believes his future story will be written. "They asked her what she was going to do when she retired, and she kind of had this funny look on her face, and she said, 'Retire? Honey, we're farmers. We never retire. We just die.' I guess I've seen too many people that when they retire, they die, whether it's just mentally or physically and mentally. I don't ever plan to retire."

Exactly what you would expect from your helpful hardware man.

Tackled for the Ultimate Loss

I can't feel a pulse," said the voice on the end of the line. It was early morning on May 6, 1999. The 911 call had come from Cowboys fullback Nicky Sualua. He said his friend had stopped breathing.

When paramedics arrived at the location of the call, the worst fears of those that recognized the address were realized. Mark Tuinei was dead.

For 15 seasons, Tuinei had methodically managed an NFL career that began on the defensive line as a free agent from Hawaii in 1983. By 1987 he was an offensive starter, twice earning Pro Bowl status to go with three Super Bowl rings. A mammoth man at 6-foot 5-inches, 320 pounds, Tuinei opened huge holes for an NFL rushing champion and protected the blind side of an All Pro quarterback. He helped both Emmitt Smith and Troy Aikman earn Super Bowl MVP status. Along the way he also helped the morale of his teammates, often hosting karaoke nights or playing pranks at the team's Valley Ranch practice sight.

But just over a year after being released by the Cowboys, Tuinei could not help himself. His former teammates initially believed the news they were hearing was another one of his pranks. It was not.

Tuinei and his wife were less than a week away from returning home to the islands where the man who shares the Cowboys record for longevity was looking forward to sharing his NFL experiences and talent with football players at his former high school. He was to become the offensive line coach at Punahou High School in Hawaii. But apparently it was Tuinei's youthful years that kept him from continuing on.

"It's a day-to-day, year-to-year battle," Tuinei told the *Dallas Morning News* in 1993 of his boyhood alcohol and marijuana use even before the drunken brawls that resulted in multiple arrests during college. "I know that I'm always going to run into trouble of some kind. I just need to make sure I handle it."

Wednesday night, May 5, apparently Tuinei took more than he could handle. According to court documents, he and Sualua traveled to a Dallas apartment where Sualua says his former Cowboys teammate was looking for heroin. According to Sualua, Tuinei had already used the stimulant Ecstasy earlier in the evening. "Mark went into the bedroom, and he said, 'Here it is.' When Mark came back to the living room, he looked as if he was passing out. Mark started having problems and stopped breathing," Sualua said in the affidavit.

Sualua told police that he performed CPR and Tuinei was alive. He then dragged the former lineman from the apartment to Tuinei's 1933 classic Ford roadster. Sualua says he drove his friend to Tuinei's house in Plano, a Dallas suburb, and that "Mark was snoring loudly." Sualua decided to gather blankets from the house and says he slept in the car with Tuinei until about 5:30 the next morning.

Then Nicky Sualua woke up.

Mark Tuinei did not.

Continuing the Climb

It is a message he shares as often as possible with the boys and girls of the south central Los Angeles community known to the world as Watts. "It's no mystery to what Watts is about. It's nothing but sex, drugs, and violence. I grew up in that environment," says James Washington of a lifestyle that is hardcore movie material to most but was his daily dose of reality. "I had five guys that I used to hang out with. Out of those five, three are dead, one is in jail and one is in a mental institute."

Washington was and is the exception.

"My dad leaving at two, my mom leaving me at four and being awarded to the state, then my grandparents coming in and becoming legal guardians, I grew up in the streets," he explains. "But as I grew up in the streets, I learned to do the right things and take the right path. The reason why I was not caught up in all the violence is that my mother being an alcoholic, my uncle being gay, my other uncle being a drug dealer, I was so determined not to be any of those things."

His determination translated into a ferocious style at the safety position for five seasons with the Cowboys. It may have simply been a reflection of the frustrations from his youth. "I strived on intimidation when I played. My personality used to be like that when I was a kid. I fought a lot," admits Washington. "I tried to change games with some of the hits that I've made. There were some that changed the whole complexity of the game. Go back and look through the five years that I was there (Dallas). When we played the San Francisco 49ers, Jerry Rice would not run the slant. When he did come inside against the Cowboys, he paid for it."

Not paying for the misfortune of his childhood has become Washington's way of life. Earning a Masters of Education from Azusa Pacific after retiring from football, he was coaching while considering a career as a junior college teacher and counselor. Again, Washington chose a path less chosen.

"God put me on this earth from something bigger than that," he realized. "I look at where the man above has taken me from nothing, molded me into this person, put me in the spotlight on Sunday and allowed me to exemplify my talents at the highest level in my business on the day where the whole world was watching. I have to be somebody special."

So Washington is working with the same aggression that allows him to wear a Super Bowl ring on each hand. Many believe his performance in Super Bowl XXVIII against the Buffalo Bills was MVP material. Emmitt Smith got the award and the accolades that go along with it. James Washington got a new appreciation for the position of decision maker as opposed to those that rely on the decision being made.

"I didn't get to drive off in the sunset like Emmitt Smith and Troy Aikman. My career ended. It wasn't planned out. I evaluated all those things, and I was determined that I didn't want to work for anyone," adds the owner of a new Los Angeles company that began buying single-family dwellings in low income areas and is now investing in multimillion-dollar buildings. "After reading different books, I figured out that as long as I worked for someone I would never be the person that I want to be. As long as someone is my boss I would never be financially wealthy. There's a difference in owning the team and playing for the team. Yes, the players on the team get paid a lot of money, but think about how much money the person that pays them has. I think that's why I stopped coaching. I loved working with the kids, but financially I don't think I was where I wanted to be."

Unless, of course, he is working with his own kids. "I've actually reached my ultimate athletically, but now I'm seeking to be the Super Bowl dad. I'm seeking to be the MVP of dads. I'm trying to be everything that I wish I would have had when I grew up."

James Washington has been where he did not want to be before. He is making up for it.

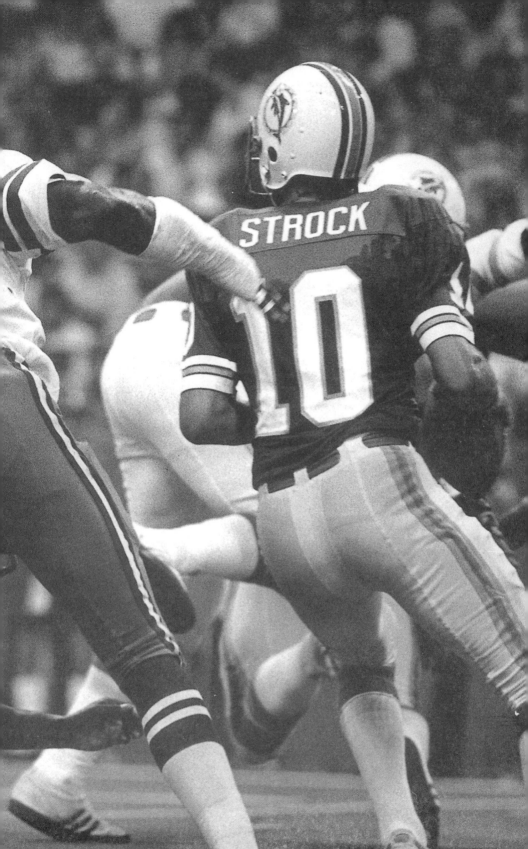